GREATER ETHIOPIA

GREATER ETHIOPIA
The Evolution of a Multiethnic Society

Donald N. Levine

THE
UNIVERSITY
OF CHICAGO
PRESS
CHICAGO & LONDON

DONALD N. LEVINE is professor of sociology at the University of Chicago. He is the author of *Wax and Gold: Tradition and Innovation in Ethiopian Culture* and the editor of *Georg Simmel on Individuality and Social Forms.*

THE UNIVERSITY OF CHICAGO PRESS, CHICAGO 60637
THE UNIVERSITY OF CHICAGO PRESS, LTD., LONDON

Printed in the United States of America

International Standard Book Number: 0–226–47558–1
Library of Congress Catalog Card Number: 73–91233

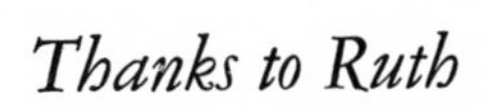

Thanks to Ruth

Contents

List of Illustrations ix

List of Tables xi

Preface xiii

1 / Conventional Images of Ethiopia 1

A Far-off Place 1

Ethiopia the Pious 3

A Magnificent Kingdom 6

Savage Abyssinia 9

A Bastion of African Independence 12

2 / Scholarly Images and Assumptions 15

An Outpost of Semitic Civilization 17

An Ethnic Museum 19

An Underdeveloped Country 22

A Complex Evolving System 23

3 / The Differentiation of Peoples and Cultures 26

Lines of Internal Differentiation 28

Lines of External Influence 30

The Peoples of Ethiopia: A Classification 33

4 / Foundations of Unity 40

Greater Ethiopia as a Relational Network 40

Greater Ethiopia as a Culture Area 46

The Ethiopian Response to Alien Influence 64

5 / Patterns of Expansion and Unification 69

Centers of Expansion before 1300 70

The Amhara Thesis 72

The Oromo Antithesis 78

The Ethiopian Synthesis 80

6 / Four Questions 87

7 / Tigrean Legacy: A National Script 92

The Kibre Negest: *A Reassessment* 92

Prologue, Narrative, and Epilogue 95
The Kibre Negest *as a National Epic* 100
A Cultural Identity Struggle 101
The Tigrean Contribution 109

8 / The Amhara System *113*
Household, Seignory, and Parish 113
The Nation as Community 117
Functional Specialization 119
Hierarchical Interaction 122
Individualistic Association 124
System Stability and Historical Change 126

9 / The Oromo System *128*
Olla, *Lineage, and Class* 129
The Agnatic Community 135
Functional Redundancy 136
Egalitarian Interaction 138
Solidaristic Association 140
System Instability and Historical Change 141

10 / Comparisons and Explanations *146*
The Question of Amhara Expansion 148
The Question of the Oromo Victories 152
The Question of Amhara-Tigrean Resurgence 155
The Question of Oromo Affiliation 161

11 / Social Evolution in Ethiopia *165*
Holistic Specialization 166
Mutualistic Specialization 169
Internal Specialization:
The Formation of Ruling Elites 171
Despecialization and New Evolutionary Potential 175
Internal Specialization:
The Creation of Free-floating Resources 179
The Present Evolutionary Situation 181
The Evolution of Ethiopian Society 183

Appendix: Roster of the Peoples of Ethiopia *187*

Notes *199*

Bibliography *211*

Index 223

Illustrations

CHARTS

1. The Peopling of Greater Ethiopia *34–35*

2. The *Kibre Negest:* Outline of Contents 94

3. System Structures and Group Action Capabilities *163*

MAPS

1. Peoples of Ethiopia: Current Distribution *36*

2. Amhara Homeland and Sphere of Influence about 1520 *76*

3. Oromo Homeland and Area of Conquests about 1700 *79*

Tables

1. Selected Pan-Ethiopian Traits: Concepts of the Supernatural, Ritual Practices, and Food Taboos *60–61*

2. Selected Pan-Ethiopian Traits: Cult of Masculinity, Aspects of Social Organization, Insignia of Rank, and Customs Regarding Personal Status *62–63*

3. Selected Structural Features of the Traditional Amhara and Oromo Systems *148*

4. Selected Historical Explananda *148*

Preface

For people in many countries the name Ethiopia is still connected mainly with the Italian invasion of 1935. A new wave of books on the Italo-Ethiopian War published in the last decade testifies to a continuing interest in that fateful event.

The usual question regarding the Italian invasion is what weaknesses in the international system permitted this aggression. One may also ask, *Why Ethiopia?* What was it that enabled Ethiopia alone among traditional African societies to retain its sovereignty until the Italians chose to exercise their anachronistic appetite for empire in the 1930s?

How much weight can one give the policies of European powers and the feats of Ethiopian emperors? Accounts of these two variables, important though they are, do not tell the whole story. To be sure, keen competition between England and France in Northeast Africa prevented either from gaining decisive supremacy there. It is also true that Tewodros II, Yohannes IV, and Menilek II presided over a reconstruction of the Ethiopian Empire that gave their people the strength to withstand repeated incursions from Egypt, Sudan, and Italy. Still, internal characteristics of Ethiopian society not commonly recognized were essential conditions for the viability of the Ethiopian state and the success of its rulers.

My objective in this work is to examine those internal characteristics from a sociologic perspective. Psychological and environmental factors will not be ignored, but their significance will be caught as they relate to structural properties of sociocultural systems. "Structure," of course, is an ambiguous term. I use it here to refer to three kinds of social facts—institutional orders, interactional patterns, and cultural codes—the meaning of which will emerge in context.

In carrying out this examination it has seemed necessary to establish certain conceptions of the Ethiopian experience as a whole which differ from those apparent in most other writings. For this reason I begin with a general analysis of prevailing images of Ethiopia, both those purveyed by popular writers through the ages and those adopted by professional scholars. My argument proceeds by developing a picture of the Ethiopian experience that draws on recent anthropological and linguistic research and articulates the factors of unity and diversity within a civilizational area that I call Greater Ethiopia. With this revised image as background, I focus on the three main ethnic groups: Tigreans, Amhara, and Oromo or Galla. My principal analytic task is to determine the main structural features of the traditional Amhara-Tigrean and Oromo sociocultural systems. This analysis affords a basis for understanding their respective historical roles and assessing their contributions to the formation and survival of an autonomous Ethiopian society. I hope that the analysis may also suggest useful generalizations about social structure in both comparative and evolutionary perspective. The concluding chapter explicitly relates that analysis to recent work on the process of social evolution.

In executing a work of this scope I have benefited immensely from the moral support and technical assistance provided by two scholarly communities: the University of Chicago and the international circle of Ethiopianists. An exemplary community of scholars, the University of Chicago has been a constant inspiration. Led by a brilliant and dedicated president, Edward H. Levi, the university has weathered the recent years of crisis in the academic world by remaining steadfast in its commitment to a scholarship that addresses serious intellectual problems and submits to demanding standards.

The opening of a magnificent research facility at the University of Chicago, the Joseph Regenstein Library, was one of the factors that led me to write this book. I wish to acknowledge in particular the help of its very able social science and African bibliographer, Jan Wepsiec. The opportunity to spend a year working in the Regenstein Library was afforded by a faculty fellowship from the Ford Foundation. Smaller grants for particular aspects of the project were kindly provided by the University of Chicago through its Committee on African Studies and the Department of Sociology's Ford Foundation Grant for Comparative Studies.

During the years when this study was conceived and carried out, Morris Janowitz, as an unusually devoted departmental chairman, provided consistent and sensitive support. The Committee for the Comparative Study of New Nations continued to provide intellectual stimulation of a high order. Other colleagues at the university who offered valuable suggestions at critical junctures are Gene B. Gragg of the departments of Linguistics and Near Eastern Languages and Literatures, Karl W. Butzer of the departments of Anthropology and Geography, Richard P. Taub of the Department of Sociology, and Victor Turner of the Department of Anthropology and the Committee on Social Thought.

To several members of the rapidly growing circle of Ethiopianist scholars I am indebted for help on a number of specialized questions which enabled me to improve the mansucript considerably. Valuable criticisms and suggestions were received from Marilyn E. Heldman, John Hinnant, Allan Hoben, Grover Hudson, Herbert S. Lewis, Charles Rosen, Rodney Ross, William A. Shack, Dan Sperber, and Shimellis Tekle-Tsadik.

Four persons—M. Lionel Bender, Harold Marcus, Asmarom Legesse, and Marcus Rosenblum—provided generously detailed commentary on each of the chapters. Lionel Bender also labored valiantly to persuade me to adopt a consistent orthography of Ethiopian words that dispenses with diacritical marks and preserves phonetic similarity as much as possible. While retaining a few old established spellings, I have generally followed the approach to transcription used by Bender and his colleagues in *Language in Ethiopia,* one which parallels the system of spellings for place names used by the Imperial Ethiopian Mapping and Geography Institute. Readers should thus be forewarned that a number of words will be spelled somewhat differently than in *Wax and Gold.*

In the new spelling of Menilek, I follow the usage adopted by the outstanding historian of the reign of Menilek II, Harold Marcus, whose critical jabs at certain portions of my manuscript were of great value in provoking me to strengthen some vulnerable points.

I owe a particularly great debt to Asmarom Legesse, with whom, in a number of seminars, jointly taught courses, and extraordinarily stimulating conversations during the last few years, I was privileged to work out many of the ideas in this volume.

To my uncle, Marcus Rosenblum of Washington, D.C., I am indebted for an especially helpful editorial critique of the entire manuscript as well as a lifetime of intellectual stimulation and challenge.

Closer to home, I have been inspired in this as in other endeavors to persevere against all obstacles by the paternal model of a sprightly octogenarian, Abe Levine. And finally to my family, Ruth, Ted, Bill, and now Rachel, I am grateful for their acceptance and enjoyment of so much of Ethiopia in our home and lives.

1

Conventional Images of Ethiopia

After the Italian invasion of 1935-36 Ethiopia came to be viewed in many parts of the world as a hapless victim of fascist aggression and a symbol of the need for collective security and international order. This was not the first time, however, that an image of Ethiopia had stirred strong sentiments in distant countries. Long before that it had aroused foreign interest for other reasons. Five types of response have been particularly prominent over the centuries. Typically Ethiopia has been looked upon as a terribly remote land; a home of pristine piety; a magnificent kingdom; an outpost of savagery; or a bastion of African independence.

A Far-off Place

For disenchanted moderns and for romantics of many times, the name Ethiopia has evoked the alluring image of a faraway land. This image has a notable ancestry. In the opening lines of the *Odyssey* Homer characterized the Ethiopians as *eschatoi andron,* the most remote of men, a phrase remembered by his readers throughout classical antiquity. Homer's Ethiopians dwelt by the streams of Ocean, "at earth's two verges, in sunset lands and lands of the rising sun."[1] Later, Herodotus chided Cambyses for ordering a march against Ethiopia without providing supplies and "without for a moment considering the fact that he was to take his men to the ends of the earth."[2] And Aeschylus had Io, the wandering woman of *Prometheus Bound,* sweep down to "a land far off, a nation of black men ... men who live hard by the fountain of the sun where is the river Aethiops."[3]

For the early Greek writers Ethiopia was less a geographical location than a state of mind. For Greeks and Romans generally, Ethiopians meant dark-skinned peoples who lived south of Egypt. At times the reference was so vague as to include peoples from West Africa, Arabia, and India. At times it was more localized, referring to the Nubian kingdom of Kush, with its capital first at Napata and later at Meroe. What was constant was that the name Ethiopian denoted a person of dark color—literally, of burnt face—and that it connoted, above all else, remoteness.

As Frank M. Snowden, Jr., has observed in his study *Blacks in Antiquity,* the classical attribution of remoteness to Ethiopians had two main rhetorical purposes. As an example of extreme variations of geographical conditions and racial features, it appeared to provide evidence for hypotheses about the effects of environment on the color, features, and life-styles of peoples living in widely separated regions. Thus Aristotle attributed the woolly hair of the Ethiopians to their dry environment and the straight hair of the Scythians (a people of the far north often cited in contrast to the Ethiopians of the far south) to the effects of a moist environment.

The other rhetorical function of classical allusions to the remote Ethiopians was to illustrate the unity of mankind, the all-inclusiveness of the human community, popular prejudices to the contrary notwithstanding. Thus did the Athenian dramatist Menander argue that a person's lineage is not relevant for determining his human worth:

> Whoever by inherent nature have no worth
> These all in this take refuge—in their monuments
> And pedigrees.... The man whose natural bent is good,
> He, mother, he, though Aethiop, is nobly born.[4]

Early Christian writers drew on biblical references as well as Hellenic conventions in constructing their image of faraway Ethiopia. Saint Augustine, like many other Christian authors, considered the Queen of Sheba referred to in 1 Kings and 2 Chronicles to have been Ethiopian and associated that with New Testament statements that "she came from the uttermost parts of the earth to hear the wisdom of Solomon." Christian apologists often alluded to the remote Ethiopians to illustrate their own form of universalism. Psalm 68 proclaimed that kings would bring presents to God in Jerusalem: "Nobles shall come out of Egypt; Ethiopia shall hasten to stretch out her hands unto God." Commenting on this and a similar verse in the Psalms, Augustine argued that the name Ethiopia was used here in a figurative sense. By Ethiopia was meant all nations, for the psalmist here "chose for special mention that people which is at the ends of the earth."[5]

It was probably in the fourth or fifth century that Hebraic and Hellenic allusions to Ethiopia began to be associated with the region now called Ethiopia, whose chief political center was then at Aksum.

When Christian writers like Athanasius (295–373) and Venantius Fortunatus (530–600) celebrated the success of apostolic efforts by noting that Christian missions had been effective as far away as Scythia and Ethiopia, they may well have had Aksumite Ethiopia in mind. The royal court at Aksum was converted to Christianity by the middle of the fourth century, and Athanasius himself dispatched the first bishop of Aksum from Alexandria. Stephanus of Byzantium, a contemporary of Venantius, showed a similar inclination to associate classical images of faraway Ethiopia with the kingdom of Aksum. In his geographical encyclopedia the *Ethnikon* he uses the Homeric phrase, *eschatoi andron,* to describe the Ethiopians, but he also records that Aksum was the capital city of Ethiopia.

The image of remote Ethiopia persisted long after the world had been mapped and the source of the Nile discovered. From the nineteenth century on, Ethiopia was considered remote in two new ways. As Western institutions changed at an accelerating rate and distances were compressed, Ethiopia came to seem removed in time as she became closer in space. Many visistors described themselves as being transported into a biblical era. Others called Ethiopia a gate into the medieval world. The current accessibility of Ethiopia by jet is advertised as an opportunity to "travel to a distant time."

Still another convention developed, that of viewing Ethiopia as remote from understanding. She was frequently portrayed as basically unknown, if not in some fundamental sense unknowable. More than one book about Ethiopia featured the word "unknown" in its title. As early as 1844 a correspondent from Cairo had written that "if Abyssinia does not become one of the most well-known countries of the world, it won't be due to the lack of interest of Europeans in this country, as for years there has been a continuous flow of travelers to this land."[6] Even so, a quarter of a century later John Hotten asserted that "about no part of the habitable world has there been such prolonged misconception and ignorance as about . . . Abyssinia."[7] A kindred point was made a century later in the preface to Dame Marjery Perham's *The Government of Ethiopia*: " 'It is a country' it was said to me by one who knows it very well, 'of which it is impossible to speak the truth.' "

Ethiopia the Pious

Three passages in the Homeric epics depict the Olympian gods as going off to feast with the Ethiopians. In book 1 of the *Iliad,* Zeus, followed by all the gods, departs for twelve days to visit the "blameless Ethiopians." Later, the goddess Iris goes by herself to the land of the Ethiopians to participate in their sacrificial rites to the immortal gods. And in the *Odyssey,* the god Poseidon "lingered delighted at the banquet side" of the far-off Ethiopians.

The Homeric pattern of portraying Ethiopians as close to the gods or of an especially pious nature is found in many later writings—pagan, Jewish, Christian, and Muslim. This image too persists despite the vague geographical identity of the subject, whether Ethiopia is taken to mean all of Black Africa, the Nubia of Napata and Meroe, the Abyssinia of Aksum, or the later Christian kingdom of Nubia. It appears in generalized descriptions and in accounts of individuals.

Diodorus Siculus, the first-century B.C. Greek historian, writes at length in this vein. Hercules and Bacchus, he notes, were "awed by the piety of the [Ethiopian] people." With no apparent incredulity Diodorus reports the Ethiopian belief that they were the first to institute religious worship, solemn assemblies, sacrifices, and other customs used to honor the gods; and that their own sacrifices were the most acceptable of all to the gods.[8] Six centuries later Stephanus of Byzantium, for whom Aksum was the capital of Ethiopia, reiterates the belief that Ethiopians were the first to introduce the worship of the gods. And one of Stephanus's contemporaries, Lactantius Placidus, elaborates:

> Certainly [the Ethiopians] are loved by the gods because of justice. This even Homer indicates in the first book by the fact that Jupiter frequently leaves heaven and feasts with them because of their justice and the equity of their customs. For the Ethiopians are said to be the justest men and for that reason the gods leave their abode frequently to visit them.[9]

An image of just and pious Ethiopians is also conveyed by the way individual Ethiopians are usually depicted in ancient literature. Both Herodotus and Diodorus mention that Sabacos, the first Nubian ruler over Egypt—in the Twenty-fifth, or "Ethiopian," Dynasty—replaced the death penalty with an order to have Egyptian offenders serve time in communal work projects. Diodorus describes Sabacos the Ethiopian as one who exceeded all his predecessors in showing homage to the gods and kindness to his subjects. Herodotus presents a vignette of another upright Ethiopian ruler. Confronting spies sent by Cambyses before his ill-fated invasion attempt, the Ethiopian king rebukes them with a small sermon: "You are liars, and that king of yours is a bad man. Had he any respect for what is right, he would not have coveted any other kingdom than his own, nor made slaves of a people who have done him no wrong."[10]

The only Ethiopian represented in any detail in the Old Testament is likewise portrayed as a man of high moral character. Ebed-melech, an Ethiopian officer at the court of King Zedekiah, responds with compassion upon hearing that Jeremiah had been cast into a pit and takes all steps necessary to liberate the prophet.[11] Noble character types also appear in later secular literature about Ethiopians. The protagonists of *Aethiopika,* the third century romance by Heliodorus —a book which had a great vogue during the Renaissance—are portrayed as particularly pious and just. Perhaps influenced by associations with *Aethiopika* Samuel Johnson depicted Prince Rasselas as an ingenuously upright and just young man, and had one of his countrymen observe that "oppression is, in the Abissinian dominion, neither frequent nor tolerated."[12]

Many Muslim references to Ethiopians are in a similar vein. A work of the highest standing in Islamic tradition, the *Sira* or biography of Muhammad by Ibn Hisham, reports that Muhammad advised his followers who were being persecuted by the Quraish in Mecca that "if you go to Abyssinia you will find a king under whom none are persecuted. It is a land of righteousness where God will give you relief from what you are suffering."[13] Muslim legends further impute piety to the Ethiopian king by saying that he declared his belief in the Prophet's mission, and several Muslim writers have eulogized the character of the Abyssinians.

Whereas these Muslim references are clearly to Aksumite Ethiopia, Christian references tended to confuse Ethiopia or Abyssinia with both Nubia and India for nearly a thousand years. Such ambiguity was reinforced by the conversion of three new Nubian kingdoms to Christianity in the latter half of the sixth century and by contemporary European ignorance about northeast Africa after the Muslim conquests of the seventh century. Late fourth-century references to Ethiopian monks may well pertain to men from the Aksumite kingdom, however, since at that time Aksum alone had been converted and monastic culture spread quickly in the Ethiopian highlands. Rufinus and Palladius reported seeing Ethiopians among the monks in the desert of Scetis in Northern Egypt and noted that many of them "excelled in virtue." One of the most celebrated Fathers of the Desert whom they describe, a tall Ethiopian named Moses, became widely known as a model of Christian virtue. One text which extols him, an anonymous Byzantine Menologion, states that the Kingdom of Heaven is not closed "to Scythian or Ethiopian. This can be seen in the case of very many others but especially in the case of Moses the Ethiopian. . . . This man whose body was black had a soul more radiantly bright than the splendor of the sun."[14]

It is likely that monks from Aksumite Ethiopia had traveled to Jerusalem from the fifth century onward. About the year 400 Saint Jerome mentioned Ethiopia as one of the countries from which monks were being welcomed daily in the Holy Land. From the thirteenth century, the continuing presence of communities of Ethiopian monks in Palestine is securely established. A number of medieval European travelers to the Holy Land reported that the Ethiopians possessed important Christian sanctuaries, including the chapel of Saint Mary of Golgotha adjacent to the Church of the Holy Sepulchre and an altar in the basilica of the Holy Sepulchre itself. Because of the rigor of their ascetic practices and the enthusiasm with which they performed the rites, Ethiopians were viewed by a number of such visitors as "the most pious of all the monks" in Jerusalem.[15] Such notices contributed to a more general image of Ethiopia as an isolated African country devoted to upholding the Christian faith. It was with this image in mind that King Henry IV of England wrote to the king of Abyssinia in 1400:

> Therefore, great Prince, we do most truly rejoice in the Lord, and give thanks to Jesus Christ, in that He has thought fit to enlarge His Church, as we hope, through the devout faith of so great a Prince and his subjects.[16]

A Magnificent Kingdom

A few passages from the classical writers suggest a contrasting image of Ethiopia—that of a significant worldly power. Pliny the Elder considered that Ethiopia had been a major power in archaic times, that it was "famous and powerful" until the Trojan wars and had formerly dominated Syria and the Mediterranean coasts. Speaking of his own times, Diodorus described Nubian Ethiopia as a wealthy and well-run polity, full of rich gold mines and ruled by powerful kings who governed by principles upheld by their devoted and deferential subjects.

Aksumite Ethiopia clearly had a reputation for being a particularly impressive state. In the latter part of the third century Mani wrote that Aksum ranked third among the great powers of the world. In Byzantium the Aksumite ruler was referred to with the rarely used honorific title *basileus*. To many Byzantine emperors Ethiopia appeared a most desirable ally. Constantius II (335–61) strove to win the Ethiopians to his side in doctrinal disputes against Patriarch Athanasius. A more successful bid for collaboration was broached by Justin I (518–27), who persuaded the Aksumite king Kaleb to go to the rescue of groups of Christians being persecuted by a South Arabian prince who had adopted the Jewish faith. Justin's successor, Justinian (527–65), sent embassies to enlist Ethiopia's aid against Persia. One of these embassies described the Ethiopian court in glowing terms: the Aksumite monarch was attended by councillors carrying gilded spears and shields and surveyed his subjects from a gold-encased, four-wheeled chariot drawn by a team of four elephants. Emperor Heraclius (575–641), faced with the threat of a Persian invasion, dispatched vessels containing a large part of his treasury to the Ethiopian kingdom for safekeeping.

The rise of Islam was to add luster to the image of Ethiopia's magnificence. Although the Arab expansion cut off communication between Ethiopia and Europe, Crusaders and other European travelers to Palestine collected and circulated stories about the Abyssinian kingdom. The imagined potency of this realm and her desirability as an ally grew phenomenally in the thirteenth and fourteenth centuries. Projecting an alliance between Ethiopia and the Crusaders, Guillaume Adam, a Dominican bishop, described the Ethiopians as *gens maxima atque potens,* a very great and powerful people, divided into five kingdoms that were so strong that one of them would be sufficient to vanquish Egypt. Niccolò da Poggibonsi reported that the sultan of Egypt feared the ruler of Ethiopia, for the latter was "the greatest Sovereign in the world." Some accounts stressed that Ethiopia controlled access to the Indian Ocean through her strategic position on the Red Sea. More often the Ethiopian king's presumed control over the headwaters of the Nile was emphasized. Some thought Ethiopia could subject Egypt to drought by withholding the Nile waters, while others fancied that the Ethiopian ruler could speed them up and inflict a flood on the Egyptians at will. The belief that the Ethiopian kingdom was particularly potent by virtue of its control over the Nile had a long career, persisting in some quarters well into the twentieth century.

The medieval image of Ethiopia as a potent ally was inflated by its confluence with a remarkable legend. The legend originated in the twelfth century, when Crusaders brought back stories about a fabulously wealthy oriental kingdom ruled by Prester John, an isolated Christian monarch battling against the infidel. In 1165 a letter purportedly sent from this priest-king was received by a number of European rulers, including the Byzantine Comnenus I and Frederick Barbarossa. These stories and letters sustained a widely shared fantasy. Prester John lived in an enchanted palace, with a magic mirror in front where he could see his vast dominions at a glance. Hundreds of counts and dukes waited on him; his butler was an archbishop, his chief cook a king. He wielded an emerald scepter and wore robes woven by salamanders and washed in fire. In his dominion there was no poverty, avarice, or strife.

At first the medieval imagination located this fabulous kingdom in Asia—now in India, now in Persia, now in China. In the 1320s, however, it began to be associated with Ethiopia, the country whose pilgrims were known from the Holy Land but whose location remained obscure. For the next two centuries geographers, historians, and chivalric poets indulged at length in portrayals of Ethiopia as the land of Prester John. The most noted Italian poet of the early Renaissance, Ludovico Ariosto, had one of his heroes soar over France, Spain, and North Africa to land in Ethiopia for a visit to the palace of Prester John (Preteianni). The chains of its drawbridges were made of gold, its columns of limpid crystal. Its ceilings and walls were studded with pearls and its rooms divided by floor lines of rubies, sapphires, and topaz. The Prester's land was the source of balsam, musk, and amber.[17]

Thanks to the legend of Prester John, Ethiopia once again became a coveted ally for European rulers long after the impulse to join her forces with the Crusaders was spent. It became the great passion of a number of Portuguese kings to reach Ethiopia and locate Prester John's realm. Portugal then could secure an invaluable post for its trade to the East as well as a strong ally in its constant battle against the Moors. Guided by this image of Ethiopia, Portuguese navigators went forth to explore the oceans.

Similar notions about Ethiopia as the land of Prester John inspired the head of the Catholic church. A medieval chronicler wrote that the pope was beside himself with joy upon learning that an Ethiopian embassy was on its way to Italy to attend the Council of Florence in 1441. The pope even recommended moving the council to Rome, so that the splendid embassy sent by the high and mighty emperor of Ethiopia should find the council sitting not in such a "paltry" town as Florence, but in the greatest metropolis of the Christian world. As concordats had recently been signed between the Roman Catholic church and the Greek and Armenian Orthodox churches, the pope was anxious to obtain a similar agreement with Prester John, who, in prestige and renown, was then surpassed by no other Christian prince. So tenacious was this image that although a European mission in the 1520s spent six years in Ethiopia without finding a trace of "Prester John," the report of the mission was entitled *Truthful Information about the Countries of Prester John of the Indies!*

The legend of the Queen of Sheba provided still another motif to embellish the Western image of Ethiopia as a fabulous kingdom. From Shakespeare to Kipling and Yeats, from Handel to Gounod, from the paintings of Piero della Francesca and Tintoretto to the doors of Ghiberti and the windows of King's College chapel at Cambridge, the story of the sojourn of the wealthy Ethiopian queen at the court of King Solomon has stirred the imagination of numerous European artists and audiences.

The flurry of international attention excited by the exploits of Emperor Menilek in the 1890s gave new life to the fabulous kingdom image. In that decade, as Harold Marcus has shown, several European writers sought to contrast Ethiopia with the rest of Africa by extolling it in superlative terms. Ethiopia was described as "a civilized nation of an immense intelligence, the only one that is civilized without wearing trousers and shoes." Its citizens were lauded as devoted patriots, its noblemen as exceptionally valorous in war and magnanimous and polite in victory. Emperor Menilek was variously depicted as a prophet, a genius, a man of "almost superhuman activity" and "astonishing" energy, and one "extraordinarily well acquainted with what is going on in the world, not only from a political, but from a general and even scientific point of view."[18] Comparable language has been used by many foreign writers to glorify the reign of Emperor Haile Sellassie I.

Savage Abyssinia

In addition to his picture of the just and pious Ethiopians of Meroe and the regions near Egypt, Diodorus sketched a set of vignettes of "the other Ethiopian nations" which he located on both sides of the Nile farther south. Most of these people, he wrote, "are entirely savage and display the nature of a wild beast. . . . They are squalid all over their bodies, keep their nails very long like the wild beasts, and are as far removed as possible from human kindness to one another; . . . and they cultivate none of the practices of civilized life as these are found among the rest of mankind."[19] Strabo held that the lives of people far removed from the temperate zone would be defective and inferior: this was clear from the modes of life of Ethiopians and their lack of human necessities. Strabo noted that one of the southernmost Ethiopian peoples was "poorly equipped for any kind of life and often, like brigands, would attack defenseless persons."[20]

Images of this sort occasionally surface in commentaries by early Christian writers. Commenting on a verse in the Psalms, "Ethiopians shall bow down before him, and his enemies shall lick the dust,"[21] Saint Augustine states that the universality of the Christian message is implied here, for it is to reach even unto the Ethiopians, whom he describes as "the remotest and most hideous of men."[22]

A number of Latin geographers, including Pliny, Solinus, and Pomponius Mela, followed their imaginations further in this direction and described Ethiopia as a land of fearful monsters. Drawing freely on these Latin authors, medieval cartogaphers depicted on maps of Ethiopia such monstrous creatures as the Blemmyes, with mouth and eyes placed in their breasts; the Himantopodes, who creep on all fours instead of walking; the Gangines Ethiopians, among whom friendship is not known; and the one-eyed king of the Agriophagi Ethiopians, who live on the flesh of panthers and lions.

When in the 1520s Europeans reached the Ethiopian highlands to see for themselves, however, they found and described a civilization at about the same level as their own. With keen admiration Alvarez describes Ethiopian architecture and painting and the Ethiopian system of justice, and he duly records the aversion of Ethiopians to such crude European customs as spitting in church. Almeida's narrative of a century later includes some secondhand reports of "barbarous customs" of some Ethiopian tribes, notably the Janjero, but the general tone of his account is appreciative, and he describes the Ethiopians as "very amenable to reason and justice . . . intelligent and good-natured . . . mild, gentle, kind, and so inclined to forgiveness that they readily pardon any injuries."[23]

Visiting in the late eighteenth century, a much more troubled time, James Bruce was so repulsed by the civil strife and bloodshed he witnessed that eventually he became obsessed with thoughts about "how to escape from this bloody country." He also wrote of observing a "bloody banquet," in which Ethiopians cut and devoured pieces of meat from living cattle. Yet so ingrained was the European disposition against viewing Ethiopia as a savage place that Bruce earned a bad name among his contemporaries because they refused to believe his gory accounts.

It was indeed only in the latter half of the nineteenth century that the image of highland Ethiopia as a savage place gained any currency, as European attitudes toward Africa hardened into arrogant ethnocentrism at best and a vicious exploitative ethnocentrism at worst.[24] Major Cornwallis Harris set the tone for this new orientation in the 1840s by describing the Amhara as "abject slaves to superstition," possessed by unscrupulous greed and possessing "neither amusements nor intellectual resources." Although he characterized King Sahle Sellassie of Shoa as a merciful, charitable, and just ruler, Harris also noted that one of the reasons the king went to war was "the insatiable love of plunder inherent in the breast of every savage."[25]

Later writers in this vein failed to match Harris's breadth of interest and balanced, if ethnocentric, reporting. Colonel William Winstanley of the Fourth (Queen's Own) Hussars flatly declared the Ethiopians to be "an uncultivated mass of mingled race . . . imbued with the characteristics distinguishing the least civilized beings."[26] A similar point of view was expressed by the Italian delegation which successfully opposed the admission of Ethiopia to the International Postal Union in 1895 on grounds that it was a "nation of primitive tribesmen led by a barbarian."[27] Lord Hindlip felt that "the Abyssinian above all things excels in cruelty, both to mankind and animals." He agreed with those who argued that "there are moral considerations which should compel all the civilized people of the world to lend their support to the crushing out of the Abyssinian power, and the substitution of a humane government in the place of Menelik's rule."[28]

This image was revived in the years after World War I, that epitome of civilized conduct, by groups in England which became alarmed by the extent of the slave trade in Ethiopia, partly for general humanitarian reasons and partly for fear that people were being abducted into slavery from British-ruled Kenya. These concerns were expressed in a series of articles that appeared in the *Westminster Gazette* and *West Africa* in 1922. A decade later, in order to build up a case for its unprovoked aggression against Ethiopia, the Italian government generated propaganda designed to prove that Ethiopia was indeed so savage, primitive, and disorganized that modern sensibilities required intervention by a European power to carry out a "civilizing mission."

A Bastion of African Independence

The ancients also had a conception of Ethiopia as a proud and independent country. Diodorus, speaking of Nubian Ethiopia, writes:

> And [the Ethiopians] say . . . that they were never brought into subjection by a foreign prince, but always remained a free people, at perfect peace among themselves. And though many, and those most potent princes likewise, have invaded, yet none have succeeded in their attempts. For Cambyses, making in upon them with mighty forces, was in danger both to have lost his life and his whole army. And Semiramis, who was so famous both for her skill and success in arms, having entered but a little way into Ethiopia, presently saw it was to no purpose to think of conquering that nation.[29]

The Nubian kingdom did remain proud and independent—until it was vanquished by Aksum, the new Ethiopia. In the middle of the fourth century A.D. the Aksumites made their last and decisive invasion of Kush and destroyed its capital at Meroe.

In consequence, they eventually inherited not only the name of Ethiopia but also the reputation for being an independent polity. Thus a seventeenth-century Portuguese historian, Luis de Urreta, explained (erroneously) the meaning of the name Abyssinia by saying that *Abassia* meant "a free and independent people (in Arabic, Turkish, and the language of the Ethiopians), who had never recognized a foreign king; such is the land of Ethiopia, as we shall relate."[30]

The image of Ethiopia as a bastion of African independence became particularly widespread in the late nineteenth century. While peoples all over Africa were being subjugated by foreign powers, Ethiopians were winning victories over a series of invaders. From their victories over invading Egyptians in the 1870s, over Sudanese Mahdists in the 1880s, and over Italians in the 1890s, Ethiopians gained a reputation as spirited fighters determined to maintain their sovereignty. It was the last of these victories in particular, that at Adwa in 1896, which called Ethiopia to world attention and prompted European states to set up diplomatic missions in Addis Ababa. The defeat of the Italians at Adwa initiated a decade of negotiations with European powers in which nine border treaties were signed.

From that time forward the image of Ethiopia the Independent was cherished increasingly by Africans and Afro-Americans. In 1892, the efforts of some Bantu Christian leaders to emancipate themselves from the authority of European missions led to the formation of an independent Black South African denomination named the Ethiopian church. In the original use of this name Ethiopia referred to all black Africans, a usage inspired by allusions to Ethiopia in Psalms and in Acts—promises of the evangelization of Africa. Later, however, leaders of the Ethiopian church movement interpreted the nomenclature to signify that the Independent church enjoyed not only the biblical apostolic succession but also a link with an actual independent Christian African monarchy.

The victory at Adwa stimulated the energies of South African blacks in the early years of the Ethiopia movement. One of its principal leaders, James Dwane, wrote Emperor Menilek asking him to look into the condition of Christian Africans in Egypt and the Sudan, and attempted to collect funds to support this cause. The image of independent Ethiopia spread so widely among the Zulus and other tribes that by 1935–36 nightly prayer meetings on behalf of Ethiopia in Natal and Zululand attracted thousands of new followers, and churches were founded with such names as the Melchizedek Ethiopian Catholic Church and the Coptic Ethiopian Church Orthodox of Abyssinia.[31]

For many secular leaders of colonial Africa, moreover, the image of independent Ethiopia was a powerful beacon and frequent source of inspiration. Nnamdi Azikiwe perceived it in this manner:

> Ethiopia is the last vestige of black autocracy. It represents the type of government which the forefathers of Africans established on this continent. . . . The continued existence of Ethiopia after its contemporaries and their descendants had vanished from political history is, and should be, an object of admiration.[32]

The threat to this symbol posed by the Italian invasion so upset Kwame Nkrumah, he recalls in his *Autobiography,* that he became motivated to work for the day when he might play a part in bringing an end to so wicked a system as colonialism. Jomo Kenyatta spoke for many Africans when he projected Ethiopia's response to the invasion: "Ethiopia, with her Emperor leading, relies on her soldiers, her courage, her traditions. There will be no concessions; Ethiopia will fight, as she always has fought, to preserve her independence against this encroachment of Imperialism."[33] Together with J. B. Danquah of the Gold Coast, Mohammed Said of Somaliland, George Padmore of

Jamaica, and others, Kenyatta formed the International African Friends of Abyssinia, a group which subsequently provided the leadership for convening the Pan-African Congress at Manchester in 1945.

Ethiopia the Independent was likewise an image to reckon with among black Americans in the West Indies and the United States. Quite as the cause of Afro-American self-assertion in the 1960s derived moral support from models of the newly independent states of black Africa, its forerunner of the 1920s was inspired by the independent kingdom of Ethiopia. Marcus Garvey stimulated the formation of a number of semireligious cults, chiefly in the West Indies, oriented to a renewed identification with Africa. Some of these took the name of "Ethiopians" and others adopted the current name of the future Haile Sellassie I by calling themselves the Rastafarians. Assertions of black pride in the United States in the 1920s occasionally took the form of a yearning to return to Africa. A group of black Americans did in fact journey back to Africa in that decade and settled in Ethiopia. Unlike Afro-Americans who went to other parts of Africa, they went not as missionaries, to convert and to teach, but in search of a homeland, to assimilate Ethiopian culture and establish roots.

Many segments of the Afro-American community responded passionately to the 1935–36 Italian invasion. An editorial in *Opportunity: A Journal of Negro Life* observed that "Ethiopia has become the spiritual fatherland of Negroes throughout the world, and from Bahia to Birmingham, and from New York to Nigeria, peoples of African descent have been stirred to unparalleled unity of thought."[34] George Edmund Haynes asserted that "Ethiopia, 'proud and free,' has become to thinking Negroes of African descent the symbol of the aspirations of black people for independence, for self-determination, and the assimilation of all that is best in modern civilization."[35] And as early as November 1935, in the *Afro-American,* W. E. B. Du Bois called the Italian attack a turning point in the history of darker groups and prophesied that it would be the last time when white men would fight, invade, and annex "colored" nations almost at will.

2

Scholarly Images and Assumptions

The images of Ethiopia surveyed in the last chapter have played a significant role at various points in world history. Notions of Ethiopia as the farthermost land in the world were invoked to advance the universalistic ideas of Greek philosophers and early Christian apologists. Muslim beliefs that Abyssinia was a just and pious country exonerated Ethiopia from the holy wars of early Islamic expansion, giving Christian Ethiopia a chance to build her strength so she could resist the Muslim onslaught when it came several centuries later—resistance which checked the sweep of Islam across Africa. The image of the fabulous kingdom of Prester John helped inspire Portuguese navigators to embark on voyages of discovery around Africa. The picture of Ethiopia as a savage place undermined the readiness of Europeans to condemn the first major fascist aggression preceding the Hitler war. The symbolism of independent Ethiopia gave hope to oppressed Africans and Afro-Americans and support to their freedom movements.

As sources of enlightenment about the Ethiopian experience, however, these images must be treated with caution. They tell less about Ethiopian realities than they do about the history of the world outside. All these images, to be sure, have had some grounding in actual observations, and all have their counterpart in the traditional beliefs Ethiopians have about themselves and their relations to outsiders; but they have never been liberated from some admixture of poetic fancy, religious aspiration, or political ambition. The Viennese classicist Albin Lesky has brilliantly analyzed the way ancient Greek conceptions of Ethiopia illustrate "that interweaving of mythical representation and rational knowledge that pervades Greek intellectual history."[1] The mythical component in foreign images of Ethiopia has shown great durability indeed. As we have seen, the basic ideas about Ethiopia that have circulated in the last two thousand years were all adumbrated in the compilations of Diodorus Siculus in the first century B.C.; and he, after all, was not even talking about the same country.

For a sound comprehension of the Ethiopian experience we must turn to a different set of images. These have emerged from efforts to relate the understanding of Ethiopia to modern developments in the scholarly disciplines.

Foundations for the disciplined study of Ethiopian society and culture were laid by two sets of travelers in the sixteenth and seventeenth centuries. On several missions to Ethiopia sent by the kings of Portugal and the popes at Rome, a number of Portuguese and Spanish clergymen collected basic information on the languages, cultures, and history of the country. During the same period small numbers of Ethiopian monks were making their way to Rome, some from Jerusalem and some directly from Ethiopia. They settled in a hospice established for them at the Vatican by Pope Sixtus IV (1471–84), near the Chapel of Santo Stefano just behind Saint Peter's Cathedral. From this center they taught interested Europeans about their languages and literature and assisted with the composition of the first Ge'ez [Ethiopic] grammars, dictionaries, and texts which were published at Rome, Antwerp, and Göttingen.

Thanks to these two groups, scholars acquired a reliable fund of factual information about Ethiopia. Introducing his translation of the first of the Portuguese records he published in Venice in 1550, the Italian humanist Ramusio exclaimed: "The journey Don Francesco Alvarez describes to the court of this great prince called Prester John deserves to be spoken of at length, for until now there has been nothing to read about the country of Ethiopia by the Greeks or Latins or any other kind of writers that is worth consideration. In his writings, such as they are, this man has to a great extent laid it open and made it clear."[2] This flourishing period of exploration and cultural exchange culminated with the work of a German scholar, Job Ludolf, commonly considered the founder of Ethiopian studies in Europe. Aided by an Ethiopian informant from Amhara province, Abba Gregorios, Ludolf compiled substantial dictionaries and grammars of both Ge'ez and Amharic and went on to construct a circumspect history of Ethiopia with an extensive commentary.

European exploration of Ethiopia virtually stopped for a century and a half after the expulsion of the Jesuits in the 1630s. It was revived by the pioneering investigations and collections of James Bruce, who was in Ethiopia from 1769 to 1771. Subsequently, in the nineteenth century a number of explorers, diplomats, geographers, and missionaries from England, France, Germany, Italy, Sweden, and Switzerland added volumes of observations and new collections of Ethiopic documents, some for publication and nearly all for preservation in European museums, archives, and libraries.

Another German scholar, August Dillmann, revitalized the scholarly tradition of Ethiopian studies in the 1850s. By the early twentieth century the study of Ethiopian culture had been institutionalized on a modest basis in a small number of academic settings in Europe and the United States. First through philology and history, then through archaeology and anthropology, and more recently through political science, sociology, and economics, Ethiopian studies have developed to the point where to say that Ethiopia is unknown or unknowable is to confess a streak of obscurantism or simple laziness.

Intellectual disciplines have their own mythical component, however. This consists of general assumptions about particular domains of experience which scholars take for granted as they busy themselves with solving specialized problems. The myths of the scholarly disciplines differ from the myths of commonsense culture in two respects: it is expected that they be related in a rigorous manner to the controlled observations and clarified concepts of the discipline and that they be subject to periodic criticism, review, and perhaps reformulation. It may be useful at this point to articulate the scholarly myths—the overarching perspectives—which have hitherto guided the world of Ethiopianist scholarship.

Three general images have dominated that world. Scholars have viewed Ethiopia primarily either as an outpost of Semitic civilization, as an ethnographic museum, or as an underdeveloped country. In this chapter I shall outline these images, examine the intellectual assumptions connected with them, and thereby prepare the way for a new image based on recent developments in sociological theory and on a fresh look at the field of Ethiopian studies.

An Outpost of Semitic Civilization

The first generations of Ethiopianist scholars saw their work chiefly as a branch of Semitic studies. They considered knowledge of Arabic, Hebrew, and Syriac the right foundation for the study of Ethiopian culture. Their academic reference group was the fraternity of Orientalist scholars; they published in such general Orientalist journals as the *Zeitschrift der deutschen morgenlandischen Gesellschaft, Journal asiatique,* and the *Rivista degli Studi Orientali.* Their contributions consisted largely of writing vocabularies and grammars of Ethiopian Semitic languages, cataloguing manuscripts, editing and translating Ethiopian texts, and examining historical source materials.

The geographical focus of these early scholars was on northern Ethiopia. Substantively their focus was on the productions of literati. Since their training was mainly in textual analysis, they naturally concentrated on Ethiopia's written traditions. Until the past few decades, moreover, few scholars anywhere were trained for the disciplined study of preliterate cultures. Their more general interests likewise favored a focus on the Semitic documents of northern Ethiopia. Some of them, like Theodore Noeldeke, Ignazio Guidi, and in our own day Marcel Cohen, have been primarily identified as comparative Semitists. Others were mainly interested in recovering archaic religious texts that had been preserved in Ethiopian Christian and Jewish monasteries.

Among the principal discoveries of this group of scholars one might mention the close relationship among the Semitic languages of northern Ethiopia—Ge'ez, Tigre, and Tigrinya; the correspondences between these and Old South Arabian languages; and other kinds of evidence linking ancient Ethiopian peoples with Sabaean and other Oriental Semitic cultures. The effect of these Semitic influences on Ethiopian languages and culture, the fact that these influences were attested by the preferred scholarly materials—written documentation—and the tendency of European scholars to affirm those aspects of Ethiopian culture which drew on Judaeo-Christian traditions produced a disposition to regard Ethiopia as an outpost of Semitic civilization.

The central features of this image are that (1) the Amhara-Tigrean peoples are identified as the "true Ethiopians" or the "Abyssinians proper," and (2) the core elements of Amhara-Tigrean culture are viewed as deriving from early Semitic influences. The consequences of this image are that Ethiopian history comes to be conceived as a process of the extension of Semitized Ethiopian culture over more and more peoples of Ethiopia; that those peoples who are not "true Abyssinians" come to be viewed as alien and inferior; and that little or no attention is given to the non-Semitic component of Amhara-Tigrean culture and to the indigenous traditions of other Ethiopian peoples.

Of recent works which embody this image most extensively, *The Ethiopians* by Edward Ullendorff might be mentioned. Subtitled *An Introduction to Country and People,* this work is actually an introduction to selected aspects of Amhara-Tigrean culture. Ullendorff's concern is overwhelmingly with those whom he calls "Abyssinians proper, the carriers of the historical civilization of Semitized Ethiopia, [who] live in the central and northern highlands." He holds that the Semites provide "the principal linguistic and cultural element" in highland-plateau Ethiopia.[3]

As a result, Ullendorff's treatment is skewed in favor of those aspects of Ethiopian culture which reflect Semitic influence. His chapter on religion devotes eighteen pages to Ethiopian religions of Semitic provenance—Christianity, Judaism, and Islam; but only one paragraph to indigenous Cushitic religions. His chapter on languages devotes only one page to the Cushitic languages, and none to the Nilo-Saharan languages, although these language families in Ethiopia exceed the Semitic languages both in number and variety and in the numbers of people speaking them. By contrast, nineteen pages are spent on the Semitic languages of Ethiopia, "since they express the 'real' Abyssinia as we know it and are the virtually exclusive carriers of Ethiopian civilization, literature, and intellectual prestige."[4] Similarly, the chapter on literature deals exclusively with Ge'ez and Amharic literature, with nary a reference to available collections of Somali poetry and Galla folk literature.

The image of Ethiopia as a Semitic outpost has informed and inspired most of the best scholarship on Ethiopia to date. Indeed, the areas which Ullendorff does include in his survey are treated with the care and polish of accomplished humanistic scholarship. In somewhat different form, this image also pervades J. Spencer Trimingham's pathbreaking survey *Islam in Ethiopia.* Moreover, this image has largely dominated what little instruction on Ethiopian culture has been available in American, British, French, German, and Russian universities.[5]

Although it continues to be useful for certain limited purposes, the Semitic outpost image suffers two serious limitations as a general orientation to Ethiopian culture. With respect to empirical adequacy, it neglects the crucial role of non-Semitic elements in Ethiopian culture. With respect to its implicit and often explicit normative assumptions, it shares the difficulties of all views which consider cultures with written traditions and world religions to be *generally* superior to nonliterate cultures.

An Ethnic Museum

Another image of Ethiopia is conveyed by the memorable phrase of one of the greatest of all Ethiopianists, Carlo Conti-Rossini, who described the country as *un museo di popoli.* The view of Ethiopia as a museum of peoples is implicit in the work of a number of anthropologists who have worked in the country. The chief assumptions associated with this view are (1) that Ethiopia is a country of extraordinary ethnic diversity, and (2) that each of its diverse peoples deserves to be studied intensively, on its own terms, as bearer of a bounded system and a unique culture.

Whereas proponents of the first perspective were largely products of the German universities of the late nineteenth century, those of the second sprang mainly from Anglo-American universities of the mid-twentieth. The geographical focus of the latter has been mainly on peoples in the southern parts of the country, and their substantive focus has been mostly on the social organization of discrete tribes. Their contribution has been to provide basic ethnographies of the relatively unknown peoples of these areas. Within the last fifteen years sustained fieldwork by a number of young scholars has produced a valuable set of intensive studies of the Dasenech and the Dorze; the Borana, Guji, Jimma, and Mecha Galla; the Gurage, Kafa, Konso, Sidamo, and Wolamo; the Harari and Somali; the Majangir and the Kimant; as well as of a number of Amhara and Tigrean communities in the northern provinces.

The accomplishments of this group by no means exhaust the ethnographic literature on Ethiopia. Information from earlier travelers and scholars was collated in volumes of the *Ethnographic Survey of Africa* published by the International African Institute. More substantial surveys, based on expeditions from the Frobenius Institut in the 1950s, appeared in the three volumes of *Völker Süd-Äthiopiens.* But the image of Ethiopia and related assumptions I am concerned with here belong primarily not to the surveyist but to the scholar who spends a long period of time investigating a single people, learning their language, assimilating some of their habits, and attempting to construct in depth a representation of their social system as a functioning whole.

I refer, in short, to the intellectual orientation of the modal Anglo-American anthropologist, staunchly antievolutionary and still more or less committed to the doctrine of cultural relativism. This doctrine holds that every culture is as valid as any other; that any cultural complex is to be examined not with respect to a presumed hierarchy of forms, but in relation to other institutions of the culture and their contributions to the group's adaptation to is environment. The Sidamo or the Dasenech, in this view, are not to be regarded as Abyssinians manqué because they lack a written tradition or a world religion, but as bearers of perfectly valid cultures in their own right.

The thrust of this view is to look for a self-sufficient, bounded system. Radical impairment of the system's integrity is viewed as pathological. Relationships with other groups outside the system are considered peripherally, if at all. More often than not, when the group is related to other groups it is not to other Ethiopians but to more distant peoples. In *A Galla Monarchy,* for example, Herbert Lewis compares the Jimma Galla with other African kingdoms like Buganda and Ashanti much more often than he relates them to other Galla tribes. Although comparisons of this sort are of course legitimate and often highly illuminating, they do tend to reinforce the assumption that the unit being compared is a self-contained, integral system.

Although the assumptions of cultural autonomy and uniqueness on the one hand and cultural relativism on the other have inspired anthropologists to create a rich library of ethnographic monographs, applying these assumptions to groups which belong to a wider system of relationships, as most groups do, tends to be misleading. To see Ethiopia as a mosaic of distinct peoples is to overlook the many features they have in common and the existence of discernable culture areas, and to ignore the numerous relationships these groups have had with one another. In particular, it leads to the erroneous view that before the conquests of Menilek II in the late nineteenth century the other peoples of Ethiopia had lived independent and self-sufficient lives, a view implicit in the opening lines of *A Galla Monarchy.* And it fails to provide any leverage for getting at the properties of the larger Ethiopian system directly. To assume that intensive study of each individual group in Ethiopia will produce a valid picture of the whole is no less futile than was the assumption of W. Lloyd Warner and his students that a reliable picture of American society could be drawn from a series of intensive studies of diverse local communities. In sum, the image of Ethiopia as a collection of distinct peoples neglects what these peoples have in common, how they interact, and the nature of Ethiopian society as a whole.

Once one begins to consider these questions, moreover, the assumption of cultural relativism must be discarded. Although it may no longer be valid to rank all cultures by a single set of criteria, it is perfectly valid to rate different aspects and dimensions of culture with respect to a variety of specific criteria. In considering the respective contributions of diverse cultures to a larger whole, valuations of this sort become indispensable. Some contribute in one area, some in another. Some contribute little, some much.

An Underdeveloped Country

In scholarly writings on Ethiopia during the last decade a third image has emerged. This is most likely to appear in work by economists, sociologists, and political scientists. Like the two images previously discussed, it has a solid empirical basis. Whereas the other views were grounded on the substantial Semitic influence upon Ethiopian civilization and on the remarkable cultural diversity of its peoples, this view starts with an assessment of Ethiopian conditions relative to more economically and politically developed nations. Finding that Ethiopia ranks low by the standard indexes of modernization—per capita income, health care, literacy, occupational differentiation, and the like—it portrays Ethiopia as a particularly "underdeveloped" country.

The geographical focus of this view is primarily on the central part of the country—Shoa province and its capital, Addis Ababa—and on the larger towns. Substantively it deals with the modernizing sector of the society, especially the school system, the modern economic sectors, and the central government. Proponents of this view have been few, but they have contributed to a basic mapping of some of the main points of change and problems connected with Ethiopia's halting movement toward economic development and social mobilization. They include studies on the modernization of Ethiopia's central administration; the weaknesses of the system of education and manpower development; and the counterproductive types of personal relationships found in Ethiopian firms and factories.

Disciplined research of this sort in Ethiopia is still at a rudimentary stage. Although much remains to be done, the limitations of the image of Ethiopia as an underdeveloped country ought also to be kept in mind. It disposes one to view Ethiopia not on her own terms but as a modern society manqué. The key point of reference is the experience of modernized societies, and Ethiopian realities are examined in relation to American or European standards. This focus on the center entails a neglect of the traditional sectors where most Ethiopians still live in ways that remain little understod. The focus on certain criteria of progress neglects the ways Ethiopia's past experience is reflected in her present and ignores sources of satisfaction available in her customary life. Such orientations unduly discredit the Ethiopian experience, leading to statements like that of Ernest Luther, who, from the viewpoint of a modern banker, finds the Ethiopians "remarkably uncreative."[6] With respect to innovative procedures and policies, moreover, it sometimes leads to artifically imposed forms which do not relate successfully to Ethiopia as a living system. A notable case in point has been the establishment of a supermodern set of civil and penal codes which do not take into account the existing forms of customary law.

A Complex Evolving System

The disciplined study of Ethiopian culture has made it possible to replace the various conventional images discussed in chapter 1 with more firmly grounded conceptions. Each of the latter has been connected with fruitful research and remains valid for future work, given the particular purposes associated with these conceptions—to study the diffusion and forms of Semitic civilization, the characteristics of a variety of distinct traditional cultures, or the problems and processes of modernization.

None of those purposes, however, is that of developing a holistic conception of the Ethiopian experience. For that, each of them is marked by characteristic deficiencies, as I have indicated. These deficiencies are not, of course, exclusively those of Ethiopian studies but are inherent in the general modes of scholarly orientation to all cultural studies. The classical orientation to the study of Great Traditions focuses on the great feats of moral action and literary expression in some exemplary cultural climate. Past cultural achievements are considered as standards of excellence against which other cultural expressions are measured and often found wanting. To some extent this orientation entails an idealization of the past.

The modernist orientation to the study of human societies focuses on certain rationalized ideals, such as egalitarian justice and scientific mastery, and the institutional arrangements and mechanisms of change needed to implement them. Such ideals provide categories of measurement in terms of which present and past societies are analyzed—categories like extent of literacy and spread of income distribution. This orientation tends to idealize the future.

The cultural relativist orientation entails no transcendent standards for societies other than the purely formal ones connected with system integrity and wholeness. Assuming that all societies in the ethnographic present are equal, it tends to idealize the here and now.

All three orientations thus exhibit characteristic normative and empirical blind spots. I have conceptualized them as pure logical types so that the rationale and structure of these orientations can be seen clearly and so that the "mythical" component of the related images may be visible.

Some scholars fit into this typology less easily than others. A few Ethiopianists have contributed importantly to our knowledge of both Semitized and non-Semitized Ethiopian cultures. Franz Praetorious composed a masterly grammar of the Gallinya language as well as grammars of Ge'ez, Tigrinya, and Amharic. Carlo Conti-Rossini wrote on the language and history of the Central Cushites as well as on numerous aspects of Amhara-Tigrean history and culture. Enrico Cerulli has carried out exemplary historical, linguistic, and ethnographic studies concerning virtually every part of the country. The work of some recent anthropologists, including Allan Hoben, Asmarom Legesse, and William Shack, has been marked by sensitivity both to the problems of national integration and to the impact of processes of modernization.

Despite these and other exceptions, it is fair to say that Ethiopian studies for the most part fall into the three types of orientation defined in this chapter, orientations epitomized by and inherent in the professional scholarly orientations of the Semitic philologist, the social anthropologist, and the development economist. Two possible ways of dealing with the shortcomings of these orientations are ignoring them and combining them. One can, on the one hand, eschew any conception at all, in the vain hope that facts will speak for themselves. But useful though factual compendia may be, they cannot generate that economical reconceptualization of the Ethiopian experience which remains one of the outstanding tasks of Ethiopianist scholarship. In the study of total societies, as in much else, Kenneth Boulding's dictum is pertinent: "Knowledge is achieved by the orderly loss of information, not by piling bit on bit."[7]

The other approach is a studied eclecticism in which one attempts to combine all three approaches, viewing the data at different points in terms of the Semitic past, the ethnographic present, and the modernist future. To some extent I followed this approach in my own earlier work on Ethiopia, *Wax and Gold*. Combining a number of deficient views, however, is not likely to produce a satisfactory synthesis. Rather, one needs to deal directly with the intellectual difficulties of each view and discover what new conception, if any, can eliminate these difficulties in principle.

Such a conception may be drawn from recent advances in general sociological theory. I refer both to the increased clarity with which total societies have come to be conceptualized as boundary-maintaining systems of action and to the more sophisticated ways in which societal evolution can now be analyzed.[8] Using this perspective one can develop an image of Ethiopia as a complex sociocultural system that has evolved through determinate stages. The original units of this system are a great number of diverse, historically autonomous societies of small scale. The crucial feature of its evolution has been the transition, still under way, from an intersocietal system to a single societal system, thanks to the development of increased adaptive capacities in some of its units.

This conception transcends the chief limitations of the three prevailing images of Ethiopia in the following ways:

1. It constrains us to take into account all of the peoples and traditions of Ethiopia, Semitized and non-Semitized, without prejudging the properties and achievements of any.

2. It constrains us to take into account indications of commonality as well as diversity among Ethiopian peoples, interconnections as well as autonomies, centripetal as well as peripheral phenomena.

3. It constrains us to view contemporary Ethiopia not as a static, undeveloped country, but as a society at a certain point in a long developmental process, the understanding of which is indispensable to knowing her future options.

Although this conception may have great theoretical appeal, one cannot assume a priori that it will be fruitful for dealing with Ethiopian realities. Is there sufficient evidence to justify treating all of Ethiopia as a single complex system? This question must be dealt with before we can carry out an elaborate analysis which takes that conception as a guiding image.

3

The Differentiation of Peoples and Cultures

The question last raised has political overtones as well as intellectual urgency. During the last quarter of the nineteenth century a series of conquests under emperors Yohannes IV and Menilek II tripled the territory subject to the Ethiopian government, adding dozens of tribes and millions of people to the empire. Traumatic though they were for most of the peoples subjugated, these conquests have been judged beneficial in several respects: they bolstered Ethiopia's position as an independent African power, greatly reduced the intertribal warfare and brigandage that had prevailed in the conquered areas, and paved the way for bringing an end to the slave trade in Ethiopia. Even so, it is not idle to raise the question whether this imperial expansion was basically *a subjugation of alien peoples or an ingathering of peoples with deep historical affinities,* especially since many of the conquered peoples still appear to chafe under the dominion of the Ethiopian state.

The first assumption has long been the popular one. The prevailing view has been that, for better and worse, the Ethiopian Empire of the twentieth century consists of a number of previously autonomous and distinct "African" tribes subordinated under an alien Semitic minority. This view is a natural consequence of beginning Ethiopian history, as scholarly convention has had it, with the supposed Semitic immigrations of the first milliennium B.C. A different view is obtained, however, if one's perspective begins not three but six thousand years ago; not in Arabia but in Africa; not with the Semitic importations but with the Ethiopian peoples at home. Such a view may justify replacing, or at least correcting, the image of an arbitrary empire composed of numerous isolated and vastly diverse subject peoples with the image of a vast ecological area and historical arena in which kindred peoples have shared many traditions and interacted with one another for millennia. I propose to refer to this latter image as Greater Ethiopia. The present boundaries of the Ethiopian state roughly circumscribe the area in question, although some of the peoples in Greater Ethiopia now straddle the borders of Sudan, Kenya, Somalia, and French Territory of the Afars and Issas; state boundaries coincide with ecological and ethnic realities here no more than elsewhere.

Of the prehistory of Greater Ethiopia very little is known. One can only hope that archaeological work in this area will become more vigorous and extensive. It does seem to be established that by the beginning of the Late Stone Age, about 9000 B.C., there were at least two distinct tool-making cultures in the area, one specializing in small stone bladelets known as the Wilton industry, the other based on long obsidian blades known as Hargeisan. The human remains associated with both these industries appear to be of a long-headed type that has been described as Afro-Mediterranean; there is no evidence of Bushmanoid or Negroid populations in the area at that time. It is not clear when and by what processes these early peoples turned from hunting and gathering to agriculture and husbandry, but by the third millennium B.C. their successors must have done so: rock paintings of human and animal figures in Harerge and Eritrea provinces indicate the domestication of cattle, and relics of hand axes, hoes, grinding stones, and decorated pottery attributed to the late third millennium B.C. in many parts of western Ethiopia reflect the rudiments of agriculture. Some recent finds suggest that agriculture and the craft of pottery were introduced from the Sudan up the Blue Nile Valley.

The analysis of linguistic distributions suggests that the proto-Ethiopians of the third millennium B.C. spoke languages derived from a single stock, that known as Hamito-Semitic or Afro-Asiatic. This ancestral language probably originated in the eastern Sahara, before the desiccation of that region. In the 1950s it was established that Afro-Asiatic was the ancestor of five major language families: Ancient Egyptian, Berber, Chadic, Semitic, and Cushitic. More recent work by Harold Fleming and others indicates that there may be six: what previously had been classified as the Western branch of the Cushitic language family should be considered a separate language family, one that has now been given the name "Omotic."[1] Since all the Omotic languages and nearly all of the many Cushitic languages are concentrated in Greater Ethiopia, this division of what had been regarded as the single language family of Cushitic into two language families of equivalent status makes it possible to speculate that the homeland of Afro-Asiatic may have been in southwest Ethiopia.

Wherever the origins of Afro-Asiatic, it seems clear that peoples speaking proto-Cushitic and proto-Omotic separated as groups with distinct languages by the fifth or fourth millennium B.C. and began peopling the Ethiopian plateaus not long after. Proto-Semitic separated at about the same time or somewhat earlier and passed over into Asia Minor. Although it seems reasonable to follow I. M. Diakonoff in assuming that the Semitic-speakers moved from the Sahara across the Nile Delta over Sinai, so that the presence of Semitic-speaking populations in Ethiopia must be attributed to a return movement of Semitic-speakers into Africa from South Arabia, a recent paper by Gover Hudson has clearly revivified the hypotheses that Semitic separated from Afro-Asiatic *in* Ethiopia and that the original route of Semitic migration into West Asia was from Ethiopia across the Bab-el-Mandab into South Arabia. Without entering into the complexities of this controversy here, we should note one aspect of Hudson's argument which is independent of the questions of the origin and migration patterns of proto-Semitic: a number of independently performed linguistic analyses indicate that the date for the presence of Semitic-speakers in Ethiopia must be pushed back much earlier than previously had been imagined, to as early as 2000 B.C. and possibly before that.

As a base line for reconstructing the history of Greater Ethiopia, then, we may consider it plausible that by the end of the third millennium B.C. its main inhabitants were dark-skinned Caucasoid or "Afro-Mediterranean" peoples practicing rudimentary forms of agriculture and animal husbandry and speaking three branches of Afro-Asiatic—Semitic, Cushitic, and Omotic.

Lines of Internal Differentiation

Whatever the extent of aboriginal unity among the proto-Ethiopians, the tremendous diversification of peoples and cultures is surely the most conspicuous phenomenon in the early history of Greater Ethiopia. By 2000 B.C. the proto-Ethiopians were beginning to separate into groups with different languages and cultures, a process that went on more or less continuously until very recent times and was accelerated by the differential impact of external forces on indigenous cultures. The main phases of this development may be reconstructed as follows.

The proto-Ethiopians divided into five core groups along lines that have remained fairly constant ever since:

1. The Northern Cushites, known to ancient Greeks as Blemmyes and otherwise as Beja, developed a single dialect cluster known as Bedawie. They lived as nomadic pastoralists in the desert lowlands near the Red Sea in northern Eritrea and southeastern Sudan.

2. The Central Cushites, speaking a dialect cluster called Agew, occupied most of the northwestern plateau highlands. Some of their ancient languages and cultures survive in small enclaves there today. The Agew practiced the plow cultivation of cereal grains.

3. The Eastern Cushites settled in and around the southern part of the Great Rift Valley in Ethiopia. They eventually separated into some two dozen tribes speaking distinct East Cushitic languages. They practiced the hoe cultivation of cereal grains and tubers, and in some areas developed remarkable forms of terraced agriculture in ancient times. A characteristic feature of the social organization of the Eastern Cushites is the *gada* system, a system in which classes recruited on the basis of generational position pass through a cycle of grades at fixed intervals.

4. The question of the origins of the Semitic-speakers in Ethiopia is, as we have seen, obscure. By the first millennium B.C. they had separated into two branches, one in the northern plateau regions and one in the central part of the country. They eventually formed seven ethnic clusters of widely varying sizes, characters, and modes of livelihood.

5. The Omotic-speaking peoples settled in the southwest, practiced the hoe cultivation of cereal grains and tubers, and organized a number of sacral monarchies. The most diversified of all the core Ethiopian populations, they divided into about fifty small societies with distinct languages and cultures.

The present distribution of Ethiopian peoples, languages, and cultures can best be understood as a function of two long-term secular processes: continuing internal differentiation within these five core proto-Ethiopian stocks, and their differential interaction with a series of intruding influences.

The most consequential endogenous changes took place among the Semites and the Eastern Cushites. The division of Ethio-Semitic into a northern and a southern branch in the first millennium B.C. was followed by significant divisions within both branches. Speakers of proto-North–Ethio-Semitic established monarchies in the first few centuries B.C. known from such sites as Yeha, Matara, and Haoulti in

Tigray and Eritrea. Their language was ancestral to Tigre and Ge'ez. The Tigre-speakers came to follow a nomadic pastoralist style of life very much like that of their North Cushitic neighbors, the Beja. The Ge'ez-speakers were agriculturalists and traders, and in the first centuries A.D. they established a major political and cultural center at Aksum. From Ge'ez was descended Tigrinya, the language of the successors to the Aksumites who will be referred to as Tigreans.[2]

The speakers of South Ethio-Semitic were more prolific. They produced some fifteen languages and dialects spoken by the Gurage people and the languages of Gafat, Amharic, Argobba, and Harari. These peoples settled on a broad belt stretching most of the way across central Ethiopia.

A major change in the constitution of the East Cushitic peoples took place toward the latter part of the first millennium A.D. when the Afar, Saho, and Somali peoples descended eastward from the southern plateau regions, evolved an independent pastoral economy, and abandoned the *gada* system. During the latter half of the present millennium, finally, the Oromo people expanded over vast areas of Greater Ethiopia and adapted in diverse ways to a number of local host cultures, a development which will be described in chapter 5.

Lines of External Influence

Although situated on high mountainous plateaus ringed by inhospitable lowland and desert regions, Ethiopia has never been totally isolated. This geographical condition has, however, moderated the flow of exogenous influences so that they could never become overwhelming. For millennia the inhabitants of Greater Ethiopia have experienced periodic waves of influence from outside peoples. Broadly speaking, one can identify three main sources of external influence: Sudanic peoples in the west, Semitic peoples to the east, and Mediterranean peoples from the north.

The earliest of these waves was brought by Negroid peoples from the Sudan. These peoples spoke languages ancestral to what have recently been classified as four branches of the great Nilo-Saharan family: Berta, Kunama, Koman, and East Sudanic. The Sudanic penetration of Greater Ethiopia took place in two widely separated periods. The first is associated with a group of peoples believed to have settled in the western and southwestern parts of Greater Ethiopia about the third millennium B.C. who are sometimes referred to as "Pre-Nilotes." Often credited with having introduced the Sudanic agricultural complex into Ethiopia, the Pre-Nilotes based their economies on the cultivation of sorghum and tuberous plants like ensete and yams. They affected the ethnic map of Greater Ethiopia in two ways: they settled and became ancestors of peoples now living on or near the western border, including the Berta, Gumuz, and Koma, and they intermixed with Omotic-speakers to form the Ari, Basketo, Dime, and Gimira-Maji groups of tribes.

A second phase of Sudanic influence is that of the Nilotic peoples, which may be located, very approximately, in the first millennium B.C. Nilotic cultures are marked by a preoccupation with cattle-raising, by the cultivation of millet, and by a dualistic form of social organization. Although they are relatively peripheral to the evolution of Greater Ethiopia, the Nilotes are represented by two tribes along the western border of Ethiopia, the Nuer and the Anyuak, and more importantly by their contributions to the formation of a number of Omotic- and East Cushitic-speaking tribes in the southwest corner of the country.[3]

The second great source of external influence was the Oriental Semites. Inasmuch as the Red Sea separates the Horn of Africa from Arabia by only twenty miles at the Bab-el-Mandab, and the surplus population of Arabia was continually looking for places to move and trade, the Yemeni Arab has been a persistent figure in Ethiopian experience. Indeed, the Arab is so much the traditional "foreigner" that in some Ethiopian languages the word *arab* is used to designate a foreign or imported object.[4] Although small groups of Arabs have been migrating to Ethiopia more or less continually for the last three millennia, however, the intrusion of Semitic cultural influence is best visualized as taking place in four distinct phases, each of which created further diversity among the peoples of Ethiopia.

The first known intrusion of Oriental Semitic influence was brought by groups of South Arabians during the second half of the first millennium B.C. These groups of immigrants have hitherto been thought of as constituting the core population of northeastern Ethiopia in antiquity and have been credited with introducing into Ethiopia a cultural complex that included Semitic language, the art of writing, architectural technology, the practice of irrigation, and Sabaean religious and political symbolism. Since, however, there is no clear evidence that any of these cultural traits appeared in South Arabia earlier than on the Ethiopian plateau, and since, as was mentioned above, Semitic language now appears to have been spoken in Ethiopia as early as 2000 B.C., that conception deserves to be modified. If the Semitic-speakers of northern Ethiopia do not represent an aboriginal Semitic-speaking population, then they must have acquired Semitic language from South Arabians so early that they developed their own advanced culture and ethnic identity well before the middle of the first millennium B.C. Even so, it is clear that there was a good deal of interaction between northern Ethiopia and South Arabia during the first millennium B.C., and it is quite reasonable to suppose that at least some elements of what may be called an Ethio-Sabaean civilization originated in South Arabia. The ethnic group differentiated by this Ethio-Sabaean culture would of course be the proto-Ge'ez-speakers.

The second stream of Oriental Semitic influence may be located in the first few centuries A.D., when there was a substantial influx of elements of ancient Hebraic culture, most probably imported by Jews then living in South Arabia.[5] These were absorbed by the Ge'ez-speakers around Aksum and by some of the Agew peoples. The Falasha, who call themselves Beta Israel, and to some extent the Kimant can be viewed as the subsequent ethnic precipitate of this phase of Oriental Semitic penetration.

From the fourth century to the sixth century, small groups of Syrian missionaries profoundly altered the ethnic complexion of northern Ethiopia by introducing Christianity to the Ge'ez-speakers. Syriac forms are prominent in the liturgy, devotional music, religious terminology, and ancient church architecture of Ethiopic Christianity. Christianity soon became a central component of the ethnic identity of the Aksumites and their descendants the Tigreans. By the end of the first millennium groups of Amhara were also beginning to embrace Christianity.

A final wave of Semitic influence entered Ethiopia through the south, affecting the eastern branch of the East Cushites and some of the peoples who had evolved South Ethio-Semitic tongues. Not long after the Afar, Saho, and Somali had moved eastward to become independent pastoralists, groups of Muslim Arabs were settling Zeila, Berbera, and other trading centers on the Somali coast. Under their influence the East Cushitic pastoralists converted to Islam. Around the twelfth and thirteenth centuries the Argobba and Harari also became Muslims. The former may well have been Amhara who embraced Islam and separated from the Amharic-speaking community enough to develop their own language, which was originally perhaps only a dialect of Amharic; the letter, speaking a language closely related to East Gurage, eventually developed the city of Harer into the major center of Islamic culture throughout the Horn of Africa.

A third set of external influences penetrated Ethiopia from diverse Mediterranean cultures. Little is known about the extent of Egyptian influence, though the stelae at Aksum and certain styles of Ethiopian jewelry, musical instruments, and lake boats have often been associated with influences emanating from Egypt. More certain is the impact of Hellenistic culture, diffused during the Ptolemaic Dynasty in Egypt (330–305 B.C.) and manifest in the use of Greek at the court of Aksum in the first centuries A.D. and the absorption of certain Greek words into Ethiopic. Subsequent Byzantine influence appears in medieval Ethiopian painting, particularly the tradition of miniatures in illuminated manuscripts. Finally, the Portuguese influence in the sixteenth century may be mentioned, an influence that some writers have connected with aspects of the architecture of the castles at Gonder.

The influences of Mediterranean cultures were of rather limited scope when compared with the impact of Sudanic and Oriental Semitic cultures. In no case can additional ethnic differentiation be attributed to the Mediterranean intrusions. What can be said is that these influences were absorbed primarily by the Aksumites and their cultural heirs, the Tigreans and Amhara, thereby accentuating in some ways the differences between them and the other peoples of Greater Ethiopia.

Keeping in mind the few basic historical processes I have just outlined helps bring some order to the stunning heterogeneity of Ethiopia's ethnic composition. This order is represented in chart 1, which shows schematically the genesis of the present distribution of Ethiopian peoples. The dates presented in that chart must be regarded as highly approximate.

The Peoples of Ethiopia: A Classification

On the basis of the preceding genetic analysis and a consideration of current regional and cultural affinities, I have developed a new classification of the peoples of Ethiopia. Since, as Abraham Demoz has sagely observed, "Ethiopia is the despair of the compulsive classifier,"[6] I have sought to escape despair by abstaining from any one principle of classification—genetic, regional, linguistic, religious, ecological, or social structural—in favor of a flexible approach which uses all of these variables, though in a necessarily imperfect manner. The classification consists of nine categories: North Eritrean, Agew, Amhara-Tigrean,

Chart 1
The Peopling of Greater Ethiopia

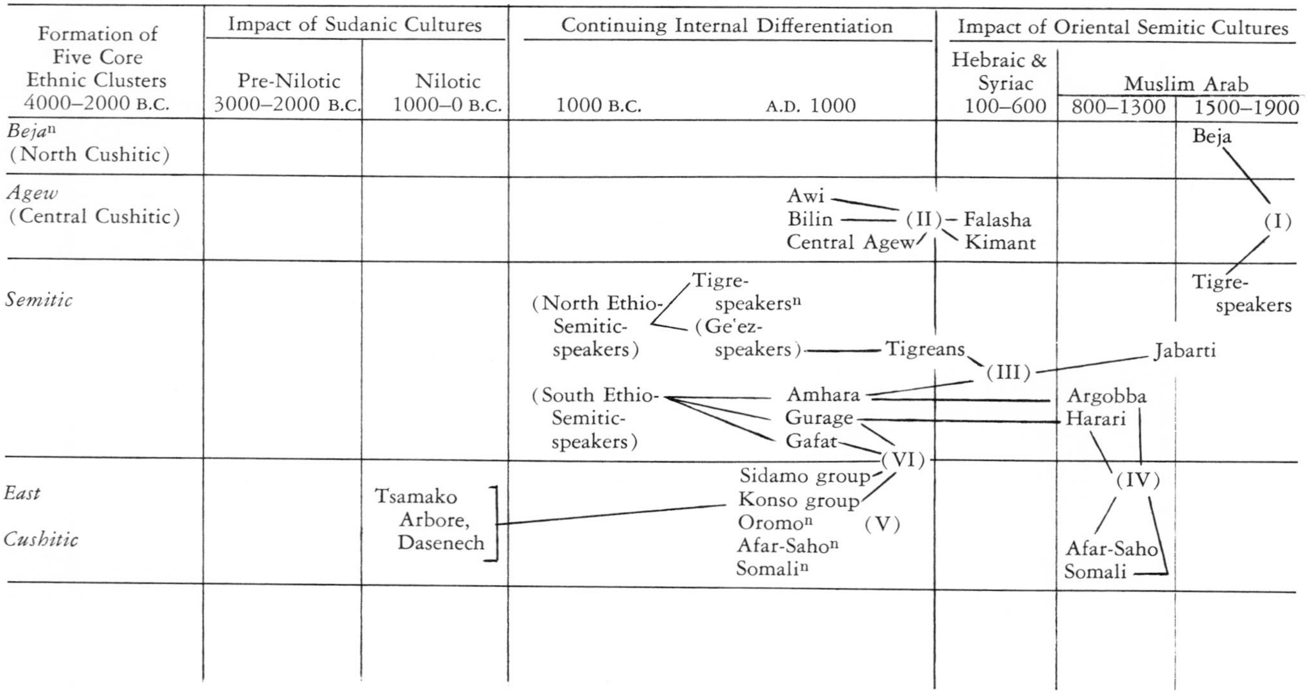

Formation of Five Core Ethnic Clusters 4000–2000 B.C.	Impact of Sudanic Cultures		Continuing Internal Differentiation		Impact of Oriental Semitic Cultures		
	Pre-Nilotic 3000–2000 B.C.	Nilotic 1000–0 B.C.	1000 B.C.	A.D. 1000	Hebraic & Syriac 100–600	Muslim Arab 800–1300	Muslim Arab 1500–1900
Beja^n (North Cushitic)							Beja
Agew (Central Cushitic)				Awi Bilin Central Agew (II)	Falasha Kimant		(I)
Semitic			(North Ethio-Semitic-speakers) (South Ethio-Semitic-speakers)	Tigre-speakers^n (Ge'ez-speakers) Tigreans Amhara Gurage Gafat	(III)	Argobba Harari	Tigre-speakers Jabarti
East Cushitic		Tsamako Arbore, Dasenech		Sidamo group Konso group Oromo^n Afar-Saho^n Somali^n (V) (VI)		(IV) Afar-Saho Somali	

Omotic	(Ancestors of Gimira-Maji Basketo Ari & Dime tribes)	Banna tribes		Kefa group, Gimira-Maji group, Ometo group, Ari-Banna group — (VII)			
	(Ancestors of Kunama, Berta, Koman group, East Sudanic group) — (VIII)	Nuer^{n} Anyuak — (VIII)	(VIII)	Caste groups (IX)			

n = adopt independent nomadic pastoralism

I = North Eritrean
II = Agew
III = Amhara-Tigrean
IV = Core Islamic

V = Galla
VI = Lacustrine
VII = Omotic
VIII = Sudanic

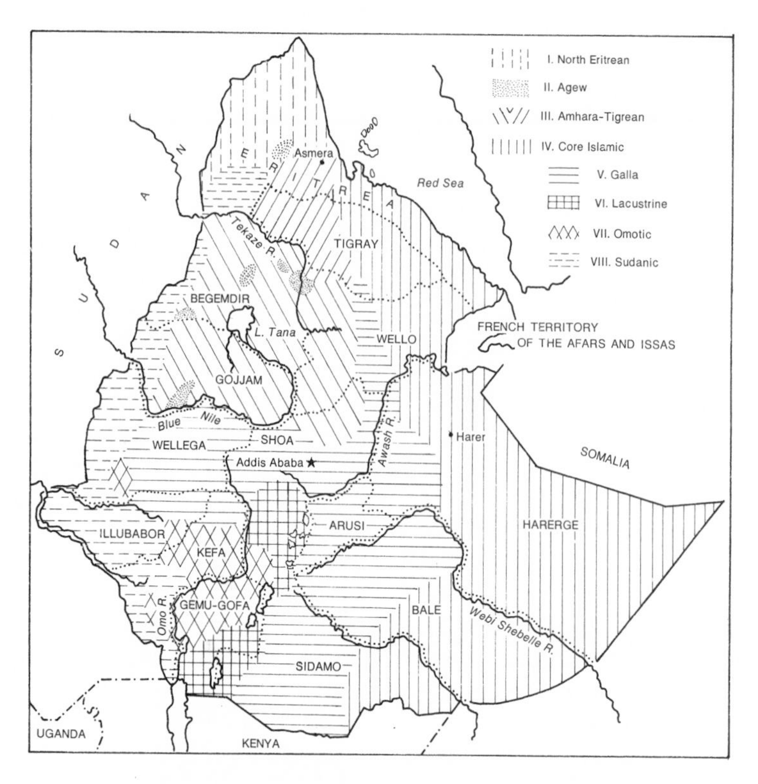

Map 1. Peoples of Ethiopia: Current Distribution

Core Islamic, Galla, Lacustrine, Omotic, Sudanic, and Caste groups. A comprehensive roster of Ethiopian peoples under this classification is presented in the Appendix. I list here the main defining characteristics of each of these ethnic categories.

I. The *North Eritrean* group consists of about a dozen small tribes residing in the triangular tip of Ethiopia. The base of this triangle runs through the town of Keren, and its sides are the Sudan border and the Red Sea. Today these tribes are Muslim, though most of them were formerly Christian. Their conversion to Islam is recent, often dating from the nineteenth century. Linguistically they divide into two groups: the Beja tribes of Beni Amer and Bet Mala speak the North Cushitic language Bedawie and often use Tigre as a second language; the others, including some originally Beja groups, speak Tigre. Most are nomadic pastoralists, herding camels and cattle. They tend to be loosely organized under weak chieftains, and most possess a hereditary class of serfs, a fact which distinguishes them from all other Ethiopian groups. Largest of the tribes is the Beni Amer, with about 60,000 people in Eritrea and an additional 30,000 across the Sudanese border. The North Eritreans all together number about 150,000.[7]

II. The *Agew* were the dominant population in the highland plateau region of northern Ethiopia before the rise of Aksum, and they remained a potent force in the region until the seventeenth century. Today small pockets of Agew remnants are dispersed over the provinces of Eritrea, Begemdir, Wello, and Gojjam. They still speak dialects of their Central Cushitic language, although most Falasha have by now assimilated Amharic or Tigrinya. Most Agew are plow cultivators and in many respects follow a style of life that closely resembles that of their Amhara-Tigrean neighbors. Only the Kimant and the Awi retain their traditional Cushitic religions; the others have adopted one of the three Semitic religions. The current population of the Agew peoples is about 170,000.

III. The *Amhara-Tigrean* group is the historical bearer of Ethiopian Orthodox Christianity and of the Solomonid monarchy. They are plow cultivators of cereal grains and keep herds of cattle, sheep, and goats. They have an ambilineal descent system and are organized in what may usefully be called a feudal system. The Tigreans, so called to distinguish them from the Tigre-speakers of group I, speak Tigrinya, and are concentrated in western Tigray province and south central Eritrea. The Amhara are located principally in western Wello, northern Shoa, Gojjam, Begemdir, and Harerge, but are also to be found in most other parts of the empire today. A third constituent of this category consists of dispersed groups of Amhara and Tigreans who converted to Islam and are collectively referred to as Jabarti. The population of group III may be estimated at about 10 million.

IV. The *Core Islamic* peoples inhabit the eastern flank of Greater Ethiopia. Converted to Islam in the first centuries of this millennium, they have lived in a state of chronic tension with the Amhara-Tigrean Christians of the Ethiopian Plateau. Three of these peoples—the Afar, Saho, and Somali—are East Cushitic–speaking nomadic pastoralists living in the desert lowland regions in the eastern parts of Eritrea, Tigray, Wello, and Harerge provinces. They are organized in patrilineal descent groups with a decentralized, segmentary political structure. The Argobba and Harari are small remnants of agricultural and trading peoples who speak South Ethio-Semitic languages. The Harari are distinguished for being the only people in Greater Ethiopia to have developed a tradition centering on a single large urban center. In their own language the term for a Harari is *ge su*—literally, "person of the city." The Core Islamic group has about 1.4 million people.

V. The *Galla* are the most widely dispersed of all the peoples of Greater Ethiopia. They comprise about a dozen tribal clusters distributed over ten provinces. Nearly all of them still speak mutually intelligible dialects of a single East Cushitic language, Gallinya. The traditional self-name of the Galla is Oromo, but this is not known or accepted by all the Galla peoples today. The Galla tribes now differ considerably in religion, style of life, and local political organization, though all of them retain some features of their traditional patrilineal descent system. The Galla number an estimated 7 million.

VI. The *Lacustrine* group of peoples is so named because they live in and around the Great Rift Valley chain of lakes. This region extends from southern Shoa southward through Gemu Gofa and the western edge of Sidamo province. The Gurage subgroup is in Shoa, the Sidamo subgroup in Shoa and Sidamo, and the Konso subgroup in Gemu Gofa. Those classified in the last two subgroups speak East Cushitic languages. The Gurage, who speak a number of South Ethio-Semitic languages and dialects divided into three quite divergent branches, are included in this category because their style of life, based on the hoe cultivation of ensete, closely resembles that of the Sidamo and their languages exhibit a fair amount of influence from the Sidamo language. All these peoples have patrilineal descent systems. Many of them have traces or even fully operational forms of the traditional system known as *gada,* based on the progression of classes through a sequence of grades. The Gurage and Sidamo subgroups are mixed in religion: some Christian, some Muslim, some pagan (a term which will be used here to refer to any of the non-Semitic traditional religions of Ethiopia). All the Konso group of tribes are pagan. The population of this cluster is approximately 2.8 million.

VII. The *Omotic* peoples are so named because they inhabit a relatively small region surrounding the Omo River in the provinces of Kefa and Gemu Gofa. As was mentioned above, they speak languages derived from what is now considered one of the six great families of Afro-Asiatic, a language family represented exclusively by these peoples. The Omotic peoples are hoe cultivators, growing tuberous plants like ensete as well as cereal grains. Most have patrilineal descent systems and were traditionally organized into small kingdoms.

Most are pagan, though the Kefa religion has long been influenced by Ethiopian Christianity, and the Bosha, formerly Christian, are now Muslim. The current population is about 1,350,000.

VIII. The *Sudanic* peoples live in enclaves scattered along the full length of Ethiopia's western border. The only ancient inhabitants of Greater Ethiopia whose languages are not descended from Afro-Asiatic, they speak languages belonging to four branches of the great Nilo-Saharan family: Koman, Kunama, Berta, and Eastern Sudanic. Their political systems are highly decentralized, although the Berta and the Anyuak traditionally had kings who performed primarily ritual functions. The Sudanic peoples are sedentary, practicing the hoe cultivation of grains. Only one of these peoples, the Nuer, has the pastoral life-style and characteristic cattle complex of the Nilotes. Their religions are mostly pagan, but the Nara were forcibly converted to Islam by Egyptians in the nineteenth century, and the Berta were converted by Sudanese Muslims somewhat earlier. The total population of this group is about 360,000.

IX. The *Caste* groups consist of a number of despised endogamous peoples scattered throughout Greater Ethiopia. Typically they are attached to particular host groups whose languages they speak and for whom they provide specialized economic or ritual services. In some instances they speak or formerly spoke their own languages or argots in secret. In some cases they appear to represent a physically distinct, often more Negroid, type than their hosts; in other cases they cannot be distinguished physically from their hosts. No estimates of the number of Ethiopians in these caste groups are available.

In addition to the nine categories of long-established inhabitants of Greater Ethiopia, a complete survey would include reference to immigrant groups of relatively recent origin who maintain a distinct identity: the Takarir, immigrants from the Western Sudan; Yemeni Arabs, found in the Rashaida tribe along the Eritrean coast and as traders throughout the country; Armenians and Greeks, long resident as traders and craftsmen; Italians, who provide a number of Ethiopia's skilled laborers; Indians, active in teaching and industrial enterprises; and expatriates of various sorts from Europe and North America.

4

Foundations of Unity

Given the complex differentiation of the Ethiopian peoples which took place long ago, what kind of unity can one ascribe to them? What sense does it make to speak of the historical experience of Greater Ethiopia as a unified whole?

I propose that the unity of the Ethiopian experience rests initially on three pervasive patterns: (1) a continuous process of interaction of the differentiated Ethiopian peoples with one another; (2) the existence of a number of pan-Ethiopian culture traits; and (3) a characteristic mode of response to the periodic intrusion of alien peoples and cultures.

Greater Ethiopia as a Relational Network

After they had separated into different tribes with distinct cultures, the peoples of Greater Ethiopia did not live as discrete isolated units. For the last two millennia, at least, they have been in more or less constant interaction through trade, warfare, religious activties, migration, intermarriage, and exchange of special services. In the conventional accounts of Ethiopian history, foreign relations—trade with Greeks, expeditions to Arabia, negotiations with Alexandria, alliance with Portugal, defense against Turks, attacks on the Fung Kingdom of Sennar, treaties with England, France, and Italy—stand out because of their high visibility; yet such relationships have been relatively brief, sporadic, and superficial. What must be brought more sharply into focus is the web of interactions which the diverse peoples of Greater Ethiopia have spun among themselves. It is this relational network, now thin and localized, now extensive and profound, but never absent, which provides the background and justification for an effort to conceptualize macroscopic Ethiopian history.

Trade, usually carried out by barter but often using indigenous forms of currency, has constituted a major form of interaction within Ethiopia for thousands of years. Ethiopians of different tribes have been brought in contact directly through local and regional markets, and indirectly through caravan traders. Given the limited resources available in each of the many ecological niches in Greater Ethiopia, the pressure of consumption needs alone makes it unlikely that any tribe could remain isolated from all others for a lengthy period. In fact, all parts of the country have developed local markets which as a rule meet once a week. These have usually been attended by members of two or more ethnic groups and often by traders from distant places. Most Ethiopians are not limited to a single market, moreover, but are familiar with a network of different markets in an area which meet on different days of the week. The numerous small societies of the Gamu highlands, for example, have long been connected by such a network of markets. Groups which do not have their own local markets, moreover, find other ways of exchanging products with outsiders. Thus the relatively isolated and self-sufficient lowland village of Silaszi, a community of the Agew of Sahalla visited by Frederick Simoons in the 1950s, has made regular contacts with other peoples in spite of its lacking a local market: itinerant Falasha come to the village for months at a time to make pots, Muslim weavers come for weeks to make garments, and ironsmiths from Lasta visit once a year to forge hoes and plowshares. In addition, the people of Silaszi periodically journey to markets in Amhara and Tigrean areas, traveling distances of two to seven days by foot, to exchange their honey, goats, and skins for spices, cloth, and iron goods.

In addition to satisfying local consumption needs, the products brought to local markets are taken by traders to progressively larger regional centers. At the regional markets, of course, people as well as goods come from more dramatically diverse backgrounds and longer distances. To the regional market at Debre Tabor, which Simoons also studied, people brought ginger from Chilga, a Kimant district (six days); wool saddle blankets from Gaint, an Amhara district (three days); cotton from the Tigrean district of Wolqait (eleven days); silverwork from Dessie, an ethnically mixed town (ten days); salt from the northern Afar region (two weeks); and coffee from the Jimma Galla (about one month).

Regional markets like that of Debre Tabor are not recent inventions. A number of very large regional markets—Aksum in the northeast, Harer in the southeast, Gonder in the northwest, and Bonga in Kefa in the southwest—served for centuries at various times in the past as trade centers for substantial parts of Greater Ethiopia. In the nineteenth century Hirmata, trading center for the kingdom of Jimma, Seqota, the capital of Lasta, and Ankober, the first royal seat of Menilek II, became extremely important centers as well. In 1905 Bieber observed that Hirmata drew some 30,000 people, and he like earlier visitors was struck by the diversity of Ethiopian peoples assembled there: Amhara from Gojjam and Shoa, Galla from all the Gibe kingdoms, and numerous representatives of the Lacustrine and Omotic groups, including Timbaro, Qabena, Kefa, Janjero, Welamo, Konta, and several others from the Ometo cluster. The market at Seqota in Lasta had contacts to the north with the Yejju and Raya Galla, and to the south with caravans coming from Gurage, Inarya, Kefa, Guma, and various southern Galla centers.

Interconnections among many of the peoples of Greater Ethiopia through the system of local and regional markets must have been established as far back as two thousand years ago. Two mineral resources used for currency and other purposes, salt bars from the Afar desert in the north and gold from the kingdom of Inarya in the southwest, have been circulated throughout Greater Ethiopia since ancient times. By the first century A.D. caravan trade connected Aksum and other northern centers with the southern and western plateau regions, the source of ivory, skins, gold, and spices. Long-distance trade routes remained active despite the eclipse of maritime trade through Aksum after the eighth century. Traditions from the Zagwe period indicate the existence of trade routes between Shoa and Angot, thence to Lalibela and north through Tigray and Bogos and eventually connecting with the Suakin-Nile routes of the Sudan. By the fourteenth century there was a well-traveled route that followed a long north-south axis, linking Hamasien, eastern Tigray, Angot, Amhara, Shoa, and points south. Meanwhile, Muslim traders had developed an extensive set of routes on an east-west axis proceeding inland from Zeila on the Gulf of Aden.

Indeed, throughout the last millennium Muslim traders played a critical role in linking the diverse reaches of Greater Ethiopia. In particular, Muslim Amhara and Tigreans known as Jabarti braved the severe hardships of caravan life in Ethiopia—attacks by bandits, oppressive tariffs, swollen rivers, steep mountains, and wild beasts—to carry their goods and, in the process, ideas and news from one region to another. As the Red Sea trade quickened in the late eighteenth and nineteenth centuries, the Jabartis found competition from itinerant Somali merchants known as Safara and from a class of Galla merchants called Afkala, who plied less sumptuous caravans in more limited territory but on a more frequent basis. In his recent articles on trade in Ethiopia, Mordechai Abir has shown how these various caravan routes fit together into an extensive trading system; how, for example, the Somali Safara penetrated as far inland as Borana country, where they waited for the feeder caravans of Konso, Arbore, and other merchants who collected ivory and other products from the Lacustrine and Omotic peoples. Abir's analysis lends support to the general argument I am developing here, particularly his suggestion that the "connection between the south and the north provided by the caravan trade must have contributed to the vague feeling which existed for centuries in central and northern Ethiopia that the borders of the mythical empire stretched well beyond the [Rift Valley] lakes to the south."[1]

One hardly needs to document the importance of warfare as a form of intertribal relations in Greater Ethiopia. Now to acquire cattle, now slaves, now to gain territory or control over trade routes, now to carry out ritual requirements or secure trophies to prove masculinity, virtually all the peoples of Ethiopia have been in hostile contact with one another, but only rarely with enemies outside of Greater Ethiopia. In such encounters, of course, they had to establish mutual understandings concerning the onset, regulation, and termination of the conflicts. Hostile groups in fact sometimes made accommodations that permitted trade to go on despite their enmities. During the times when Galla, Gurage, and Sidamo tribesmen were engaged in chronic warfare, they made market pacts which prevented hostilities from occurring within the market area and guaranteed safe conduct for travelers en route. For similar reasons Konso markets were located in neutral territory outside their towns, which were often at war with one another. James Bruce described another form of such accommodation, in which warring groups established trade relations by sending their children to one another as hostages. Bruce also noted that despite the absence of security in northwestern Ethiopia while he sojourned there, alert traders were able to penetrate south as far as Inarya and Kefa, taking myrrh, beads, cloths, and rock salt and returning with slaves, civet, wax, hides, and ginger.

The spread of Christianity and Islam established other kinds of ties. Although conversions were sometimes secured by force, notably in the reigns of Zera Ya'iqob in the 1450s and Yohannes IV in the 1870s and during the *jihad* of the 1530s, more typically they came about peacefully, through channels opened up by traders and by the need for diplomatic alliances. Between the eighth and sixteenth centuries Orthodox Christian monks converted groups of Beja nomads in the north, Agew peoples in the northwest and central regions, the kings of Welamo and Kefa in the near southwest, and many other groups; remains of churches throughout the south which antedate the sixteenth-century Galla invasions bear witness to their far-reaching activities. Wherever Christian churches were established, parishioners were integrated into a nationwide calendar of ritual observances and a far-flung decentralized system of religious instruction that included specialized centers of learning spread over Tigray, Amhara, Begemdir, Gojjam, and northern Shoa.

These same centuries saw Islam spread from the Somali coast to Ifat in eastern Shoa, south of that line to the states of Dewaro and Bale, and as far west as the kingdom of Hadiyya. Some Muslim colonies were established as far north as Tigray. These peoples became linked to the center of Islamic learning at Harer. They also became integrated into the Islamic system of pilgrimages, including pilgrimages to Muslim shrines in southern Ethiopia, and into a network of Muslim slave trading (that later would spur a resurgence of Muslim expansion in the nineteenth century).

The effect of Christian and Muslim missionary activity was thus to crisscross Ethiopia with lines of supratribal alliance and to bring most Ethiopians into the arena of competition between the two religions. Some peoples converted to one and then to the other. Many peoples, notably the Amhara, Galla, Gurage, and Tigreans, came to divide their allegiance between both. Relations between the two groups of religionists have often beeen antagonistic, particularly since the sixteenth century, but there have been numerous kinds of accommodation between them. Since both Islam and Christianity in Ethiopia have been highly syncretistic, moreover, their followers have not found it impossible to join in common religious observances. Muslims and Christians have reportedly taken part in one another's holiday ceremonies in Gonder and Shoa. The major pilgrimages in Ethiopia provide a particularly dramatic vehicle for such communion: huge numbers from both faiths attend the annual sacrifice at Lake Bishoftu, a fertility rite of pagan Galla origin, and go on the annual pilgrimage in honor of Saint Gabriel at Kulubi in Harerge province.

More intimate relationships among different ethnic groups in Ethiopia have been formed through processes of migration and intermarriage. Settled or nomadic, the Ethiopians are great travelers. To find new land, go on hunting or raiding expeditions, seek fortune at a royal court, escape enemies, study at a religious center, carry on trade, or make a pilgrimage, Ethiopians have long been accustomed to moving from one part of the country to another, in many cases to settling there. The Amarro, Janjero, Konta, and other peoples have plausible traditions concerning the immigration of Amhara settlers who came from the north several centuries ago, and the Welamo trace one of their dynasties to Tigrean immigrants. The Galla, as has been mentioned, migrated and intermixed with dozens of other peoples in Greater Ethiopia. The kingdom of Kullo was colonized by refugees from Dewaro in the sixteenth century. Ali Derar, a mountain in Jimma, is named after a sheik who migrated from Tigray in the eighteenth century, at which period groups of Gurage were found as far north as Gonder. Kefa minstrels have plausible traditions of origin from northern Agew immigrants who intermarried with and taught their art to a few noble Kefa clans. When, before and during the period of Menilek's expansion into southern Ethiopia, numerous Tigreans left their homelands because of famine, overpopulation, and soil desiccation and migrated south to settle in Sidamo and Kefa provinces, they were following a long-established Ethiopian custom.

Although most groups in Ethiopia appear to have norms of some sort against tribal exogamy, it is not clear how seriously these were or are followed. Certainly the historical practice has been to tolerate a good deal of intertribal marriage, at all levels of society. Omotic peoples, Cushites, and Semitic-speaking Ethiopians have intermarried heavily among themselves, and to a lesser extent with Negroid peoples, Oriental Semites, and Europeans. Intermarriage has long been a means of solidifying a national elite in Ethiopia. Zera Ya'iqob and other medieval Amhara kings took wives from the daughters of Muslim and pagan notables. Amhara and Galla frequently intermarried at the Gonderine court in the eighteenth century. Within the last century, the rift between Yohannes IV and Menilek II was to have been healed by an arranged marriage between their children, and Emperor Haile Sellassie I married the daughter of an originally Muslim Galla king from Wello.

In the course of their interactions over the centuries, many Ethiopian groups established interethnic relationships involving special kinds of dependency. The result is a subtle and extensive network of interdependencies that has yet to be examined in a systematic way. First, a number of endogamous pariah groups live in a kind of symbiotic relationship with their neighbors. As ritual experts, hunters, potters, tanners, or smiths, they provide indispensable services for their hosts, whose languages they have adopted. Similar patterns of interdependence exist between distinct tribal groups. The Dorze must procure the *kalacha,* a phallic forehead-ornament worn as a symbol of rank by their elected assembly leaders, from the Konso. Similarly, the Guji depend on the Derasa to provide the *kalacha* needed for their ritual leaders. Centuries of warfare between Amhara and Falasha were followed, after the defeat and dispersal of the latter in the early seventeenth century, by a pattern of interdependence whereby the Amhara came to rely on the Falasha for clay pots, leather goods, and silver work. Averse themselves to the desert climate, trade, and non-agricultural labor, Christian Amhara have traditionally depended on Afar to mine the desert salt, on Muslims to carry on trade, and on Gurage and others to provide labor. Still other groups have come to be widely appreciated for the special services they perform, such as the minstrelsy of the Wello Amhara and the skilled weaving of the Dorze.

Some mention should be made, finally, of the importance of Amharic and Gallinya as media of communication among the peoples of Greater Ethiopia. As early as the 1620s it was observed that in spite of the enormous linguistic complexity of the land anyone who knew Amharic could find in all parts of the country people with whom he could converse intelligibly.[2] Gallinya subsequently came to play a similar role for those not reached by Amharic, particularly for traders in the southern part of the country.

Greater Ethiopia as a Culture Area

Through these various forms of interaction Ethiopians of diverse traditions became acquainted and developed customs for relating to one another. If their images of each other often contained pejorative stereotypes, such stereotypes were nonetheless invaluable for providing modes of reciprocal orientation that enabled them to trade, fight, worship, and negotiate with one another.

These interethnic contacts, moreover, did not take place among total strangers. The fact is that the peoples of Greater Ethiopia are relatively homogeneous in a number of respects. Some of the culture traits they share may derive from a common aboriginal proto-Ethiopian culture, some may represent similar adaptive responses to similar situations, and others probably reflect a coalescence of traits deriving from prolonged interaction in the distant past. Whatever their origins, there seems to be a sufficiently large number of pan-Ethiopian culture traits that one can plausibly refer to Greater Ethiopia as a culture area, alluding thereby to that remarkable "tenacity of the attachment of cultural qualities to the soil" of which Alfred Kroeber wrote, that "stylistic set or faculty, at once absorptive and resistive, that for thousands of years, however inventions might diffuse and culture elements circulate, succeeding in keeping China something that can fairly be called Chinese, India Indian, Egypt Egyptian."[3] And Greater Ethiopia, we may add, Ethiopian.

To describe Greater Ethiopia as a culture area is to draw attention to a set of themes which appear in numerous variations among the traditions of the Ethiopian peoples. Few if any of the peoples of Ethiopia make use of all of those themes, but most exhibit most of them. Indeed, one of the more fruitful ways of characterizing the differences among Ethiopian peoples is to show how they elaborate these common themes in different ways and to varying degrees. In this section I shall identify a number of such "pan-Ethiopian" themes from the following domains: beliefs about supernatural beings; ritual practices; food taboos; the cult of masculinity; aspects of social organization; insignia of rank; and customs regarding personal status and the home.

Nearly all the peoples of Greater Ethiopia believe in a single supreme deity. Without exception this deity is associated with the sky and is conceived as masculine. In a few cases he is believed to be accompanied by a female deity, usually an earth goddess, but generally speaking the "pagan" as well as the Semitic religions of Ethiopia are monotheistic.

The names given to this preeminent sky-god vary considerably, but most of them are related to one of three glosses: *waq, tosa,* and *zar.* The first of these is prevalent among the East Cushitic peoples, including the Afar and Somali (Waq), Saho (Wak), Galla (Waqa), Timbaro (Waha), Hadiyya (Wa'a), Sidamo (Magano), Konso and Burji (Waq), Tsamako (Muqo), and Dasenech (Waq), and also appears among the Gurage (Waq), Gamu (Waga), and Majangir (Waqayo). Names for the supreme deity that are cognates of *tosa* appear among a number of the Omotic peoples, including the Basketo (Tsosi), Welamo (Tosa), Gofa (Tsuossa), Kullo (Tosa), Zala (Tsosa), Amarro (Tsose), and Male (Tsosi). The third set of names is found throughout the western regions, among Agew peoples including the Bilin (Jar) and Kimant (Adara), Sudanic peoples including the Mao (Yere) and the Koma (Yere Siezi), and Omotic peoples including the Kefa (Yero), Anfillo (Yere), Bencho (Char), Nao (Yero), and Chara (Yero). That Amhara culture is not sui generis but must be viewed as part of the broader culture area of Greater Ethiopia is indicated, dramatically and paradigmatically, by the fact that cognates of all three of these names have been used by the Christian Amhara to designate various supernatural forces. *Wuqabi* signifies a special guardian spirit which Amhara believe to be appointed by God to watch over every person until his "water" (life-force) is spent; *tosa* is an Amharic term for that which afflicts a person as a curse; and *zar* refers to a kind of spirit believed to possess persons until placated by special offerings.

The supreme deity of the various religions of Ethiopia is conceived as remote and inaccessible, and as having relatively little direct import for human problems. Of far greater significance for Christian and Muslim Ethiopians are their various saints. Among these, Saint Gabriel is revered by Christians, Muslims, and Jews alike. Still more widespread are beliefs in a number of active spirits which are localized in certain trees, waterplaces, and hilltops. Such genii loci include the Maryam of the Mensa, a female spirit thought to dwell in large sycamore trees; the Aymba Qole of the Kimant, whose abode is on a certain hilltop where there is a single huge tree; the *eqqo,* elemental spirits which the Kefa locate in trees and running water; the Talehe of the Welamo, a spirit of the Omo River; the Afar spirit localized in the volcano atop Mount Ayelu; and the malevolent spirits called *agannint* which the Amhara locate in waterplaces. Cognate words are used to refer to one or more classes of localized spirits in a number of languages: Kimant: *qole;* Amharic: *qolle;* Galla: *qollo;* Kefa: *qolo;* and Welamo: *qolte.*

Throughout Greater Ethiopia there are beliefs that certain physical symptoms are caused by named spirits which take possession of a victim. Among the Mensa a demon called *waddegenni* enters young women and makes them sick. Among the Gurage *zitena* refers to a form of spirit possession that produces serious and often fatal illnesses. The term *zar,* already mentioned, is the most widely used name for this intrusive spirit: belief in *zar* possession appears among the Amhara, Tigreans, Falasha, Kimant, Arsi Galla, and, in cognate form, among the Somali (*sar*) and the Hadiyya (*jara*). Often associated with this concept is a shamanistic practitioner who exorcises the spirit or performs special services by entering into a trance brought on by possession. *Zar* cult shamans and their counterparts are widespread in Ethiopia; among the Sheko, for example, *kai* spirits take possession of the shaman and enable him to serve as a medium between his clients and the *kai*.

Belief in the powers of the evil eye, often attributed to malignant men who transform themselves into hyenas or other animals at night, is also pan-Ethiopian. Such powers are usually attributed to members of low-status groups, though among the Somali it is the chief's glance that is called the "burning eye" and credited with destructive powers. The Konso believe that a *koima,* a man with the evil eye, can cause food to stick in the throat, crops to dry up, and children and calves not to suckle. The Amhara *buda* blights his victim's crops or animals or "drinks his blood" through the magic power of his evil eye; the *buda* concept is also found among the Kimant, Falasha, Kefa, and Sidamo. Precautionary measures are often taken to protect individuals and their loved ones from the evil eye: Falasha women wear strings of charms around their necks, Mekan leave a narrow strip of hair growing from forehead to neck to protect boys from the evil eye, Konso set up carved figures near crops or cover possessions to guard them against such witchcraft, Sidamo keep alert at night and raise occasional shouts to scare off those with evil eyes, and Amhara keep their children away from strangers. It is widely believed—by Kimant, Amhara, Konso, Kefa, and others—that persons with the evil eye attack because they are envious of others' possessions.

Among the Mensa and other Tigre-speakers the theme of the evil eye is linked with another pan-Ethiopian theme: belief in the special powers of the serpent. Mensa legend relates that in olden times people died at a glance from a large white serpent with big eyes which was known as Heway. Elsewhere in Ethiopia the serpent is not only credited with special powers but venerated as well. Tigreans believe that their ancestors worshipped serpents and that serpents stand by guarding the monasteries of Tigray at present. In a number of Aksumite king lists the first name is that of King Arwe, the Serpent. The high priests, or *qallu,* of the Borana and Arsi Galla are believed to have descended from the union of a maiden and a serpent. Serpents figure prominently in many Ethiopian myths of origin or creation. The Janjero associate a gigantic serpent believed to live in Mount Bor—which was a preferred place for offering human sacrifices until the Amhara outlawed that practice at the beginning of this century—with the creation of the world and consider its anger to be the cause of earthquakes. The Sidamo regard the serpent as the moral hero in their "Garden of Eden" myth: at a time when the human race lived without troubles and never knew death, Magano, the supreme deity, appeared among them as a tired wayfarer begging for water; his request was flatly refused by a woman, but the serpent offered him milk. As a consequence, Magano punished humanity by subjecting them to afflictions and mortality and rewarded the serpent by granting him immortality. The association of the serpent with fertility is common: Mensa men, for example, traditionally refrained from killing serpents during the period of their wives' pregnancies in order to avoid complications. Many peoples have cults that involve the special breeding and veneration of serpents. Such customs have been reported for the Borana, Guji, Arsi, Derasa, Konso, Gidole, Gawwada, Mocha, Maji, Chara, Welamo, Zala, Koma, and Mekan. The Chara, for example, raise serpents inside their homes, feed them milk and other foods, and accord them sacred respect. The Gawwada king is reported to carry on privileged conversations with a large serpent which is kept in the roof of the royal palace.

In contrast to Nilotic peoples like the Nuer, most peoples in Greater Ethiopia observe a cycle of religious ceremonies held according to a ritual calendar, not just when they fear that mystical danger threatens. Fixed schedules of ceremonies are found among pagan groups like the Borana and Guji Galla, the Konso, Dorze, and Welamo, as well as among the followers of Semitic religions. Celebrating the beginning of the solar new year with bonfires is an ancient custom. The Amhara-Tigrean festival of Mesqel, which commemorates the finding of the True Cross with bonfires, was based on this pre-Christian observance. This accounts for the popularity of the Mesqel festival among non-Christian Ethiopians. The pagan Dorze have thus elaborated the Mesqel festival into a holiday of enormous proportions.

Pilgrimages constitute another common feature of the sacred calendars of Ethiopians. Earlier in this chapter I mentioned the importance of pilgrimages as a means of bringing together Ethiopians of diverse ethnic groups; here I wish to make the point that the very inclination to go on pilgrimages is a notable pan-Ethiopian trait. Octennial pilgrimages to the Abba Muda shrine were a central part of the life of the Galla before their great dispersal and still are important for the Borana. Even after the dispersal, numerous Galla tribesmen traveled enormous distances to make that pilgrimage. They also established other shrines for pilgrimages in the new regions, such as the big sycamore on the slopes of Mount Bokkaha. The Afar, after each year's rainy season, journey to the shrine on Mount Ayelu to pray for health, prosperity, and success in war, and they maintain other pilgrims' shrines as well. The Somali make pilgrimages to the tombs of their saints each year on the anniversary of the saint's death. Amhara and Tigreans make pilgrimages to particularly renowned church-shrines each year on the relevant saint's day. Hidar Tsion, the celebration of the church of Saint Mary of Zion in Aksum in the month of Hidar, has long been a major occasion for pilgrimages, and in this century the pilgrimage to the church of Saint Gabriel at Kulubi in Harerge province on Saint Gabriel's Day in the month of Tahisas has achieved comparable importance. The Muslim Gurage have developed a shrine in honor of a contemporary saint, Shehotch, which, like the shrine of Sheik Hussein, attracts pilgrims from many parts of southern Ethiopia. Among the peoples of the southwest, the Konta make pilgrimages to sanctuaries where their *kallicha* ritual experts are buried; the Majangir make pilgrimages to the shrines of their ritual experts, the *tapa,* while they are still alive; and Sidamo elders have traditionally gone on pilgrimages to two venerated places, Mount Bensa and the River Logida.

Animal sacrifice is a major component of ritual practice in Greater Ethiopia. Such sacrifices are usually carried out on prescribed occasions with prescribed types of animals, the preferred victims being cattle, sheep, and goats. A vestige of this custom persists among the rural Amhara, who sacrifice a specific type of sheep or chicken on the first day of the new year, and in *zar* cult ceremonies among the Amhara, in which goats are often sacrificed. The ritual sacrifice of animals occurs in all the other groups of Ethiopian peoples in our classification.

Another widely diffused custom is the use of grass for ritual purposes. Grass is used in purification rituals among the Dorze, and Guji as well as Dorze place grass on the floor in ceremonies to exorcise spirits. The Amarro, Mao, and Tirma peoples make devotional offerings of grass, and the Konso use a kind of creeping grass in religious rituals. The Mensa and kindred peoples use blades of grass in a ritual at their betrothal ceremonies. In observance of the new year, Amhara strew freshly cut grass on the floors of their homes, while children make and distribute wreaths of grass. Amhara also weave rings and headbands of grass at Easter. Grass figures as a symbol of authority among many people in southern Ethiopia.[4] The Gurage place handfuls of a special kind of grass at the feet of their chieftains during installation ceremonies.

The use of sacred trees for devotional purposes is a conspicuous pan-Ethiopian theme. Mensa pray to a giant sycamore called *chaggarit.* Kimant, Shangama, and Majangir worship in sacred groves. Sidamo grease the bark and roots of their sacred trees with butter, and Guji require that some offering be left when one passes one of their many sacred trees. Afar rub the feet of a newly installed sheik with earth from the root of the *shola* tree, a tree mystically associated with their ancestors. Konso erect sacred dead juniper trees (*ulahita*) in honor of their warrior grade. Gurage create shrines outside their villages by designating certain *zegba* trees as sanctuaries of Waq. In Amhara culture this motif appears in two forms—the institution of the *adbar,* a tree considered sacred to the local spirits of each area, at which propitiatory sacrifices are made once a year, and the sacred sentiments associated with the groves of cedar trees customarily planted around Orthodox Christian monasteries.

The dispensation of rain is one area in which the sky-god of Ethiopian religions has a direct impact on human lives, and all the peoples of Greater Ethiopia have some procedures to propitiate him and secure the right amount of precipitation. Many tribes maintain a specialized role of rainmaker; this is so for the Nara, Koma, Suri, Arbore, Tsamako, Dasenech, Burji, Welamo, Gofa, Zala, and Hadiyya. Among the last two, and probably others, this office was hereditary within a certain lineage and invested with exceptional importance. Among other tribes, including the Kimant, Arsi, Guji, Gurage, Konso, and Mao, rainmaking is one of the functions of high-ranking ritual specialists. In still other tribes it is clan heads, chieftains, or kings who are endowed with rainmaking powers: rainmaking is a traditional duty of the Afar sheiks, of Somali chieftains in the pre-Islamic state of Somali society, and of the heads of particular clans among the Beni Amer, Janjero, and Sheko. The Sheko clan head bears the title of *irubab,* "father of rain," and is thought to have the power of starting or stopping rainfall by contracting or extending his legs. Among the Amarro the king brings rain by placing his right foot in a stream outside the royal compound. In some cases large numbers of people are involved in the rainmaking rituals. The Somali conduct an elaborate ten-day ceremony before each rainy season which includes communal prayers for rain, Koranic recitations, and the sacrifice of animals contributed by each tribal section. Among some of the Mecha Galla, ululating women carrying food and foliage form a grand procession to a central place where they sit and chant prayers for rain. In Amhara culture the *debtera,* a group of lay choristers affiliated with the church, are thought to possess magical formulas which bring or stop rainfall, and there may also have been some earlier tendencies to endow chieftains with rainmaking powers: local traditions relate that an eighteenth-century ruler in Menz was deposed because there had been too little rain during his first few years of office.

In the area of food taboos, two items are nearly pan-Ethiopian. A taboo on pork is observed not only among the Judaic Falasha and most Muslim tribes, as one would expect, but among many other Ethiopian peoples. The ban on pork is considered a central norm of their *Christian* religion by Amhara and Tigreans. It is also found among a number of pagan tribes, including the Kimant, the Borana and Guji Galla, the Sidamo, and the Janjero. The peoples of Ethiopia also exhibit what has been described as a distinctively Cushitic aversion to fish, an aversion which Cerulli has linked with the Cushitic tendency to regard waterplaces as abodes of supernatural beings. Evidence of taboos on or strong aversion to fish has been reported for tribes in all parts of Greater Ethiopia, including the Beni Amer, Kimant, Amhara, Somali, Borana, Konso, and Welamo. Among the Mao, individuals who are particularly gifted in communing with their household spirits are forbidden to eat fish. The Sidamo and the Kimant traditionally laid particular emphasis on the sinfulness of eating fish, the latter group, according to Bruce, on the grounds that one of their ancestors, the prophet Jonah, was swallowed by a whale or some other great fish [*sic*].

Although the use of wild animals for food is generally disparaged in Ethiopia, hunting is highly esteemed as a way to demonstrate male courageousness. Indeed, masculine aggressive prowess as displayed by killing wild beasts and human enemies represents a preeminent value in most of the cultures of Greater Ethiopia.[5] The killer typically enjoys a privileged status marked by special insignia and perquisites. After killing a man, for example, an Arsi Galla is entitled to wear a copper ring in his ear. Among the Konta, one who killed an elephant received a silver earring which entitled him to take part in royal councils. Hadiyya custom has it that the killer of an enemy of a large beast has the right to a gift from every woman he meets. Many peoples set up formal occasions at which the killer can boast of his achievements, and they distribute rewards according to the number and fierceness of the beasts and humans he has slaughtered. They also cultivate special genres of verse which are sung to goad the killer and celebrate heroic exploits; some examples will be presented in chapter 10. The deeds of great warriors are recounted at their funerals, and stelae are often erected to commemorate them. The Mensa and the Afar plant as many stone slabs as the number of people the deceased has slain. Konso place phallic stelae known as *daga deeruma,* "stones of manhood," on the graves of men who have killed an enemy in battle. In what admittedly can be no more than pure conjecture, the huge stelae of ancient Aksum have been thought of as commemorative stones of this sort. Although in some instances the explicit association with virility may be unconscious or forgotten, moreover, the use of many other kinds of phallic symbolism is conspicuous throughout southern Ethiopia, from the phallus-shaped sticks of the Derasa and the phallic clay roof ornaments atop Konso men's clubhouses to the phallic head ornaments worn by certain officeholders among the Borana, Guji, Konso, Kefa, Dorze, and others.

The Ethiopian cult of masculinity differs from the Latin cult of *machismo* in two respects. The former does not emphasize sexual prowess, nor is it complemented by the idealization of woman for distinctively feminine qualities. In this matter the Galla are atypical, for at least the pagan Galla entertain a fair amount of public boasting about sexual accomplishments and a relatively benign view of women. The general Ethiopian pattern, however, is to associate the highest values exclusively with masculinity and to conceive of the virtues of masculinity almost exclusively in terms of aggressive capacity. Although in some groups the distribution of wealth and power keeps women from a wholly subordinate position, nearly all the peoples of Greater Ethiopia consider women generically inferior, express little if any appreciation of distinctively feminine traits, and harbor many idioms of contempt for alleged female atributes. The Bilin reportedly regard women as property, not human beings, and liken women to hyenas. A classic Harari writing, the *Kitab al-Fara'id,* states that all human knowledge can be formulated in four thousand precepts, which in turn can eventually be reduced to four, the first of which is: Do not trust women.[6] Gurage consider the woman to be inherently immoral, and a constant source of contamination of men unless she performs cleansing rituals after childbirth, menstruation, and sexual intercourse. Kefa males regard women as weak, sharp-tongued, and lazy, and highly dangerous both because they may infect men during their menstrual periods and because of their avid sexual desires which rob men of their strength. Konso males consider women socially unstable, and are particularly fearful that they may rob men of vitality by seducing them into too much sexual activity. The Amhara depreciate women's activity and talk as inferior, and disparage women's character as unreliable and treacherous. In their ritual greeting to men, Sidamo women customarily demean themselves by likening their position to the earth on which men tread. Another indication of the relative status of women in Ethiopia is the general practice of excluding them from participation in public assemblies or important rituals, though a few tribes, like the Welamo, Gurage, and Mecha Galla, have some ceremonies in which women alone participate.

The emphasis on masculinity appears in other aspects of social organization. The family systems of nearly all the peoples of Ethiopia are strongly patriarchal, and patrilineal descent is the dominant principle in organizing rights and relationships in most Ethiopian tribes. The patriarchal theme is expressed in the practice of polygyny, which is common among the pagan as well as the Muslim peoples, and in the custom of the levirate, which is also widely practiced (although not, it is worth noting, by the Falasha). Patrilineal descent groups of varying genealogical depths organize the bulk of social relationships in segmental societies like those of the Afar, Somali, Gurage, and Kefa, and in those of the Borana, Guji, Sidamo, Dasenech, and others where they are complicated by cross-clan solidarities formed by a generation-grading system. Even among the Amhara, whose ambilineal descent system is so untypical for Greater Ethiopia, there is a bias toward male primogeniture in the allocation of some rights and positions. Many Tigrean communities, moreover, deviate from the ambilineal pattern by allocating land-use rights through patrilineal descent groups.

Although dualistic organization, in the form of a division of societies into two exogamous moieties, has been reported for societies as far apart as the Kimant, Borana, Male, Banna, and Sheko, the number is not so great as to justify calling this a pan-Ethiopian feature. In some instances which have appeared to represent dual systems, like the Kefa division into "high clans" and "low clans," the divisions appear to constitute a pattern of stratification into two social classes rather than a moiety system.[7] However, a pattern of stratification comparable to the Kefa division between high- and low-ranking descent groups can be identified as more generally characteristic of Ethiopian tribes. The Afar division into Asaimara ("Red") and Adoimara ("White") can be glossed as a division into "noble" and "commoner" clans. Most of the North Eritrean peoples distinguish between a stratum of nobles and one of serfs (*tigre*), and the Leqa Galla divide into lineages of higher and lower status known as Boran and Gabaro, respectively. In these cases, as in that of the Kefa, the stratification patterns are attributed to the conquest of one people by another. Among other peoples, including the Kimant, Somali, Borana, Dorze, and Gurage, distinctions of status among lineages take the form of assigning greater prestige to certain patrilineal descent groups. Among the Amhara the division between nobility and commoners has sometimes been connected with a loosely conceived sort of clanship; this has been true to a certain extent in this century among the Shoa Amhara.

Most Ethiopian societies have also distinguished two other status groups, slaves and caste groups. Slavery was widespread in Greater Ethiopia until the 1930s, and today ex-slaves, children of former slaves, and de facto slaves in some regions occupy social positions much like their predecessors'. Slaves were acquired by conquering other peoples, by taking captives in war, or in slave-raiding expeditions. Although Sudanic tribes like the Nara (=Barya), Kunama, and Berta (=Shanqella) were heavily raided for slaves—so much so that the word Barya came to signify "slave" in Amharic and perhaps other tongues—members of any ethnic group were liable to be consigned to slavery by more powerful members of other tribes, if not their own tribe. Within some tribes, like the Kefa and the Berta, slavery was a form of punishment for wrongdoing. Most of the North Eritrean tribes, including the Bet Juk, Habab, Marya, and Mensa, were noted for condemning their fellow tribesmen to slavery on the slightest pretext.[8] Between tribes, Borana made slaves of Konso, Afar made slaves of Amhara, Kefa made slaves of most of their neighboring tribesmen, and Amhara and Tigreans, while not supposed to enslave fellow Christians, had slaves from many non-Christian groups.

Caste groups represent another pan-Ethiopian social phenomenon. As Herbert Lewis has observed, if the term caste can be used for any social formation outside the Indian context, it can be applied as appropriately to those Ethiopian groups otherwise known as "submerged classes," "pariah groups," and "outcastes" as to any non-Indian case. Lewis has noted that these groups meet the commonly assumed criteria for caste and, except for not adhering to the Hindu religion, exhibit all the defining characteristics of caste listed by Edmund Leach: (1) endogamy; (2) restrictions on commensality; (3) status hierarchy;

(4) concepts of pollution; (5) association with a traditional occupation; and (6) caste membership ascribed by birth.[9]

The occupational specialties of the Ethiopian caste groups include hunting, fishing, smithing (iron, silver, gold), tanning, pottery-making, and weaving. One or more of these activities is regularly despised by the associated host group; tanning tends to be despised most frequently. Members of caste groups are also despised and often feared as sources of pollution because of their eating habits, frequently because they eat wild boar, hippopotamus, or canine meat. Caste group members are typically associated with supernatural forces, as bearers of the evil eye, magicians, or ritual experts.

If one were to construct an ideal type of the pan-Ethiopian stratification pattern, then, it would consist of four strata: high-ranking lineages, low-ranking lineages, caste groups, and slaves. This pattern is fully actualized in a number of tribes, such as the Dorze, who distinguish *bairo* (high-ranking clans), *gedos* (low-ranking clans), *degala* and *mana* (caste-group tanners and potters), and *aile* ("ex"-slaves). An analogous quartet of categories appears among the Amhara, Afar, Somali, Borana, Leqa, Sidamo, Kefa, Janjero, and other peoples. In all other cases except a few of the Sudanic tribes, three of the four categories are present.

A related area of pan-Ethiopian traits which Eike Haberland has taken the lead in exploring is that of insignia of authority. The royal drum, known in Amharic as *negarit* and in some other instances by a cognate term (Kefa: *negarito;* Sheko: *negara*), is one such symbol. The *negarit* was sounded whenever Amhara-Tigrean monarchs left their camps or palaces to go to war, to church, or simply to journey. The Kefa drum was beaten when the king began to eat, proclaimed laws or summons to war, or went on procession. The high priests of the Borana possess sacred drums which are believed to have descended with them from heaven. Among the Konso sacred drums which symbolize peace and harmony are circulated from town to town in a fixed cycle, and such drums are beaten at the end of each grading cycle.

The ring stands out as the most important symbol of royalty in Greater Ethiopia. This appears to have been true in ancient Aksum and the medieval Amhara kingdoms as well as among more than two dozen Omotic kingdoms. Made of gold, silver, iron, or even grass, such rings are worn on the ear or the finger but most commonly as armbands. Installation ceremonies usually consist of the placing on of the official ring. A number of tribes without kings similarly use rings as insignia of authority: the high priests of the Borana wear sacred arm-rings, Gurage clan chiefs are invested in office by having silver bands and rings made of sheep tendons placed around their arms, Konso lineage priests put on five iron bracelets when they assume office, and Marya restrict the wearing of gold and silver armbands to their chiefs and nobility.

Among animals, the lion is commonly associated with royalty in Greater Ethiopia. More important still is the honeybee and its products. Haberland has observed that the bee is symbolic of good fortune in all of Ethiopia and has documented a number of associations between bees and royal authority: the use of bees as oracles to determine new kings by landing on the chosen person, a custom recorded for the Zagwe King Lalibela and among the Janjero, Sheko, Basketo, and Male; restriction of honey or honey wine to royal consumption; rubbing the royal corpse with honey; restriction of beeswax candles to use at the funerals of kings; burial of kings in cylindrical beehives; and punishment of lese majesty by wrapping the offender in cloths soaked in beeswax and setting him afire.[10]

A number of customs regarding personal status can also be identified as pan-Ethiopian. The act of conferring personal names is regarded as highly significant by most Ethiopians, and usually this is done in a ritual which is deferred for some months or even years after the person is born. In some cases the attainment of fully adult status involves acquiring a new name: Galla and Hadiyya men and women become known as "father of" and "mother of" their firstborn sons; Amhara women are sometimes given new names upon marriage; and Dasenech men acquire both paternity-names and ox-names. Chieftains frequently acquire new names when they assume office. Circumcision is required throughout Greater Ethiopia, usually either at eight days or in connection with a transition rite in a grading cycle. Clitoridectomy is also required in most tribes.

Differences in hairstyle are used to indicate a number of status distinctions: between virgins and married women, boys and men, males in different *gada* grades, nobility and commoners, insiders and outsiders. The status of killers is indicated by such means as smearing the hair with butter (Hadiyya), dying the hair with red ochre (Sidamo), or wearing ostrich feathers in the hair (Somali). Among Amhara the status of outlaw (*shifta*) is indicated by a wild, bushy growth of hair. Wives of Dorze assembly leaders are known by a headdress in which the hair is combed high straight above the forehead in the form of a shield. In traditional Gurage life "poor men" had completely shaven heads; "common" men wore small plaits at the back or hanging from a central plait; elderly "rich men" wore a full growth of hair.[11]

As a final category of pan-Ethiopian traits let me mention similarities in the construction of homes. Most sedentary peoples in Ethiopia have homes that are round—rectangular houses in parts of Eritrea, Tigray, and Harerge being the chief exceptions—with cylindrical walls of wattle and daub and a conical thatched roof. (Nomadic peoples usually build oval huts made of curved sticks covered with mats or camel's hair cloth.) They typically decorate their houses with clay or wooden ornaments, frequently phallic in shape, placed atop the roof.[12] Similar ornaments are placed atop Orthodox Christian churches and Falasha synagogues. The center mainstay pole, moreover, is commonly regarded as an object of special significance. All Galla tribes venerate the mainstay pole, which they call *utuba mana.* Even Galla who are seminomadic designate one of the poles in each of their temporary structures as *utuba mana,* and leave it standing when they break down their huts to move elsewhere.[13] The Kefa offer sacrifices of beer and chicken blood at the foot of their central post, or *gimbo,* during holidays. Similar rituals at the foot of the central post are performed by Guji, Dorze, and others. The Zala construct their homes by first erecting the center post and then pausing while the head of the family pours a libation of beer and sprinkles cow dung around it, praying all the while to Tsosa. The Kembata hold a ceremony at the center post after a house is raised. The central mainstay pole in Gurage houses has been described as the focus from which the social, ritual, and economic life of the homestead radiates, and its erection is similarly a major ritual occasion. In what may or may not be a faint reflection of such attitudes, the Amhara regard the part of the home around the mainstay pole (*meseso*) as a kind of inner sanctum, a place for the most intense and gratifying convivial experiences; and among Tigreans the word for the central post, *amdi,* has overtones of a highly respectful nature.

This survey has of necessity been highly selective, both in the number of peoples referred to and in the number of traits discussed. In tables 1 and 2 I have sought to provide a somewhat fuller picture of the distribution of most of the traits that were mentioned. These tables are incomplete in two respects, however: the number of peoples shown as possessing each trait is limited to two for each of the categories in

Table 1

Selected Pan-Ethiopian Culture Traits: Concepts of The Supernatural, Ritual Practices, and Food Taboos

	I	II	III	IV	V	VI	VII	VIII
Concept of a supreme male sky god	Beni Amer Mensa	Falasha Kimant	Amhara Tigrean	Afar Somali	Borana Mecha	Sidamo Konso	Kefa Dorze	Kunama Majangir
Cognate of *waq* used for deity or spirit		Kimant	Amhara Tigrean	Afar Somali	Borana Guji	Gurage Konso	Gamu	Majangir
Cognate of *zar* used for deity or spirit		Bilin Kimant	Amhara Tigrean	Somali	Arsi	Hadiyya Dasenech	Kefa Chara	Mao
Concept of genii loci in trees, waterplaces, or hilltops	Mensa	Kimant Kunfel	Amhara	Afar Somali	Arsi Guji	Sidamo Konso	Kefa Dorze	Gumuz Mekan
Belief in spirit possession	Mensa	Falasha Kimant	Amhara Tigrean	Somali	Borana Mecha	Gurage Sidamo	Sheko Dorze	Kunama Mekan
Belief in evil eye	Mensa	Falasha Kimant	Amhara Tigrean	Somali	Borana Guji	Gurage Konso	Kefa Dorze	Mekan
Belief in special powers or sacredness of serpents	Mensa		Tigrean		Guji Leqa	Sidamo Konso	Chara Maji	Koma Mekan

Annual calendar of	Beni Amer	Falasha	Amhara	Afar	Borana	Gurage	Dorze	Gumuz
religious ceremonies	Mensa	Kimant	Tigrean	Somali	Guji	Konso	Welamo	
Ritual bonfire at	Mensa		Amhara	Somali	Mecha	Gurage	Kefa	
solar new year (mesqel)			Tigrean			Hadiyya	Dorze	
Importance of			Amhara	Afar	Arsi	Gurage	Konta	Majangir
pilgrimages			Tigrean	Somali	Borana	Sidamo		
Ritual sacrifice	Beni Amer	Falasha	Amhara	Afar	Borana	Sidamo	Kefa	Gumuz
of animals	Mensa	Kimant		Somali	Guji	Konso	Dorze	Mao
Use of grass for	Mensa		Amhara		Guji	Gurage	Dorze	Mao
ritual purposes			Tigrean		Mecha	Konso	Amarro	Tirma
Veneration of	Mensa	Kimant	Amhara	Afar	Borana	Gurage	Kefa	Gumuz
sacred trees			Tigrean		Guji	Konso	Gamu	Majangir
Rainmaking rituals	Beni Amer	Kimant	Amhara	Afar	Arsi	Arbore	Gofa	Koma
	Mensa			Somali	Mecha	Konso	Ubamer	Mao
Taboo on pork	Mensa	Falasha	Amhara	Afar	Borana	Sidamo	Janjero	
		Kimant	Tigrean	Somali	Guji			
Taboo on fish	Beni Amer	Kimant	Amhara	Somali	Borana	Sidamo	Welamo	Mao
					Mecha	Konso	Dorze	

Table 2

Selected Pan-Ethiopian Traits: Cult of Masculinity, Aspects of Social Organization, Insignia of Rank, and Customs Regarding Personal Status

	I	II	III	IV	V	VI	VI	VIII
Special status accorded	Mensa	Kunfel	Amhara	Afar	Arsi	Hadiyya	Dorze	
to killers	Marya		Tigrean	Somali	Borana	Konso	Konta	
Special genre of songs	Mensa	Bilin	Amhara	Afar	Borana	Gurage	Kefa	
to praise warriors	Marya		Tigrean	Somali	Tulema	Konso	Dorze	
Use of stelae or stones	Beni Amer		Tigrean[a]	Harari	Arsi	Sidamo	Janjero	Kunama
to honor brave heroes	Mensa			Afar	Borana	Konso	Gamu	
Strongly pejorative	Beni Amer	Bilin	Amhara	Harari		Gurage	Kefa	
image of women				Somali		Konso	Dorze	
Exclusion of women from	Beni Amer			Afar	Borana	Sidamo	Kefa	Nara
public assemblies				Somali	Guji	Konso	Dorze	Kunama
Importance of patrilineal	Beni Amer	Kimant	Tigrean	Afar	Guji	Gurage	Kefa	Mao
descent groups	Mensa			Somali	Mecha	Sidamo	Dorze	
Custom of levirate	Beni Amer			Afar	Borana	Gurage	Anfillo	Gumuz
				Somali	Guji	Burji		Koma
Presence of caste groups		Agew of Lasta	Amhara	Argobba	Borana	Gurage	Kefa	Mekan
		Falasha	Tigrean	Somali	Mecha	Konso	Dorze	Suri
Division of lineages into	Beni Amer	Bilin	Amhara	Afar	Borana	Gurage	Kefa	
categories of high/low status	Bet Asgede	Kimant	Tigrean	Somali	Leqa	Derasa	Dorze	

Drums as insignia of authority	Bet Asgede Mensa		Amhara[a] Tigrean	Afar	Borana	Konso	Basketo Welamo	Suri
Arm rings as insignia of authority	Mensa Marya		Amhara[a] Tigrean		Borana Guji	Gurage Burji	Kefa Sheko	
Bees/honey associated with rituals or royalty		Agew of Lasta[a]	Amhara	Harari	Guji		Dorze Kefa	
Naming ritual occurs months/years after birth	Mensa	Falasha Kimant	Amhara Tigrean		Borana Guji	Konso Dasenech	Amarro Shangama	
Practice circumcision	Beni Amer Mensa	Falasha Kimant	Amhara Tigrean	Afar Somali	Borana Guji	Gurage Konso	Dorze Gamu	Kunama Mao
Practice clitoridectomy	Beni Amer	Falasha	Amhara	Afar Somali	Leqa	Gurage Sidamo	Anfillo Kefa	Kunama Mao
Hair styles used to indicate status	Beni Amer Mensa		Amhara Tigrean	Somali	Borana Guji	Gurage Konso	Dorze Sheko	Koma Suri

[a]In historic times.

our classification, and when no name is listed in a category it cannot be clear whether that reflects the absence of the trait in question or merely that it was not described in the literature available to me. I have referred to a trait as "pan-Ethiopian" if its presence could be securely attested in five or more of the ethnic group categories.

This survey of pan-Ethiopian traits is by no means exhaustive. It does not include all the traits identified by other authors as having a broad distribution in Ethiopia, such as the construction of rock-hewn churches,[14] the custom of wearing amulets to ward off evil spirits,[15] the use of *gebeta,* a board game played by moving pebbles over rows of holes on clay or wooden boards,[16] and other insignia of rank discussed by Haberland. I have not mentioned probable pan-Ethiopian traits whose presence could not be determined for more than three or four of the ethnic group categories, such as the striking similarities in the chants and gestures employed in mourning ceremonies among such disparate peoples as the Amhara, Sidamo, and Dorze. I have said almost nothing about forms of political organization, conflict resolution, folklore, and musical culture; in these and other areas future investigations may well uncover many more pan-Ethiopian traits.

Enough material has been presented, however, to justify conceiving of Greater Ethiopia as a culture area. Some of the traits listed have affinities with other culture areas: some with Nilotic, or West Sudanic, or Bantu cultures of Africa, others with Semitic cultures of North Africa and the Near East. Others appear to be distinctively Ethiopian. The point here is not to establish exclusively Ethiopian characteristics. What I have demonstrated is that the image of Ethiopia as a Judaeo-Christian Semitic core surrounded by a hinterland of disparate African tribes must be replaced by an image which acknowledges that the peoples of Greater Ethiopia have long shared many features of a deeply rooted cultural complex.

The Ethiopian Response to Alien Influence

Besides possessing a substantial number of common cultural elements, the peoples of Greater Ethiopia exhibit a characteristic mode of relating to foreign intrusive influences—a mode which may be called "creative incorporation." This tendency was adumbrated some years ago by Enrico Cerulli while surveying the history of Ethiopian written literature. In all periods of their literary history, Cerulli notes, Ethiopians have been heavily influenced by foreign writings—by Greek, Syrian, Arabic, and European sources. This extreme receptivity, however, has never taken the form of passive, literal borrowing. "Rather, one can say that it is precisely a typical Ethiopian tendency to collect the data of foreign cultural and literary experience and transform them, sooner or later, to such an extent that even translations in Ethiopic are not always translations, in our sense of the term; but they frequently contain additions, supplementary material, at times misrepresentations of the original, at other times simply the insertion of new materials in such quantity that the literal sense of the original is completely lost."[17] Cerulli goes on to note that once these foreign inspirations have been absorbed and transformed, the resulting contents and styles are quickly canonized. They become part of a tenaciously conserved native tradition.

One can readily extend Cerulli's point to cover other kinds of foreign influence. In recent years art historians have begun to identify a number of Byzantine and European paintings which served as models for Ethiopian miniatures. Here too pronounced receptivity is accompanied by a tendency to transform the foreign sources. Marilyn Heldman has interpreted the portrait of King David playing his harp in the Psalter of Belen Sagad as an example of this phenomenon. Having identified the model for this painting as a miniature in an old Greek Psalter, she notes a number of respects in which the Greek model was transformed: the personification of melody in the original has been changed into an Ethiopian court attendant, the harp has become an Ethiopian instrument, the *begena,* and the insignia of kingship have been transformed into the Ethiopian umbrella, fly whisk, and earring.[18] The Hebraic and Syriac musical ideas in Ethiopian liturgical chants and the Portuguese (or Indian) forms in the Gonderine architecture must be viewed as foreign influences which have undergone similar transformations. Whatever the stimuli, Ethiopian responses reveal a recurrent pattern that indicates neither nativistic rejection nor slavish adherence to imported forms, but a disposition to react to the stimulation of exogenous models by developing and then rigidly preserving distinctive Ethiopian versions. Only when foreign influence increased until it threatened to undermine the capacity of Ethiopians to shape their own culture—the most notable instance being the attempt to subordinate Ethiopian Orthodox Christianity to the Roman Catholic Church in the seventeenth century—was it stubbornly resisted.

This pattern of creative incorporation has been discerned in the earliest instance of alien contact, that between the Pre-Nilotes and the proto-Ethiopians. It is in this manner that G. P. Murdock interprets the response to the intrusion of Sudanic culture in the third millennium B.C.: the proto-Ethiopians "stood their ground, apparently by adopting agriculture and a sedentary mode of life from the culturally more advanced Negroes."[19] Murdock's reconstruction indicates that the proto-Ethiopians neither succumbed to the aliens nor abruptly repulsed them, but responded in a mode of creative incorporation. They not only adopted the Sudanic agricultural complex—based on the cultivation of sorghum, millet, and cow peas—from the Pre-Nilotes, but went on to improve the crops thus introduced, produced important new varieties, and experimented with wild plants in a search for new crops. As a result, highland Ethiopia ranks as one of the world's important minor centers of origin for cultivated plants, contributing eleusine, teff, nug, garden cress, coffee, fenugreek, castor, and safflower. Similarly, after obtaining cattle, sheep, and goats of Egyptian origin through the Sudanic peoples, proto-Ethiopians proceeded to domesticate the donkey and later to cross it with the horse to produce mules. For such achievements the proto-Ethiopians, the ancient Agew in particular, have been judged by Murdock to be "one of the culturally most creative peoples on the entire continent."

It is in response to the various streams of Oriental Semitic influence that this pattern has exhibited itself most clearly and most fatefully. Although significant groups of Ethiopians were highly receptive to the Judaic, Syrian Christian, and Muslim Arab intrusions, what stands out in each instance is the way Oriental Semitic culture was adapted so that Ethiopian autonomy and sense of identity were preserved throughout. In each of these experiences, the Ethiopians neither subordinated themselves to the intruder nor attempted to annihilate him, but evidenced a highly receptive disposition—an inclination to adopt attractive elements of the alien culture and subsequently to transfigure and rework them into a distinctive Ethiopian idiom.

In the area of religious beliefs this pattern is conspicuous. The response to representatives of Judaism, Christianity, and Islam was to adopt their central beliefs and symbols, but to incorporate them in such a way that the resulting belief systems strongly reflected indigenous traditions. Elohe, Egziabher (the Christian god) and Allah were adapted in a manner that permitted continued belief in the sacral significance of stones, trees, waterplaces, and serpents and in the efficacy of rainmakers and the evil eye. Pre-Semitic deities like Waq and Zar were not eliminated, but were transformed into special spirits.

Comparable adaptations took place in contacts between Ethiopians who followed Semitic religions and pagan tribes, and even in contacts between pagan tribes: the Nao called their deity Kai before their subjugation by the Kefa; afterward they embraced the Kefa deity Yero and relegated Kai to the position of a localized spirit.[20]

Although this Ethiopianization of the Semitic religions has been noted by earlier observers, it has usually been interpreted as evidence of the superficiality with which Ethiopians have assimilated them. From the perspective proposed here, one can interpret it instead as an effort by Ethiopian peoples to maintain their traditional cultural orientations relatively intact by absorbing and transfiguring only as much of the Semitic religions as suited their purposes.

It is particularly noteworthy that groups within five of the seven categories of peoples into which I have divided the descendants of the proto-Ethiopians have embraced the Semitic influence to the extent of incorporating it into the marrow of their self-conceptions. The Falasha, Agew of Lasta, Kimant (II) and the Tigreans and Amhara (III) believe their ancestors were Jews, and the ruling strata of the Afar and Somali tribes (IV), the Yejju Galla (V), and some of the North Eritrean tribes (I) claim descent from Arabs. This pattern is repeated internally by groups within the two other categories which claim descent from Semitized Ethiopians: the Gurage (VI) trace their origin to Tigrean colonists, and traditions of both the Kembata (VI) and the Kefa (VII) maintain that their royal lineages are descended from one of the Solomonid Amhara monarchs. In all cases, however, these beliefs about Semitic origins are used as means of ancestral ennoblement *to confirm the superiority of the respective Ethiopian tribes as Ethiopians,* and are certainly consistent with the notion that they are superior to both Jews and Arabs. The Somali, who have had the most extensive and continuous contact with Arabs, are no exception. As Trimingham notes, "they are extremely proud of being Somali and though they may delight in the fiction that they are descendants of the Prophet or his companions and have constructed elaborate genealogies, they do not consider themselves Arabs, and inter-marriage with Arabs today is almost unknown."[21] In the Sudan, by contrast, conversion to Islam was typically accompanied by an overwhelming Arabizing influence. The peoples of Greater Ethiopia have tended to respond to the periodic intrusion of alien cultural elements, whether Sudanic agriculture, Mediterranean literature, Byzantine art, or Semitic religions and genealogies, in a mode that upholds their sense of cultural autonomy, continuity, and creativity. In chapter 7 I shall analyze an example of this pattern that has special historical importance.

To have similar orientations and traditions and to be part of a complex relational network is not, however, to belong to a single society. Even today, one can scarcely speak of the diverse peoples of Greater Ethiopia as composing a single national society. They remain organized in relatively discrete, autonomous, local social systems, under the umbrella of what is still aptly called the Imperial Ethiopian Government. Yet they are much closer to constituting a national society today than they were in the past. We turn now to examine the processes which led to the degree of national unification that does currently exist.

5

Patterns of Expansion and Unification

The previous chapter presented grounds for considering Greater Ethiopia a sufficiently unified ecological and cultural area to justify treating it as a legitimate object for holistic analysis. Let us now consider what factors transformed this entity from a congeries of loosely related units into an emerging single societal system.

About the year 1300 it would have been difficult to predict such a transformation. Greater Ethiopia at that time consisted of well over fifty separate societies, each with its own language, religion, and customs. Each was proudly independent. None of them had established a preeminent position beyond a fairly circumscribed local area.

Most of these groups never developed ambitions beyond the struggle to survive and to live in ways hallowed by their cultural traditions. Some of them did not survive. The kingdoms of Inarya, Fatigar, Dewaro, and Bale have vanished. Historically significant peoples like the Bosha, the Doba, and the Gafat have been annihilated or assimilated or, like the Argobba, Baiso, Belaw, and Gidicho, have dwindled to remnants of a few hundred persons. Countless places with names important at that time, like Kuelgora, Waz, Kelat, and Segah, have disappeared.

It is remarkable that so many of those diverse groups did survive. Protected by mountains and waterways and oriented chiefly to their local exigencies, most of them have remained stationary, living in or near the circumscribed territories of their earlier habitats. They remained strong enough to protect themselves against hostile neighbors but not so aggressive as to engage in sustained territorial expansion.

Were this true of all the surviving groups, Ethiopia today would indeed be no more than a museum of peoples, and would doubtless have succumbed to European rule in the nineteenth century. As it was, a small number of these groups had the motivation and capacity to expand. Two of them, the Amhara and the Oromo, laid the foundations for Ethiopia's transformation into a polyethnic national society.

Chapter Five

Centers of Expansion before 1300

Although the decisive expansions began in the fourteenth century, it should be noted that before 1300 there were four known centers of expansion which were of consequence for the eventual shape of Greater Ethiopia. These early expansions stemmed from the Aksumites, the Beja, the Agew, and the Somali.

A small group of Ge'ez-speaking people established at Aksum a kingdom which flourished from the first to the sixth century A.D. and continued to play a significant role in northern Ethiopia until the tenth century. Through a series of wars the kings of Aksum extended their boundaries in all directions. At various times they established their dominion over the Beja in the north, the Saho in the south, and the Nubians in the west. At two different periods they crossed the Red Sea to become masters of Yemen. Of more enduring importance, they consolidated a monarchical tradition and a Christian culture that would survive transplantation to the south despite the destruction of Aksum as a political center.

The Muslim Arab conquests, although not directed against the Aksumites, weakened them by cutting Aksum off from trade and contact with Yemen, Egypt, and the Greco-Byzantine world. What is more, the Arab expansion indirectly stimulated three minor waves of ethnic expansion within Greater Ethiopia.[1] The first of these was the Beja, nomadic pastoralists speaking North Cushitic who had lived for thousands of years along the Red Sea coast. It was characteristic of Beja life to be moved periodically by the poverty of their land and the pressure of enemies to invade new territories in the Red Sea region. In response to the expansionist pressures exerted by Muslim Arabs from Egypt, the Beja moved south in large numbers during the late seventh and eighth centuries and took possession of most of the territory that had been under Aksumite control in the north.

In reaction to the Beja intrusion, the Aksumites sought to extend their dominion more effectively over lands and peoples farther south. They penetrated central Ethiopia in an effort to subjugate the pagan and Judaized Agew and to convert them to Christianity. For a while they were successful, and a revitalized Aksumite kingdom extended its control to the port of Zeila and resumed a thriving trade with Yemen. In pushing southward away from the Beja, however, they provoked the hostility of the Agew. In the 970s the latter lashed back with a campaign in which Aksum was sacked, her churches were burned, and most of her royalty were killed. This warfare opened the gate for a northward expansion of some of the Agew tribes. As the Beni Amer of Eritrea are the ethnic precipitate of the southward Beja migration of the eighth century, so their neighbors thirty miles to the east, the Bilin people, are the descendants of Agew tribesmen who migrated north after the fall of Aksum in the tenth century.[2]

By that time Muslim Arabs had established a ring of coastal centers around the Horn of Africa, which facilitated a stream of Arab immigration into coastal areas then occupied by the Somali. Some of these Arabs settled and became founders of Muslim lineages. Demographic pressure from the increased immigration and quite possibly a series of droughts in the region stimulated a sustained expansion of Islamized Somali tribesmen from the eleventh to the fourteenth century. Moving southward along the coast and down the valleys of the Webi Shebelle and its tributaries, the Somali subjugated or displaced indigenous Bantu cultivators and Bushmanoid hunting and fishing people and established their presence in the vast area of the Horn which they have occupied ever since.

Expansions like those of the Somali, Agew, and Beja were essentially quests for new territory. The peoples they conquered were either killed, enslaved, or forced to move elsewhere. Living under highly decentralized forms of political organization, they had neither the interest nor the capacity to integrate diverse peoples under a common authority. In contrast, the Aksumites, whose rulers in periods of political prosperity called themselves "King of Kings," enjoyed holding sway over diverse peoples, receiving tribute from them, and bringing them into a single cultural orbit.

The ideal of a Christian state that had been instituted at Aksum, though dimmed by the hardships encountered in the wake of the Muslim Arab conquests and their repercussions, never died. Precisely where the post-Aksumite kingdom was centered at the beginning of the twelfth century is not known, but in 1135 the imperial center was reestablished by an Agew king in the province of Lasta. He and his descendants ruled as the Zagwe Dynasty for 135 years. Although relatively quiet politically, this appears to have been a period of vital missionary activity, as well as a time for the construction of a number of remarkable monolithic churches.

According to Ethiopian tradition, the sole survivor of Aksumite royalty, Ambasa Widim, fled south to Menz after the sack of Aksum and fathered a line of descendants who eventually "restored" the

Solomonid Dynasty in 1270. Whatever the literal truth of this story, it accurately reflects the reality that the traditions of Aksum underwent a period of quiescent development in the south before their triumphant resurgence in a new form.

The Amhara Thesis

Credit for revitalizing the effort to provide a political and cultural center for Greater Ethiopia goes to a group living in a region called Amhara. Situated in what is today the southwestern part of Wello Province, the historical Amhara region was bounded on the west by the Abbai (Blue Nile) and its tributary the Bashilo River; on the north by the regions of Angot and Lasta; on the east by the escarpment leading down to the Danakil Desert, and on the south by the Wanchet River, reached through a mountain pass so precipitous that it is known as Ahiyya Fejj, Destroyer of Donkeys.

During the first millennium A.D. the inhabitants of Amhara were Agew peoples who developed a distinct South-Ethio-Semitic tongue, *amariñña* or Amharic, quite possibly through a process of pidginization and creolization.[3] The composite character of this language made it preeminently qualified to become the national language of Ethiopia. Combining features distinctive of both the northern and southern branches of Ethiopian Semitic, it also incorporated a large component of Cushitic vocabulary and syntax. A recent survey of the languages of Ethiopia notes that Amharic is a particularly "typical" Ethiopian language, possessing six of the eight phonological markers and sixteen of the eighteen grammatical features identified as characterizing the broader Ethiopian language area.[4]

Many of the Agew in this region were converted to Christianity in the centuries right after the Beja invasions, if not before. As early as 870 A.D. two important churches were built at Lake Hayq.[5] One of the last kings of Aksum is believed to have lavishly endowed one of these, the Church of Saint Stephen, and to have built himself a palace nearby.

The earliest descriptions of Amhara, from the sixteenth and early seventeenth centuries, refer to it as a large region, containing several subject provinces, all of which speak Amharic. It is described as more mountainous than the rest of the empire, but with fertile hills and valleys, full of fields of barley, wheat, and millet and rich with honey and horned cattle. Until the Muslim invasion of the 1530s, it figured as the nucleus of the Abyssinian kingdom, a region where the royal palace and residences afforded the maximum amount of security.

It was a pretender from Amhara, Yikunno Amlak, who ended the Zagwe Dynasty by leading an expedition in which he killed its king and acceded to the throne with the name of Tesfa Iyesus, Hope of Jesus. Claiming descent from the ancient rulers of Aksum and beyond that from King Solomon and the Queen of Sheba, Yikunno Amlak established in 1270 what is known as the Solomonid Dynasty. The kingdom he appropriated was not insubstantial, but neither was it vast in extent or very secure. Zagwe resistance soon flared up in Lasta. Farther north, the Beja and Bilin tribes endangered communications with the Nile Valley and the Red Sea. In the northwest, the Falasha were building a strong independent kingdom. In the west and southwest the independent kingdoms of Gojjam, Damot, and Hadiyya flourished. A string of aggressive Muslim states had been firmly established in the southeast: Bale, Dewaro, Fatigar, and the greatest threat of all, Ifat. The nomadic Afar were restive in the east. Dozens of independent pagan kingdoms occupied the far southwest.

Under the kings of Amhara, as Yikunno Amlak and his successors were called by contemporary Arab writers, the Amhara sphere of influence expanded considerably. The great breakthrough of Amhara political expansion occurred during the reign of Amde Siyon (1314–44), aptly called the founder of the Ethiopian state. On becoming king, Amde Siyon drove a wedge south and conquered the vast kingdom of Damot. Immediately after, he subjugated the neighboring kingdoms of Hadiyya and Gojjam. Thus strengthened, he turned eastward to subdue the hostile Muslim states of Ifat and Fatigar, went on to defeat the other Muslim sultanates of Dewaro and Bale, defeated Falasha troops in the north which had been mobilized to support the Muslim cause, and annexed other parts of Shoa, including the fractious province of Menz. His achievement was immense, his reputation great: an Arab writer of the 1340s described him as the ruler over ninety-nine kings!

Amde Siyon established a pattern followed by several successors. Throughout the rest of the fourteenth century and most of the fifteenth century they consolidated and extended the authority of the Solomonid monarchy. Beja tribes in the north were subdued; Agew lands in the northwest were incorporated; the port of Zeila was occupied; and many pagan tribes in the southwest, including the Kembata, Janjero,

Kefa, and Welamo, were brought under the imperial authority. The zenith of Amhara power was attained under Zera Ya'iqob (1434–68). His expeditions to the south had a profound and lasting impact on the peoples of those regions. Many of them still have legends which recall that period. Among the Sidamo, for example, his reign is still remembered as a Golden Age. Even among the remote Maji, who live in the southwesternmost part of Greater Ethiopia, he is remembered under the name Seraqo.[6]

The Amhara expansion was not merely an extension of brute power. Political subjugation was accompanied, and often preceded, by a diffusion of Amhara cultural influence in such spheres as language, religion, moral values, and political style. The Amhara language spread to become the mother tongue of peoples in the provinces of Shoa, Gojjam, and Begemdir, as well as most of Wello. In other regions which maintained their mother tongues, numerous Amharic words entered the local vocabulary. Amharic became a lingua franca for the elites of all the regions in the Amhara sphere of influence.

The official religion of the Amhara kingdom, Monophysite Christianity, had a major impact on the beliefs and practices of indigenous pagan religions. To some extent that influence was imposed: Zera Ya'iqob, in particular, insisted that his subjects abandon their pagan rites for Christian ones, and ordered them to wear a tattoo condemning the devil and affirming belief in the Trinity. But the major responsibility for converting other Ethiopians to Christianity seems to have been borne by a number of remarkable Amhara monks who went as missionaries to the pagan lands armed with little more than a cross. Many of these, like the sainted Tekle Haymanot, were disciples of Iyesus Moa, abbot of the Lake Hayq monastery. Impressed by these formidable personalities, men who became known as miracle workers, slayers of dragons, and powerful preachers, a number of pagan Agew and Omotic peoples fused their traditions with Christianity and succumbed to the mystique of Amhara Christian supremacy. Years before Amde Siyon led his armies into Damot, Saint Tekle Haymanot had so impressed its king, through such deeds as uprooting the trees where demons lived, driving out possessing spirits, and remaining implacable despite threats of death, that the king and all his people submitted to baptism.

The main thrust of Amhara missionary activity was to replace pagan animistic beliefs and ritual practices. Thus one missionary during the time of Amde Siyon, Saint Ewostatewos (Eustathius), founder of an important monastic order, is celebrated for having destroyed twelve sacred groves of trees dedicated to pagan deities. But the Christian missions also had an impact on certain areas of morality. Major battles were waged, over centuries, to eliminate polygamy and the practice of castration to make eunuchs.

The spectacle of a strong, expansive monarchy, animated by a faith promulgated by heroic missionaries and celebrated with the colorful pomp and ceremony of Ethiopian Christian processions, so impressed a number of subject or neighboring peoples that they came to imitate certain aspects of Amhara political culture as well. Eike Haberland has recently sought to specify the particulars of such influence. He sees it in the change in the character of some of the Omotic monarchies, a movement from the archaic pattern of a sacred office which passively symbolizes the well-being of the land toward more active royal participation in administration and military activity, and from an attitude of indifference to political history toward a more historically conscious sense of the kingdom, reflected in the development of oral traditions of king lists and related memories. His most concrete evidence is drawn from the vocabularies of the Omotic kingdoms, many of which adopted Amharic terms to designate features of their political order presumably influenced by the Amhara example—terms such as royal hall, councillor, proclamation, tax, and royal drum, as well as Amhara insignia of kingship, notably the royal umbrella.[7]

The Solomonid expansion of the fourteenth and fifteenth centuries promoted the integration of Greater Ethiopia in two respects. It broadened the base of support for the political and cultural center of an emerging Ethiopian state by increasing the number of people in the highland plateau regions who identified with the Solomonid kingdom and its Monophysite Christian religion. Beyond Tigray, Lasta, Angot, and Amhara, the only areas sustaining a precarious identification with this center during the Zagwe dynasty, the core territory of the kingdom was extended to many other areas which came to speak Amharic: to Menz and the rest of Shoa, to Gojjam and Damot, to Wegera and Dembiya, and subsequently to Agew Midir and Semien. Second, beyond this central region, often called "historic Abyssinia," it influenced a wide area of peripheral kingdoms and peoples by impressing them with the grandeur of the imperial center and the power of its religion.

At the end of this period, serious obstacles to the continued expansion of Amhara power were posed by two adversaries, the Turks and

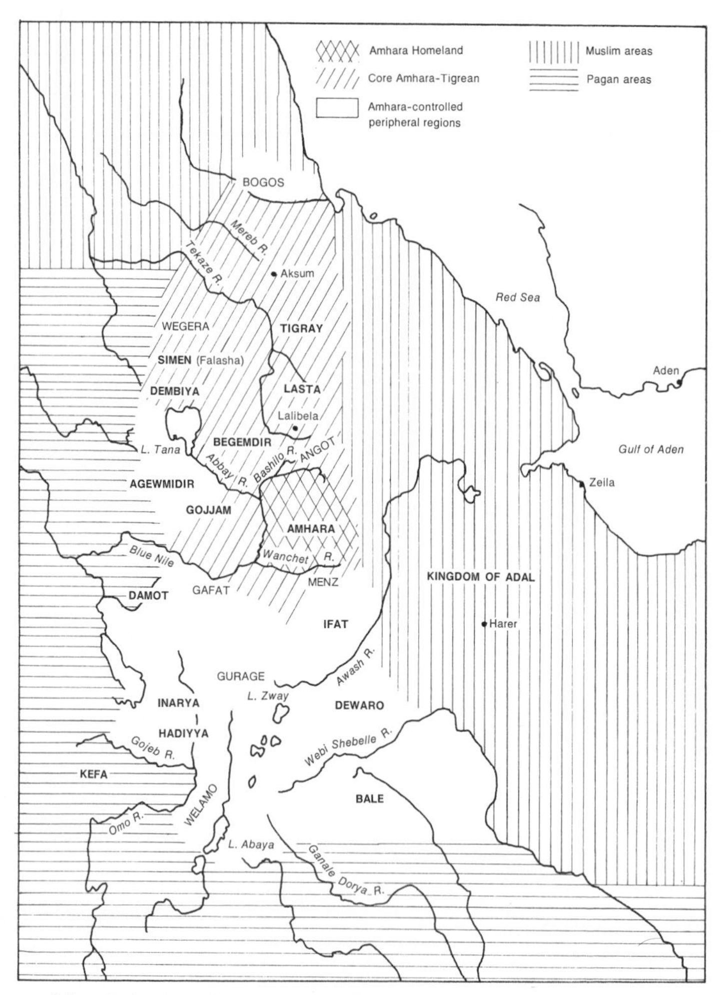

Map 2. Amhara Homeland and Sphere of Influence about 1520

the Galla. By 1520 the Turks had emerged as the greatest military power in the world. Their conquests of Syria, Egypt, and the Arabian coasts brought them to the doorstep of Ethiopia. They proceeded to supply firearms to great numbers of Afar and Somali tribesmen, who, led by a charismatic figure from the sultanate of Harar, Ahmad Grañ, launched a *jihad,* a Muslim holy war, against the Solomonid kingdom. The *jihad* devastated Shoa, Amhara, Lasta, and parts of Tigray. It was halted only when Grañ was killed by a combined squad of Ethiopians and Portuguese matchlockmen. The Turks themselves invaded the north in the 1550s. They succeeded in establishing lasting control over the coastal towns of Massawa and Arkiko, but were pushed back from the interior by Ethiopian forces.

Conventional histories of Ethiopia stress the epochal character of the destruction wrought in the Abyssinian kingdom by the invasion of Ahmad Grañ's forces, and the accidental nature of their rout, which prevented Ethiopia from becoming a totally Islamic state. Both points are misleading, however. Although the small expedition of Portuguese matchlockmen who killed Grañ in 1543 certainly helped to put a quick end to the *jihad,* it is likely that sooner or later the Abyssinians would have prevailed. Grañ's home base, the sultanate of Harer, had been impoverished by his campaigns and racked by internal dissension. The morale of his nomadic followers, accustomed to life on the deserts and steppes, was being eroded by the formidable altitudes and rainy seasons of the highland plateaus. Turkish expansionism in the Horn of Africa was being checked by the Portuguese, who by 1540 had secured their control over the open waters of the Indian Ocean. And Abyssinian cultural orientations, as I shall argue in detail below, gave the Amhara-Tigreans a kind of staying power with which the ad hoc assemblage of Grañ's followers could scarcely compete over the long run.

The consequences of the *jihad* were indeed serious—it had been, as J. S. Trimingham describes it, "devastating in its destruction, irresistible in its ferocity, and appalling in its cruelties"—but the result was far from a fatal disruption of the Abyssinian state. The rest of the sixteenth century saw the Amhara kingdom recoup its strength in many ways and expand as before. Emperor Galawdewos (1540–59) quickly reoccupied the provinces of Dewaro and Fatigar, reasserted control over the Gurage—who paid him an annual tribute of gold figurines, many hides, and a thousand head of cattle—and reconquered the Hadiyya and other kingdoms in the southwest. Sertsa Dingil (1563–97), in a brilliant series of campaigns, decisively put an end to Harer as a military power, to Turkish expansion in Eritrea, and to the independence of the Falasha kingdom. He also forced the peoples of Inarya and Bosha to undergo baptism and become Christians. Despite continued harassment and attempted invasions from foreign Muslim centers in subsequent centuries, the Solomonid kingdom reestablished sufficient security to contain external Muslim threats thereafter.

What did prevent Abyssinia from returning to the pre-*jihad* status quo and produced an irreversible change in the face of Greater Ethiopia was a series of invasions by an East Cushitic people from the south who moderated the Muslim-Christian antagonism by weakening the positions of *both* parties.

THE OROMO ANTITHESIS

The warfare between the Amhara kingdom and the Afar and Somali tribesmen under Grañ was in some respects a clash between similar antagonists. Both were groups of Semitized Ethiopians, adherents of a Semitic religion and followers of political leaders who sought legitimacy through identification with Semitic ancestors. By contrast, the expansion of the Oromo represents a novel element in the politics of the empire—the assertion of a pagan, purely African force. And a remarkable force it was. Their rapid spread over the area of present-day Ethiopia and Kenya during the sixteenth century constitutes one of the great expansions in history, comparable in magnitude, as Asmarom Legesse has observed, to the conquests of the Fulani of West Africa and the Nguni of southern Africa.

Although earlier scholars believed that the Galla migrated from Arabia by way of the Horn of Africa, a preponderance of evidence now supports the argument that the Oromo homeland was in southern Ethiopia, somewhere between the middle lakes of the Great Rift Valley and the Bale plateau. Although it is likely that the Oromo had earlier followed a primitive agricultural style of life, perhaps on the Bale plateau, at the time of their great expansion they were nomadic pastoralists.

The first Galla movements for which we have any documentation occurred during the 1520s, when they invaded Bale; in the next decade they crossed the Webi Shebelle and invaded Dewaro. During the apex of Muslim expansion under Grañ, then, the Galla had already made serious inroads into Muslim territory in southeast Ethiopia, another reason the *jihad* was vulnerable over the long run. In the 1540s and 1550s they penetrated northward to invade Fatigar and Shoa. One group then branched eastward and in 1567 made devastating raids in the Harer region. Other tribes pushed farther north to invade the Amhara region, and beyond that Angot and Begemdir. In the last decades of the century they went farther into Begemdir, Dembiya, and Gojjam. Still another division of the Galla carried its invasion toward the west. They moved up the Great Rift Valley to the province of Waj, and subsequently spread to the Gibe River region, to Damot, and into Gojjam. In most of the territories penetrated during the sixteenth century, the Galla still remain.

In contrast to the Amhara expansion, the timing and style of the Oromo expansion were not calculated to extend political dominion. The Galla did not seek to gain recognition for a central authority, to collect tribute, or to impose a national religious culture. Their expansion was triggered by two motives: a need to carry out ritually prescribed military expeditions against enemies and a search for new land

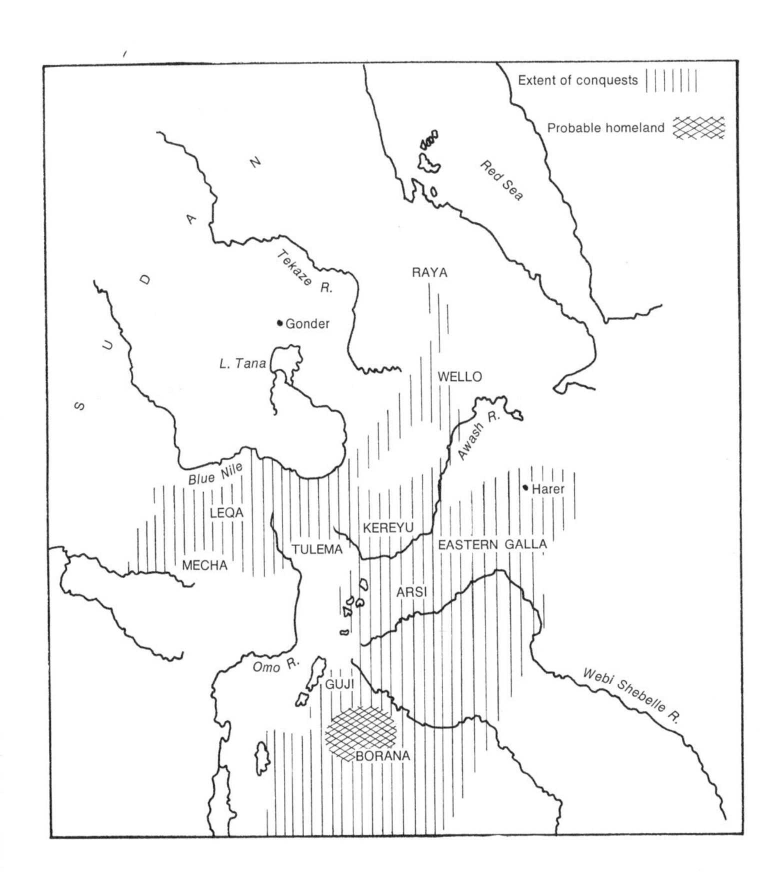

Map 3. Oromo Homeland and Area of Conquests about 1700

to accommodate a rapidly growing population. Its timing was dictated not by the stategic considerations of imperial power, but by a cultural calendar which stipulated that raids against some new enemy should be carried out every eight years. Its style was not to stay and rule but, initially at least, to hit and run: attack the enemy by surprise and carry off the most booty in the shortest time. When population pressures, the increasing distance of raids, and other considerations prompted the Galla to stay and settle, they were more inclined to adopt the culture of their new neighbors than to spread their own.

In some ways the Galla expansion resembles that of the Somali. Both were nomadic pastoralists moved by demographic pressures to conquer new lands. But whereas the Somali encountered indigenous peoples of inferior technology and power who were easily subdued, the Galla encountered a variety of peoples with more specialized technologies and strong social organizations. To survive in this new setting, the Galla were forced to make a number of very diverse adaptations in the regions where they settled. In one sense, the story of the various accommodations between the Galla and the other peoples of Greater Ethiopia is the story of the making of modern Ethiopian society.

The Ethiopian Synthesis

Although the full history of this process has yet to be written, its general phases and patterns can be suggested. I shall deal first with Galla accommodations to other peoples in the south, then discuss the central issue of the types of relationships established between Galla and Amhara in the north.

The first few decades of expansion established a broad Galla zone which permanently divided the southern half of Greater Ethiopia. We know little about the peoples who were annihilated, absorbed, or displaced by this initial sweep. Presumably the South Ethio-Semitic-speaking peoples—Argobba, Selti Gurage, Gafat, and Amhara—suffered extensively. But the Galla could not penetrate everywhere they wished. They were contained within this zone by many peoples who stubbornly resisted their incursions.

On the west, Lacustrine and Omotic peoples such as the Konso, Derasa, Wolamo, Sidamo, Gurage, and Kefa stood their ground, effectively preventing an Oromo takeover; expansion on the east was checked by the Somali and the Afar. In subsequent centuries these peoples became "traditional enemies" of the Galla. Although some territorial loss was associated with these hostilities—notably the continuing penetration of southeast Ethiopia by Somali at the expense of the Galla—for the most part a kind of equilibrium was established. Periodic reciprocal raiding became the dominant form of interaction. In this relatively stabilized situation, moreover, there developed, as was noted earlier, more peaceful relationships among the antagonistic tribes. An early instance of this accommodation was the negotiation of a treaty in 1568 between the eastern Galla and the *amir* of Harer, whereby the former agreed to stop their hostilities and were induced to attend the markets in Harer territory. Eventually proximity to Harer city, which became a vital center for the diffusion of Muslim culture despite its political demise, and perhaps the example of the Somali and Afar, stimulated most of the Galla in this region to convert to Islam. Indeed, some of the eastern, Barentu Galla tribes have so acculturated to their Somali neighbors that they have assumed a Somali genealogy and are counted as members of the Ogaden Somali family by the Somali themselves. The Kereyu tribe of the Galla is likewise reported to have adopted many aspects of the culture of their Afar neighbors.

The Galla experienced comparable accommodation and acculturation in relation to their enemies in the southwest. I have already mentioned the convention whereby hostilities were renounced when Galla tribesmen attended markets in the Gurage region, and the existence of trade and ritual relationships which different Galla tribes established with both the Konso and the Derasa. The Otu branch of the Guji Galla has assimilated Sidamo culture so thoroughly that many now speak only the Sidamo language. The southern Guji disparage their northern kinsmen by calling them "half-Sidamo" or "half-Derasa." Galla who settled in proximity to the Gurage adopted the ensete plant culture of their neighbors and have come to resemble them so much that they are referred to as "half-Gurage" by other Galla. The Galla tribes who settled in the Upper Gibe region, impressed by the monarchical forms of the Inarya and Bosha they conquered or by the neighboring Kefa kingdom, reorganized their entire political system; during the eighteenth and early nineteenth centuries, they formed a number of kingdoms of their own. These kingdoms were also converted to Islam in the nineteenth century. In short, before the conquests of Menilek in the late nineteenth century, the southern part of Greater Ethiopia was primarily a scene of multidimensional interaction between the Galla and their enemy-trader-host-comrade tribes to the east and west.

The picture in the north was just as complicated. During the latter half of the sixteenth century the Galla spread north and west, over Shoa, Amhara, Angot, Begemdir, Damot, and Gojjam. At times they were checked by Amhara forces. They suffered stunning defeats by troops under Sertsa Dingil in 1569, at Lake Zwai in 1573, and in both Gojjam and Begemdir in 1578. But they kept on coming. The seventeenth and eighteenth centuries saw a protracted struggle between Amhara and Galla, now one side winning, now the other. By the end of this period the Galla were solidly enough established to play a crucial role in working out the destiny of the empire.

They became influential in two ways: by establishing independent enclaves in the heartland of the Solomonid kingdom and by entering directly into the mainstream of Amhara life and politics. A string of Galla enclaves emerged in the central part of the country, elongating northward, as it were, the central zone previously established in the south. The nomadic invaders borrowed enough culture from their hosts to make an adequate adaptation to the new environment but maintained a distinct identity, political autonomy, and some crucial ingredients of their traditional culture. In Shoa the Tulema Galla adopted the plow cultivation of grains and, somewhat later, Monophysite Christianity from the Amhara, but they maintained Gallinya as their mother tongue. To the north, the Wello and Yejju Galla tribes adopted many Amhara practices and the Amharic language as well, but kept their separateness by becoming Muslims during the eighteenth century. Beyond them, the Raya Galla maintained more elements from their pastoral way of life, but were influenced by Tigrean neighbors and immigrants to learn the Tigrinya language.

Galla efforts to establish a separate presence west of these enclaves were never successful, but it was in those areas that they became most fully integrated into Amhara life. Despite repeated attempts to cross the Blue Nile and conquer Gojjam province, they were consistently defeated in that region. Most of them fled after such skirmishes; but many joined the victorious army and became soldiers of the Amhara king. Some doubtless remained to settle in Gojjam, but they were largely absorbed by the host people and are remembered today in Gojjam mainly through records of Galla names in some parish genealogies.

Although the Galla also failed to establish a separate ethnic enclave in Begemdir province, they intruded there even more successfully by becoming part of the imperial court at Gonder. As in the south, where a state of chronic enmity opened the way to pacific relations between the Galla and other peoples, so the chronic enmity between Galla and Amhara opened the way to special kinds of alliance. The opening wedge was for particular Galla groups to become allied with dissident Amhara figures. Early in the reign of Emperor Iyasu I (1682–1706), for example, a cousin of the king made an attempt to usurp the throne. His family had taken refuge among the Galla in order to escape the customary banishment of the king's relatives to a mountain fortress. When it began to look as though Iyasu's religious policy was to favor the theological doctrines of the monks of Debra Libanos against that of the followers of Saint Eustatewos, two of the latter began to stir up seditious sentiments among the people of Damot and neighboring areas. One of these monks, Kasmati Wali of Damot, was himself of Galla origin. They mobilized great numbers of Galla to support the pretender. Iyasu learned of the plot in time to hasten to the Blue Nile with such forces that the Galla were overawed and lost their spirit.

In the eighteenth century, however, the Galla were more successful in this kind of undertaking. Young Bakaffa had taken refuge among the Yejju Galla after his escape from the mountain prison, and when he became king (1719–29), the Galla were welcomed at his court. He not only recruited a regiment of Galla soldiers, but employed a Galla as Master of the Palace and surrounded himself with a Galla praetorian guard. Although he had Amharic Christian names as well, the name by which he was chiefly known, Bakaffa, was itself a Gallinya name, meaning "inexorable." After this episode, the Galla position at the imperial court steadily grew in significance. Bakaffa's son Iyasu II (1730–55) married a woman from the Wello Galla. Their son Iyoas I (1755–69) insisted on speaking Gallinya at the court, gave numerous official posts to Galla men, and permitted his two maternal uncles to play major roles in his regime.

What is more, Iyoas's reign initiated a century of relative disorganization in northern Ethiopia, commonly known as the Era of the Princes (Judges). The great Galla expansion had reduced the Abyssinian kingdom to a fraction of its former size. Galla enclaves between Shoa and Amhara and Tigray disrupted communications among the core Abyssinian highland provinces. Galla personnel at the imperial court had confused and demoralized the central regime. There ensued a period of extreme decentralization and bloody civil wars in which Galla strength waxed through the ascendancy of a new political element, the Yejju Galla dynasty. The founder of this dynasty was Ras Ali I, "the Great," who gained the governorship of the provinces of

Amhara and Begemdir and assumed control over the Gonderine emperor, by then a mere figurehead. Ali's position was transmitted through several generations of his descendants, all of whom affected a conversion to Christianity in order to legitimate their authority but who clearly favored Muslims, and at times openly supported Islam against Christianity.

With Galla nobles ruling the core provinces of Amhara and Begemdir, controlling of the puppet emperors at Gonder, and even penetrating parts of Tigray and Gojjam provinces, the Amhara expansion seemed eclipsed once and for all. So it would have been, but for three contrary developments.

A local dynasty of Amhara rulers in northern Shoa, originating in the district of Menz, successfully pursued a policy of steady reconquest and settlement of Shoa province throughout the eighteenth and early nineteenth centuries. By the reign of Sahle Sellassie (1813–47), who called himself king of Shoa, most of this province was under Amhara rule. Annual expeditions went out to the Galla territories to collect tribute and punish withholders. Galla-Amhara accommodation proceeded apace. Nearly all the Galla of Shoa Province became Christians, and intermarriage between Galla and Amhara became relatively frequent.

Reunification in the north was more sudden and dramatic. The process was triggered by an external threat, the attempted invasion of Ethiopia from the west by Egyptian forces under Muhammad Ali. A young man named Kasa, a nephew of the chief of the frontier district raided by Muhammad Ali's men in 1837, was roused by that event to a mission to strengthen Ethiopia so it would not be vulnerable to such attacks. He and many of his countrymen were alarmed by the possibility of collusion between the Egyptians and the Muslim Yejju Dynasty within Ethiopia. The result of Kasa's determination became visible in 1855 when, after defeating the last Yejju Galla ruler and the other great feudal lords as well, he took the throne as Emperor Tewodros II.

A third development may be mentioned, one which rendered the Galla vulnerable to the aggressive policies of Sahle Sellassie and Tewodros. This was the tremendous differentiation experienced by the Galla themselves in the wake of their invasions. Although most Galla continued to speak Gallinya, they were spread so far over Greater Ethiopia as to prohibit any effective communication. More important, they had adopted radically different cultures: some were now Christians, some Muslims, and others remained pagan; some were now plow cultivators, some hoe cultivators, and others remained nomadic pastoralists. They had divided into numerous tribes which were as likely to fight one another as to fight other ethnic groups. This precluded concerted defense on a pan-Galla basis.

One axis of division among the Galla tribes was that some were inclined to identify with the Abyssinian monarchy. The pattern of Galla-Amhara alliance at the level of the royal court was continued by Tewodros, who married Tewabech, daughter of the Galla chief he would defeat in 1853. A major new alliance was forged by Emperor Yohannes with a Wello Galla chieftain, the Imam Muhammad Ali, whom he baptized in 1882 as Mikael. The latter accompanied Yohannes in campaigns against the Sudanese, and the Wello Galla cavalrymen were known as some of the emperor's best soldiers. As early as 1871 Menilek integrated Wello Galla soldiers with his Amhara troops, and one of his key officers, Ras Gobena, was Galla in origin. Ras Gobena, supported by numerous Galla nobles and soldiers, in fact carried out much of the work of conquering other Galla tribes for Menilek. An important chieftain of the Leqa Galla, Moroda Bakere, who allied himself with Ras Gobena and participated in Gobena's battles in the western regions, later submitted to Menilek's suzerainty, taking the Amhara name Gabre Egziabher and receiving the title Dejazmatch. Moreover, although many Galla groups valiantly opposed these conquests, in some Galla quarters the conquests were welcomed as a way to put an end to their own troublesome intertribal fighting. These instances of Galla submission to and alliance with Amhara-Tigrean authorities did much to strengthen the Ethiopian state on the eve of the battles with Italy in the mid-1890s. To defend Ethiopian soil against the Italian enemy Galla troops fought side by side with Amhara and Tigrean forces.

Warfare between Galla and Amhara had gone on more or less continuously for 450 years. Like the conflict between the Amhara and the Muslim sultanates of the east which preceded it, it was terribly destructive of human life, economic resources, and artistic treasures. But as a consequence of this protracted struggle, the Amhara were able to complete in the nineteenth century what they had been incapable of doing in the fifteenth. By the end of Zera Ya'iqob's reign in 1468, the Solomonid empire was so vast that it was no longer viable, given the administrative resources then available. A period of feudal distintegration was inevitable in any case. Both indirectly and directly, the Galla intrusion constituted a major factor in the nineteenth-century unification. It did so indirectly as a stimulus, in that the growth of Galla power in the north, through enclaves and intrigues, spurred the rulers of Shoa and the emperors Tewodros and Yohannes to respond in heroic measure to the challenge of unifying the country. It did so directly both by providing a far-flung cultural corridor through which the multifarious peoples of Greater Ethiopia could more readily be connected and by Galla-Amhara-Tigrean military alliances which enabled the Ethiopian state to dominate all the peoples in Greater Ethiopia and prevail over external enemies from the Sudan and from Italy.

6

Four Questions

In one sense the question which opened this book has been answered. Ethiopia was chosen for invasion by fascist Italy because it was the only traditional society that survived the Scramble for Africa. It was able to survive—to hold Egypt and Sudan at bay, play power politics with England, France, and Russia, and inflict a punishing defeat on Italy in 1896—because of a sequence of developments that had occurred over three thousand years. First, the diverse peoples of Greater Ethiopia had come to constitute a loose intersocietal system by virtue of sharing similar cultural traditions and engaging in many kinds of interactions. Second, many of these peoples became integrated into a single polyethnic imperial system through the efforts of the Aksumites and later the Amhara, who established a single political authority over vast territories. Third, this process was disrupted but then revitalized by the Galla, who both stimulated and participated in the national resurgence and provided a certain amount of social cement to connect the many peoples at the periphery of the empire. By the time of the European appropriation of the African continent, consequently, Ethiopia possessed a traditional order fully capable of governing and defending itself.

The answer thus far has been a genetic one. Although it does not exhibit the detail usually expected of a historian, its logic has been one of the historian's principal methods of explanation: to proceed from antecedent to significant consequent events so as to demonstrate how the later events were conditioned by the earlier ones. For the comparative student of societies, however, such an answer often serves chiefly to raise other kinds of questions. Instead of seeking the genetic explanation of a particular phenomenon, comparativists are likely to be more concerned with explaining it in terms of generalized abstract properties.

To carry out this mode of explanation we must identify certain factors (dependent variables) whose variation can be linked to other factors (independent variables) in a determinate way. A set of dependent variables can readily be generated in the present inquiry by raising questions about the major formative experiences in Ethiopian history which have been outlined. Four aspects of that account seem particularly problematic.

1. *What enabled the Amhara to carry out their far-reaching expansion in the fourteenth and fifteenth centuries?* The medieval expansion of Amhara power has no parallel in Ethiopian history. Lacking the techniques and stimulation which Aksum derived from the Sebaeans and the Hellenistic world, lacking the weaponry which Yohannes and Menilek acquired from European powers, the Amhara rulers from Amde Siyon to Zera Ya'iqob established their dominion over many peoples with roughly comparable technologies. For all their success in battle, the Oromo never established a single government for all their own tribes, let alone a regime over other peoples. The closest parallel to the Amhara expansion in the past millennium is that of the Kefa kingdom in the late eighteenth century, but that was an empire of much smaller scale and shorter duration.

Two scholars have already made observations which touch on this question. J. Spencer Trimingham attributes the success of the Amhara expansion to an impulse for religious survival, a "desperate response from the vital element of Abyssinian Christianity" to the threat from hostile pagan peoples.[1] More recently, in his extremely well researched reconstruction of this period based on new documentary material, Tadesse Tamrat has stressed an economic motive, the desire of Amhara rulers to gain control of the lucrative trade carried on by Muslims in the Ethiopian interior.[2] Whether the Amhara expansion was mainly reactive or proactive, however, the question remains: What gave the Amhara the capacity to carry out their political expansion so successfully?

2. *What enabled the Oromo to defeat the Amhara so regularly in the sixteenth and seventeenth centuries?* Unlike the followers of Ahmad Grañ, whose Turkish firearms gave them a decisive advantage over the Amhara, the Oromo were technologically inferior to the Amhara when their expansion began. They came on foot and had no weapon better than a wooden spear. Only in the 1550s did they acquire horses, presumably from the Somali, and iron spears. And their switch to cavalry was a mixed blessing: Oromo on horseback were handicapped in regions like Amhara where foot soldiers had better maneuverability on tortuous mountain passes. In any case, the Amhara

had superior horses as well as (by then) some firearms, helmets, and coats of mail. Yet the Oromo took possession of more new territory in a hundred years than the Amhara had conquered in two centuries.

To some extent the Galla victories can be explained by the weakness of the Amhara resulting from Grañ's *jihad.* Yet I have already shown that the *jihad* did not cause enough disruption to leave the Amhara helpless before the new invader. Indeed, this factor is not even mentioned by our most valuable contemporary source, an Amhara monk named Bahrey who wrote a *History of the Galla* in the 1590s. Bahrey himself raises with genuine consternation the question I pose here: "How is it that the Galla defeat us, though we are numerous and well supplied with arms?" Three answers are suggested by his work. Some wise men, he reports, attribute the Galla victories to divine intervention: God was punishing the Amhara for their sins. Being a devout Christian, Bahrey does not openly repudiate this interpretation; but he devotes much more of his text to presenting naturalistic explanations. His second answer is sociological. The Abyssinian nation is divided into ten social classes, most of which take no part in war and do not hide their fear. Only the tenth group "is composed of those who carry the shield and spear, who can fight, and who follow the steps of the king to war. It is because these are so few in number that our country is ruined."[3] Bahrey's third point concerns the motivation of the Galla:

> If they have killed men or large animals, they shave the whole head, leaving a little hair in the middle of the skull. Those who have not killed men or large animals do not shave themselves, and in consequence they are tormented with lice. That is why they are so eager to kill us.[4]

Bahrey was right, I believe, to look for the explanation of the Galla victories in the contrast between Amhara and Oromo social patterns. There is something to be said for his point that because of the greater development of functionally specialized classes among the Amhara they were able to mobilize a much smaller proportion of able-bodied men for battle than the Galla. Even so, a highly motivated and well-organized special military force can sometimes prevail over a general manpower levy.

Bahrey's suggestion that the Galla were more strongly motivated to win in battle than the Amhara seems more promising. Emperor Sertsa Dingil, who reigned when Bahrey wrote, made a similar point when he reportedly ascribed the victories of the Galla to their firm determination on going into battle to either conquer or die, and the routs and defeats of the Amhara to the "exact opposite" disposition.[5] Perhaps an explanation for these opposed orientations can be found in social patterns more basic than the Galla's putative desire to get rid of lice.

3. *What enabled the Amhara-Tigreans to spring back in the nineteenth century and establish their hegemony over a vaster empire than ever?* From 1800 to 1850 the Solomonid monarchy was weaker than at any previous time in its history. Warfare among feudal lords raged unchecked. Islam was spreading rapidly in the south and the far north. The Yejju Galla Dynasty was undisputed master of the core provinces of Amhara and Begemdir. External Muslim threats were being revived. The Christian community was weakened by the eruption of bitter doctrinal disputes. In this situation, nevertheless, emperors Tewodros, Yohannes, and Menilek stimulated an unparalleled upsurge of Amhara-Tigrean strength. How was this possible?

4. *What enabled the Galla to contribute so effectively to the integration of Greater Ethiopia in the nineteenth and twentieth centuries?* Selective affiliation with other groups was not the only response possible in their situation. Conceivably, the Galla could have reunited to oppose the Ethiopian state with all their might, or they could have withdrawn to a wholly isolated self-centered and self-contained condition. As it was, from the 1870s onward significant numbers of Galla joined forces with Amhara and Tigreans on behalf of new dynastic or national goals. Those who resisted or remained outside the national center adapted to the polyethnic situation of Greater Ethiopia in various ways, establishing trading relationships with other tribes, incorporating many non-Galla into Galla communities, and assimilating the cultures of many groups near whom they settled. Whereas the typical pattern of Amhara settlement among other peoples was to establish a defended enclave devoted to the maintenance and propagation of Amhara culture, the Galla adapted so readily to other cultures that different Galla groups came to be designated, as we have seen, as half-Gurage, half-Derasa, Gallinya-speaking Amhara, and so on. What accounts for this apparently pronounced capacity of the Galla for expansive social affiliation?

The foregoing questions suggest that to account for the main formative experiences in the evolution of Ethiopian society we must isolate and examine four aspects of the historical actions of the

Amhara and Galla peoples. On two of these variables, the capacity for political domination and what may be called regenerative capacity, the Amhara have been shown to rank high and the Galla relatively low. On the other two variables, military ability and capacity for social affiliation, the Galla rank high and the Amhara, by comparison, not so high. How can these differences in collective capacities be explained? Without presuming to account for all of the variation in question, I shall seek to identify certain "structural" properties of the traditional social systems of the two peoples which can be shown to have promoted or inhibited the capacities in question.

Generally speaking, "structure" refers to those aspects of phenomena which cannot be described or understood solely with reference to the properties of elementary units. For many social scientists it has become customary to divide the universe of facts amenable to structural analysis into two spheres, the social and the cultural.[6] In both spheres, the concept of structure has many meanings. In order to avoid the complexities of attending to the full range of structural issues, I shall limit my analysis to three types of structural properties, those which seem particularly relevant to explaining the differences between Amhara and Galla actions which have just been cited.

Broadly speaking, structural analysis can proceed on three levels. It can delineate the properties of a system as a whole, the nature of the relations between a whole and its parts, or the character of relations among parts. My analysis of the traditional Amhara and Oromo systems will deal with selected issues on each of these levels.

First I shall consider that part of the cultural code of each society which defines the identity of a total community: its boundaries, its mythical past, and its future project.

Second, I shall deal with part-whole relations by considering one aspect of the institutional order, namely, the extent to which different institutionalized role-complexes perform specialized functions for the total system.

Third, I shall examine relations among parts by considering the typical ways in which interaction processes are patterned.

After a close look at one complex within the Amhara cultural system in the next chapter, this structural analysis of the two systems will be carried out in chapters 8 and 9. How that analysis contributes to answering the four questions raised above will be considered in chapter 10, and in the concluding chapter I will discuss the significance of all this for understanding the evolution of Ethiopian society.

7

Tigrean Legacy: A National Script

The medieval efflorescence of Amhara power and culture was predicated on a set of developments that took place long before the Amhara emerged as major actors on the Ethiopian scene. I refer to the role of Aksum, which served as a seedbed for the germination of elements which would later become firmly rooted in Amhara consciousness. After Aksum ceased to function as a political center these elements were transplanted to the Amhara homeland, where they flowered with unusual durability.

The achievements of Aksum can be identified as a specifically Tigrean contribution to Ethiopian nationhood, for present-day Tigreans are the direct descendants of the inhabitants of the Aksum plateau, and their language, Tigrinya, was already spoken in Aksum by the second half of the first millennium A.D. A major bequest of the ancestral Tigreans to Amhara culture was a national script. I use this ambiguous term advisedly, for they created a national script in three senses.

They developed the Ethiopic script, an indigenous form of writing that made possible the elaboration of a Great Tradition in Ethiopia and the formation of a stratum of literati.

They also created a national script in the dramaturgic sense. By this I refer to the set of motifs and directives that orient every societal community. Like the script of the playactor, the societal script provides a sense of the actor's identity, indications of significant past experiences, and guidelines for future actions.

Finally, as a major work in the Great Tradition and principal repository of the societal script, they created a particularly hallowed literary script, the *Kibre Negest.*

THE *Kibre Negest*: A REASSESSMENT

The *Kibre Negest* is often described as the foremost creation of Ethiopic literature. Its central narrative has held the imagination of northern Ethiopians for a thousand years. For centuries observers have commented on the extraordinary popularity of the *Kibre Negest* among Amhara and Tigreans. Abba Gregorios reported to Job Ludolf in the 1650s that the *Kibre Negest* was a work "of very great authority" among his countrymen, and somewhat more than a century later James Bruce noted that "its reputation in Abyssinia is immense." In the 1840s Rochet d'Héricourt observed that the legend of the Queen of Sheba, the central story of the work, "dominates the fastnesses of Ethiopia." The depiction of this legend in a conventionalized sequence of forty-four pictures, moreover, has long been one of the most widely enjoyed creations of Ethiopian painting.

It is surprising, then, that the question of the role of the *Kibre Negest* in Ethiopian culture has not been taken very seriously. One reason for this neglect may be its literary quality: to many readers the *Kibre Negest* has seemed little more than a hodgepodge. In this chapter I shall challenge that interpretation and argue that the *Kibre Negest* is a truly unified epic which has served a variety of important cultural functions, including the provision of a societal script for the Amhara-Tigrean peoples.

To be sure, the *Kibre Negest* is in many respects a composite work. The product of many hands, the final redaction was completed early in the fourteenth century by six Tigrean scribes. The principal redactor, a chief priest of Aksum named Yishaq, claims that he merely translated an Arabic version of the work into Ethiopic, although the text incorporates many oral and written traditions from Ethiopia as well as from the Near East. Quotations and allusions are drawn from a potpourri of identifiable sources: from thirty-one books of the Old Testament and twenty books of the New Testament; from Chaldean Targums, the Talmud and Midrashim, rabbinic commentaries, and the Antiquities of Josephus; from Koranic stories and commentaries; from Old and New Testament apocryphal writings, including the Syriac Book of the Bee, the Book of Adam, the Book of the Cave of Treasures, Wisdom of Solomon, Ascension of Isaiah, the Book of Enoch, Jubilees, the Legends of Mary, and the Testament of Reuben; from the writings of patristic authors including Origen, Cyril of Alexandria, Gregory of Nyasa, Gregory of Nazianzus, Severus, and Epiphanias; and from other Ethiopic works including the Synaxarium and the Life of Hanna.[1]

Even when the content is original, the literary style of many passages of the *Kibre Negest* reveals its composite origin. As David Hubbard has shown in splendid detail, the style of the epic moves back and forth shamelessly among the styles of Old Testament wisdom writings, New Testament parables, rabbinic exegetical argumentation, Koranic lamentation, Koranic use of historical illustration, apocryphal biography, patristic homily, and patristic allegorical interpretation.

It is this composite character that has most impressed students of the *Kibre Negest* and has surfaced in general descriptions of it. Wallis

Chart 2
The *Kibre Negest:* Outline of Contents

- I. Prologue—chapters 1–18
  - A. Question: Wherein lies the greatness of kings?—2
  - B. Sacred primacy of Tabernacle of Zion—1, 10–11, 17–18
  - C. Elect genealogy and God's convenant—3–9, 12–16
- II. Central Narrative: Book within a Book––19–94
  - A. Ethiopian monarchy connected with the chosen lineage—21–43
    1. Visits of Tamrin the merchant and Makeda, Queen of Ethiopia, to King Solomon—21–28
    2. Seduction of Makeda and birth of Menilek—29–32
    3. Menilek acknowledged as Solomon's legitimate descendant—33–34
  - B. Moralizing glosses
    1. Polygamy attacked; Solomon's polygamy exonerated—28B–29A
    2. Contra kings not of Israelite lineage—348
    3. Proclamation of moral commandments by Zadok—40–42.
    4. Pro authority of kings and clergy—44
  - C. Ethiopians take possession of the Tabernacle of Zion—45–63
  - D. Enhancement of status of Ethiopian kingdom—63–83
    1. Decline and fall of Solomon—63–67
    2. Prophecy of descent of Mary and Christ through Solomonic line—68–71
    3. Misguided reign of Solomon's second son and successor, Rehoboam—70
    4. Reign of Solomon's third son, Adrami, as king of "Rome"—72–73
    5. Semitic ancestry of other kings—74–83
  - E. Moralizing gloss—criticism of the Jews—69
  - F. Establishment of Menilek's kingdom—84–94
  - G. Criticism of Christian heretics (Nestorians)—93B
- III. Epilogue—95–117
  - A. Old Testament stories parelleling gospel events—96–98
  - B. Defeat of Satan and omnipresence of God—99–101
  - C. Coming of Christ and wickedness of Jews—102, 106–11
  - D. Significance of the holy ark—103–5
  - E. Ultimate triumph of Ethiopia—113–17

Budge describes the *Kibre Negest* as "a great storehouse of legends and traditions," and Ullendorff calls it "a gigantic conflation of cycles of legends and tales."[2]

The result has appeared uneven and disjointed to most commentators. Rochet d'Héricourt considered its central narrative to be "confused, tangled, and devoid of interest."[3] Walter Plowden belittled the *Kibre Negest* as a "rubbish of invented tales, or imperfect and incoherent statements."[4] In more measured language a number of more scholarly readers have rendered similar judgments. Cerulli observes that the *Kibre Negest* consists of four different parts which are markedly unequal in artistic quality. Introducing the first publication of the complete text of the *Kibre Negest* in 1905, Karl Bezold held that "the question of the literary unity of the book . . . should be answered in the negative." Following Bezold, David Hubbard divides the book into three parts and argues that they were inserted at different periods. Hubbard also describes the first part as broken by interruptions and notes that the third part could readily be expunged.

The first cautious steps toward a reversal of Bezold's judgment were taken by Cerulli himself when he observed that a variety of inspirational subjects embodying varying degrees of expressive intensity may well serve the overriding objective of the work—that is, to exalt the Solomonid Dynasty. In alluding to this political motive Cerulli expresses what has become the prevailing view of the function of the *Kibre Negest:* that its chief purpose was to add legitimacy to the line of kings which gained ascendance with Yikunno Amlak in 1270. One need not accept this view, however, to see Cerulli's point and carry it further. A new appreciation of the *Kibre Negest* may be reached by looking not at the diversity of its contents but at its overall structure. In its inner form the *Kibre Negest* reveals a fully realized aesthetic unity.

Prologue, Narrative, and Epilogue

The general form of the *Kibre Negest* is that of a book within a book. Its central narrative, chapters 19 through 94, is presented as a manuscript purported to have been discovered by an archbishop of "Rome" (Constantinople) in the Church of Saint Sophia. The narrative is flanked by a prologue of eighteen chapters and an epilogue of twenty-three chapters.

The prologue and epilogue consist, as it were, of a number of antiphonal statements between a chorus and a solo. The "chorus" takes the form of the "318 Orthodox Fathers," an allusion to the 318 bishops of the Council of Nicaea (A.D. 325). The solo speaker is named Gregory, a conflation of two historical personages: Gregory the Illuminator, who lived at the time of (but did not attend) the Nicene Council, and Gregory Thaumaturgus, who died half a century earlier. The bishop who is said to have discovered the manuscript of the central narrative is Domitius, who did attend the Nicene Council. The setting of the book thus may be dated in the fourth century A.D., and the actions of the book within the book take place more than twelve centuries earlier, about 960 to 930 B.C., during the reigns of Solomon and Rehoboam.

The issue which animates the work as a whole is raised near the very beginning, when Gregory says:

> When I was in the pit I pondered over this matter, and over the folly of the Kings of Armenia, and I said, In so far as I can conceive it, in what doth the greatness of kings consist? Is it in the multitude of soldiers, or in the splendour of worldly possession, or in the extent of rule over cities and towns? This was my thought each time of my prayer, and my thought stirred me again and again to meditate upon the greatness of kings.

The question is never answered head on. But the prologue indicates that the "greatness of kings" has to do with two things: possession of a sacred emblem—the Tabernacle of Zion—and connection with an elect genealogy, with whom God made a covenant. The entire prologue is concerned exclusively with these two motifs and the rest of the epic works out their implications and destinies.

The opening lines of the epic state forthrightly that these two themes are to be its central subject:

> The interpretation and explanation of the Three Hundred and Eighteen Orthodox Fathers concerning splendour, and greatness, and dignity, and *how God gave them to the children of Adam,* and especially concerning the greatness and splendour of *Zion,* the Tabernacle of the Law of God, of which he Himself is the Maker and Fashioner, in the fortress of His holiness before all created things. . . [Emphasis mine]

The sacred primacy of the Tabernacle of Zion is celebrated in the first, middle, and closing chapters of the prologue. We are told that Zion was the first thing to be created by God; that it was the place where the Father, Son, and Holy Spirit agreed to create Adam; that the heavenly and spiritual Zion became incarnate in two respects, through the likeness of the Tabernacle which Moses made out of wood, and through the "Second Zion," Mary, mother of Christ.

The other chapters of the prologue describe the generations of the elect line, from Adam through Noah and Shem through Abraham to Jesse and David, and God's covenants with Noah, Abraham, and their descendants. God promises Abraham to "bring down the Tabernacle of My Covenant upon the earth . . . and it shall go round about with thy seed, and shall be salvation unto thy race." The prologue closes by joining the themes of Zion and the Chosen People even more closely:

> Unto David will I give seed in her [the Tabernacle]
> And upon the earth one who shall become king
> And moreover in the heavens one from his seed
> Shall reign in the flesh upon the throne of
> the Godhead.

The dynamic of the central narrative is thus established. If royal glory comes from descending in the line of King David and from possessing the Tabernacle of Zion, how can this glory be associated with the kings of Ethiopia?

The first objective is attained through the events described in chapters 21 to 43, the second through those in chapters 45 through 63. As Cerulli rightly observes, these two sections have the highest literary merit of the whole epic. They contain the heart of the plot and the most intense dramatic episodes.

The first episode begins with the visit of Tamrin, a wise merchant, to King Solomon. Overwhelmed by Solomon's wisdom, Tamrin returns to his queen, Makeda, the Queen of Sheba, and tells her "how Solomon administered just judgment, and how he spake with authority, and how he decided rightly in all the matters which he enquired into, and how he returned soft and gracious answers." Makeda at length makes the trip to Jersualem herself and is similarly impressed. She decides to adopt Solomon's religion: no longer to worship the sun, but "the Creator of the sun, the God of Israel; [and the] Tabernacle of the God of Israel." Before leaving Solomon's court, Makeda agrees to dine with him, and then to spend the night at his palace provided that he swear not to take her by force. Solomon makes her swear a counter oath not to take by force any of his possessions. It is an oath she is forced to break when, parched with thirst after the highly spiced food

Solomon deliberately had served her, she takes a goblet of water. Solomon thereby becomes freed from his oath and works his will with her. On returning to Ethiopia the queen gives birth to a son, who in the extant manuscripts is named variously as Beyne-Lekhem or Ibna el-Hakim, but in oral versions of the story is always called Menilek. On reaching manhood Menilek journeys to Jerusalem, where he is recognized by his father and crowned as king of Ethiopia with the name David II.

In the second main episode, Menilek returns to Ethiopia with the firstborn sons of the nobles of Israel, including Azariah the son of Zadok the priest. Unable to tolerate the thought of being separated from the Tabernacle of Zion, Azariah replaces it with pieces of wood and spirits it away. Menilek, Azariah, and their companions, animals, and wagons are then raised above the ground and fly across the Red Sea back to Ethiopia before the theft of Zion is discovered and Solomon's men give chase.

Through Solomon's crafty seduction of Makeda and Menilek's clandestine abduction of the Ark of the Covenant, the Ethiopian king now has special claims to glory. These claims are enhanced in the succeeding section, chapters 64 to 83, a collection of short narratives which relate: the corruption of Solomon by the daughter of Pharaoh and his subsequent downfall; a prophecy of the descent of Mary and Christ through the Solomonic line; the misguided reign of Solomon's second son and successor, Rehoboam; the reign of his third son, Adrami, as king of Rome [Constantinople]; and accounts of the Semitic ancestry of several other lines of royalty, including the kings of Medyam, Babylon, Persia, Moab, Amalek, and Philistia. The combined effect of these stories is to enhance the importance of Semitic ancestry for royalty. "For as God sware He gave . . . an exalted throne and dominion to the seed of Shem" (chap. 83)—a state which Ethiopia is about to achieve when Menilek returns and is crowned. Moreover, it implicitly celebrates the Ethiopian king over all the other Semitic kings, because Menilek is the firstborn of Solomon's three sons who become kings, and because the tales of nearly all the other kings involve wickedness or moral corruption. Only Adrami is presented in morally favorable light, enhanced by the prophecy of the coming of Christ in the immediately preceding chapter.

The final section (chaps. 84–94) of the book within a book describes the triumphant return of Menilek to Ethiopia, his mother's abdication, his coronation, and his institution of a new moral order. The

Semitic line is now enthroned in Ethiopia, sharing glory with none but the descendants of Solomon who rule in Rome: "for the kings of Ethiopia and the kings of Rome were brethren and held the Christian faith" (chap. 93). But the final glory must be reserved for Ethiopia, for we read that, 130 years after the time of Constantine, "Satan, who hath been the enemy of man from of old, rose up, and seduced the people of the country of Rome, and they corrupted the Faith of Christ, and they introduced heresy into the Church of God by the mouth of Nestorius." The manuscript ends with the established supremacy of the glory of the Ethiopian king, who promptly sets out to wage war, protected and blessed by possession of Zion, receiving tribute from the kings of Egypt, Medyam, and India—feared by all and fearing no one.

In chapter 95, which begins the "epilogue," the word returns to the chorus of 318 bishops and Gregory. They heartily affirm the validity of the manuscript which has just ended. When that story begins, the Jews are the chosen people; when it ends, the mission has been transferred to Ethiopia. It is the task of the epilogue to celebrate that reversal: to add legitimacy to the story, to carry the reversal further, to infuse the whole conception with prophetic certainty and apocalyptic grandeur.

The reversal is accentuated in the epilogue by its focus on the coming of Christ and the salvation of Christians, on the one hand, and the wickedness of Jews on the other. The warm sympathy for the Jews which marked the central narrative can now be discarded for the tables have been turned. The use of Old Testament prophecies as proof texts for the coming of Christ parallels the use of Solomonic ancestry to legitimate Ethiopian kings: Jewish symbols are used to discredit the Jews and glorify Ethiopians. The reversal is climaxed in the last two chapters, which allude to military expeditions against Jews. In those expeditions the kings of Ethiopia and "Rome" collaborate, an allusion to the sixth-century alliance between Kaleb of Ethiopia and Justin I of Byzantium. Even so, Rome's defection from the orthodox faith is also prophesied in the closing chapters, whereas Ethiopia by contrast "shall continue in the orthodox faith until the coming of our Lord." Gregory must finally conclude:

> Thus hath God made for the King of Ethiopia more glory, and grace, and majesty than for all the other kings of the earth because of the greatness of Zion, the Tabernacles of the Law of God, the heavenly Zion.

Chapter Seven

THE *Kibre Negest* AS A NATIONAL EPIC

We must conclude, then, that in spite of the great diversity of its material and the uneven quality of its parts, the overall structure of the *Kibre Negest* appears highly unified. All elements of the epic conspire toward a common end.

We may now ask, what is the cultural significance of this work? Is this coordination of literary elements mere propaganda, as Cerulli and others have suggested, a device to confirm the legitimacy of the usurping dynasty from Amhara? Is it so, as Conti-Rossini flatly asserts, that the *Kibre Negest* "has no other purpose than that of demonstrating the usurpation of Yikunno Amlak to be nothing more than a just act of vindication"?[5]

Evidence of many kinds contradicts that interpretation. For one thing, the date of the final redaction of the *Kibre Negest* is now believed to have been around 1320, half a century after the Solomonid usurpation, when the position of the Amhara dynasty was quite secure. More important, the redactors were not Amhara but Tigreans, and their patron was no Amhara ruler but a Tigrean lord named Ya'ibike Igzi. Far from being a devoted champion of the new dynasty, Ya'ibike Igzi attempted to rebel against the reigning Solomonid monarch, Amde Siyon, for which affront the king had him destroyed.

There are clear indications, moreover, that the central story of the *Kibre Negest* was current at least in oral tradition long before the Amhara usurpation. A passage in the history of the Coptic patriarch Philotheus shows that the Ethiopian legend ascribing the origin of Menilek I to the union of Solomon and the Queen of Sheba was known in Cairo as early as the tenth century. A work written in 1208 by an Armenian Christian records the belief that Abyssinians possessed the Ark of the Covenant and that the Queen of Sheba came to Solomon from Abyssinia. The allusion to Ethiopia's alliance with Byzantium in the epilogue convinced Budge and other scholars that much of the material of the *Kibre Negest* dates from a time when memories of this alliance were relatively fresh, around the year 600. In what is perhaps the most persuasive reconstruction of the origins of the *Kibre Negest* to date, moreover, Jean Doresse proposes that the Aksumites adopted the core ideas of the Solomonic saga from the Judaized legends of the South Arabian kingdom of Himyar in the course of their occupation of Yemen in the sixth century.

Historical evidence apart, the internal character of the work makes clear that much more is at stake here than the fortunes of a particular dynasty. On the contrary, I would argue that the *Kibre Negest* is more fruitfully viewed as a national epic, a work which in various ways embodies orientations developed by a stratum of Tigrean literati at a point when they had attained a working synthesis of diverse cultural ingredients and were ready to advance a firm conception of Ethiopian national character and purpose.

The *Kibre Negest* is a national epic in three respects. First, most simply and obviously, it contains a myth of the founding of the Ethiopian nation. It is thus a national epic in the conventional, dictionary sense: an imaginative work that embodies a conception of crucial formative events in the national history. As such it has aptly been compared with the Aeneid, another effort to glorify one nation's beginning by linking it to an earlier, prestigious nation's history and epic.

Second, it can be seen as expressing central psychological conflicts which members of the society typically experience in the course of growing up. This aspect of the work will be discussed in a separate publication.[6]

Third, it is the literary expression of what Talcott Parsons has referred to as a complex of *constitutive symbolism* and that is included in what I have referred to above as a societal *script:* a body of symbols that provides specialized cultural legitimation both for the societal enterprise as a whole and for privileged positions within the society.[7] To follow the inner logic of the epic from this perspective is to observe the dialectical resolution of the Tigrean struggle to create a viable national identity.

A Cultural Identity Struggle

Whatever the reasons may have been for Yishaq's disclaimer that he merely translated the *Kibre Negest* from an Arabic text into Ge'ez, the fact remains that the work itself is suffused with patriotic feelings and serves from first to last to glorify the land of Ethiopia and proclaim a proud Ethiopian identity. Several passages praise the country in a characteristically Ethiopian manner. The *Kibre Negest* repeatedly compares Ethiopia with Judah, a land flowing with milk and honey, a land of undisputed attractions; but whenever the comparison is made, Ethiopia appears the fairer. Thus, when asked to stay on and settle in Judah, the headmen of Tamrin the merchant reply:

> Our country is the better. The climate of our country is good, for it is without burning heat and fire, and the water of our country is good, and sweet, and floweth in rivers; moreover the tops of our mountains run with water. And we do not do as ye do in your country, that is to say, dig very deep wells in search of water, and we do not die through the heat of the sun; but even at noon-day we hunt wild animals, namely, the wild buffaloes, and gazelles, and birds, and small animals. And in the winter God taketh heed unto us from year to the beginning of the course of the next. And in the springtime the people eat what they have trodden with the foot as in the land of Egypt, and as for our trees they produce good crops of fruit, and the wheat, and the barley, and all our fruits, and cattle are good and wonderful.

In a similar, but more poignant, situation, Solomon pleads with young Menilek to remain with him in Jeruslaem. The reply could be that of a twentieth-century son of the Ethiopian soil, rejecting the fleshpots of Europe to return home to live out his bittersweet destiny:

> Though thou givest me dainty meats I do not love them, and they are not suitable for my body, but the meats whereby I grow and become strong are those that are gratifying to me. And although thy country pleaseth me even as doth a garden, yet is not my heart gratified therewith; the mountains of the land of my mother where I was born are far better in my sight.

And Menilek's chief companion on the return trip to Ethiopia, Azariah the priest, utters similarly appreciative words, words which Ethiopians could most naturally be expected to put in the mouth of this archetypical expatriate:

> We say that God hath chosen no country except ours, but now we see that the country of Ethiopia is better than the country of Judah. And from the time that we have arrived in your country everything that we have seen hath appeared good to us. Your waters are good and they are given without price, and you have air without fans, and wild honey is as plentiful as the dust of the marketplace, and cattle as the sand of the sea. And as for what we have seen there is nothing detestable, and there is nothing malign in what we hear, and in what we walk upon, and in what we touch, and in what we taste with our mouths.

The intensity of the protests suggests that the land of Judah had indeed exerted some attraction for Ethiopians. The issue, of course, is not the territory, with which Ethiopians probably had little acquaintance before the Diaspora, but Judaic culture, with which ancient Tigreans had a good deal of contact. In effect, the *Kibre Negest* is a record of the process of working out some of the mental conflicts engendered by that contact, a process that can profitably be analyzed in the terms of Anthony Wallace and Raymond Fogelson's seminal paper "The Identity Struggle."[8]

The identity struggle denotes a complex process in which one tries to maintain or restore a favorable self-image. This process consists of efforts to minimize the discrepancies between real and ideal identities and to maximize the distance between feared and real identities. These efforts take such forms as employing mechanisms of defense like denial, repression, projection, or rationalization; reconstituting the self through such devices as religious conversion, prophetic inspiration, or psychotherapy; or acting outwardly so as to change the kinds of communication one receives from significant others. Although these concepts were devised to deal with psychological processes within the individual, they apply to collective behavior as well.

It may be postulated that a protracted identity struggle must have been set in motion by the sustained confrontation between the Northern Ethiopians and the intruding Oriental Semites. This would not have been so had the Ethiopians defined either themselves or the Semites as inferior people. Instead the ancient Tigreans conceived of themselves as superior people and at the same time perceived the Jews, Arabs, and Syrians as superior in certain respects. Impressed by aspects of Oriental Semitic culture, they may have associated the lighter skin color of its bearers with their achievements. Such a conflict demanded resolution.

Two passages in the *Kibre Negest* allude to these issues. Shortly after the headmen of Tamrin the merchant have eulogized the land of Ethiopia, they add the following qualification: "But there is one thing that ye have wherein ye are better than we are, namely wisdom, and because of it we are journeying to you." And just after Azariah the priest finishes his eulogy of Ethiopia he adds, "But there is one matter that we would mention: ye are black of face. I only mention this because I have seen it, and if God lighteth up your hearts there is nothing that can do you harm." This seems to imply that if God does not light up the hearts of the Ethiopians, their black skin puts them at a disadvantage.

These issues must have been posed time and again in the experience of the ancient Tigreans. Repeatedly they confronted aliens who impressed them because of certain cultural superiorities associated with a lighter skin color. It is possible that they adopted writing and religion from the Sabaeans; it is certain that they adopted many elements of Hellenistic, Judaic, and Syrian Christian cultures. Christianity may even have exacerbated a sensitivity to differences of skin color, for early church fathers were enamored of imagery that associated blackness with sinfulness. Gregory of Nyasa went so far as to say that Christ came into the world to make blacks white, and that in the Kingdom of Heaven Ethiopians become white. That such ideas were internalized by blacks is suggested by the remarks attributed to the ascetic Father Moses the Ethiopian, who derided himself as a "sooty-skinned black man" and once rebuked an archbishop for being white only outwardly but still black inwardly.[9]

Ethiopians could simultaneously acknowledge what they perceived as the superiority of an alien culture and assert their own indomitable sense of superiority by following the response pattern which I described in chapter four as one of "creative incorporation." In the *Kibre Negest* this pattern is exemplified by the way the Tigrean literati dealt with a sequence of four identity conflicts.

The first of these conflicts is triggered by the perception of Judaic religion as superior. This is symbolized in the *Kibre Negest* by the extent to which the Ark of Zion is glorified. The reaction of a proud people to this perception was one of anxiety about being inferior to the Jews with respect to religion. The narrative resolves this conflict by working out a new image of the Ethiopian self based on an identification with the intrusive culture. The Ethiopians can then say that, because they have abandoned their old beliefs and superstitious practices and have embraced the God of Israel and his commandments, they are equivalent to the Jews.

Conversion to Judaism, however, produces an even more distressing identity conflict. It entails accepting beliefs about the descendants of Ham set forth in the Old Testament. The *Kibre Negest* makes it clear that Judaized Ethiopians must have chafed under the biblical curse placed upon them as Hamites. Thus an officer of King Solomon attempts to undermine young Menilek's commitment to his native land by reminding him that "when the sons of Noah—Shem, Ham, and Japhet—divided the world among them, they looked on thy country with wisdom and saw that, although it was spacious and broad, it was a land of whirlwind and burning heat, and therefore gave it to Canaan, the son of Ham, as a portion for himself and his seed forever." Another passage in the epic notes that "by the Will of God the whole of the kingdom of the world was given to the seed of Shem, and slavery to the seed of Ham."

Simple acceptance of Judaic beliefs would thus *exclude* the Ethiopians from the covenant with God and condemn them to the status of slaves. As this was intolerable, conversion was not enough. *The Tigreans had to deny that they were the Hamites of the Old Testament.* They did this by portraying their elite as having been descended from the elite of Judah, even as Menilek was descended from Solomon and David. They used this genealogy to replace an older Ethiopian tradition which held that the kings of Aksum were in fact descended from Ham—through Aethiopia and Aksumawi, his son and grandson!

Having defined their rulers as Semites, the Tigrean scribes could now appropriate the divine covenant with the sons of Shem. This act is anticipated in the story of Solomon's dream in chapter 30:

> And after he slept there appeared unto King Solomon (in a dream) a brilliant sun, and it came down from heaven and shed exceedingly great splendour over Israel. And when it had tarried there for a time it suddenly withdrew itself, and it flew away to the country of Ethiopia, and it shone there with exceedingly great brightness for ever, for it willed to dwell there.

The reversal of roles is actualized by the transfer of the Ark of Zion from Jerusalem to Ethiopia by Menilek's retainers. By this fateful deed the curse on the "Hamites" is lifted once and for all. The Ethiopians now become the chosen ones, while henceforth the Jews are to be excluded. When Menilek is told that the Ark now belongs to him and his people, he has an intense emotional reaction.

> He was perturbed, and laid both hands upon his breast, and he drew breath three times and said, "Hast thou in truth, O Lord, remembered us in Thy mercy, *the castaways, the people whom Thou hast rejected,* so that I may see Thy pure habitation, which is in heaven, the holy and heavenly Zion? . . . He hath crowned us with His grace." [Emphasis mine]

This ascension to the Jewish role would have been sufficient to restore a favorable self-image for the Ethiopians had not another group of Semites convinced some Ethiopians of the superiority of the Christian religion. Although in the early centuries it may have been possible for some Christian communities to conceive of themselves as followers of a kind of reformed Judaism, over time political and psychological forces in the Christian world made it difficult to maintain a keen sense of identification with the Jews. At some point the Judaic component of Ethiopian identity had to be played down. This denigration could not be blatantly accomplished in the central narrative of the *Kibre Negest,* which after all was devoted primarily to the task of establishing that identity. So when the Jews are first chided, in chapter 69, in the form of a prophecy by the angel Gabriel, they are not categorically condemned:

> But Israel will hate their Saviour, and will be envious of Him because He will work signs and miracles before them. And they will crucify Him, and will kill Him, and He shall rise up again and deliver them, for He is merciful to the penitent and *good to those who are His chosen ones.* And behold, I tell you plainly that *He will not leave in Sheol His kinsmen of Israel.* [Emphasis mine]

In the epilogue, however—once the new regime under Menilek has been firmly established and the Ethiopians stand in secure possession of the Ark and God's covenant—then a more scathing repudiation of the Jewish component of the new identity can be expressed. From the vantage point of Christian superiority, the verdict on the Jews in chapter 115 is noticeably harsher:

> And the Jews shall weep and repent when it shall be useless to do so, and *they shall pass into everlasting punishment;* and with the Devil, their father who had directed them, and his demons who had led them astray, and with the wicked shall they be shut in. [Emphasis mine]

Having now established that their superiority over the Jews is based on their identity as Christians, the Ethiopians can deny their Jewish identification with clear conscience.

A final phase of the Ethiopian identity struggle is initiated by the consciousness that they are not the only Christian power in the world. As we have already noted, Byzantine Christian rulers attempted on several occasions in the fourth and sixth centuries to influence Aksumite policy. The Ethiopian Christians were doubtless aware that their theological doctrines had been repudiated by the Byzantine church at the Council of Chalcedon. These events may well have stimulated anxieties about whether Ethiopia was inferior to Byzantium. That issue was firmly settled, in chapters 93 and 113 of the *Kibre Negest,* by accounts and prophecies which condemn the "Roman" Christians for having forsaken the orthodox faith and followed the heretical teachings of Nestorius. The Ethiopians thus emerge as the sole authentic bearers of Christianity, the *only* people in the world now favored by the God of Solomon.

The *Kibre Negest,* then, can be seen as a condensation of the complex identity struggles which the Tigrean elite experienced over a period of centuries. The confused and incoherent statements which earlier European commentators found in it were in fact the expression of the actual conflicts involved in this process. The conflicts in question were never resolved once and for all. But the *Kibre Negest* blended the diverse components of an Ethiopian self-image into a working synthesis that could define a national mission and legitimate the privileged positions of those responsible for bearing this mission.

Its appeal transcends the claims of any parochial loyalties in Ethiopia. It glorifies no tribe, no region, no linguistic group, but the Ethiopian nation under her monarch.

It declares this nation superior to all others—to the Persians, Moabites, and other alleged Semitic peoples, because of the corruption of their rulers and the fact that Menilek was the firstborn of Solomon's sons; to the Jews and other Christians; and a fortiori to all who were not of Semitic descent or Christians.

It thus provides a mandate for the Ethiopian kingdom to expand its dominion in the name of the Lord of Hosts. The message is clear: no sooner is Menilek instated as king of Ethiopia (chap. 92) than he embarks upon conquest (chap. 94):

> And after three months they rose up to wage war from the city of the government. . . . And the Levites carried the Tabernacle of the Law, together with the things that appertained to their office, and they marched along with great majesty . . . . And the other mighty men of war of Israel marched on the right side of it and on the left, and close to it, and before it and behind it, and although they were beings made of dust they sang psalms and songs of the spirit like the heavenly hosts . . .
>
> And on the following morning they laid waste the district of Zawa with Hadiya, for enmity had existed between them from olden times; and they blotted out the people and slew them with the edge of the sword. Any they passed on from that place and encamped at Gerra, and here also they laid waste the city of vipers that had the faces of men, and the tails of asses attached to their loins.

This passage expresses the tremendous sense of mission with which the Solomonid expansion was charged. It contains a very contemporary reference indeed: Emperor Amde Siyon had attacked and conquered Hadiyya just a few years before the final redaction of the epic.

The *Kibre Negest* also highlights the special status of those entrusted to lead this mission. Chapter 44 gives specific advice about the deference expected toward kings: "It is not a seemly thing to revile the king, for he is the anointed of God. It is neither seemly nor good." If the king does well, God will favor him; if not, "retribution belongeth to God."

The royal authority, moreover, is to be confined to males. In two separate passages, Queen Makeda insists that women should never reign again in Ethiopia, but only men.

In addition, the epic affirms that "the people must not revile the bishops and the priests, for they are the children of God and the men of His house." The priests have the duty to instruct men with wisdom and rebuke them for sins. The priests are also given a mandate to rebuke the king for any royal misconduct they have witnessed.

Indeed, the clerical mandate is spelled out in much detail. Polygamy is to be fought and monogamy upheld. The nakedness of close relatives is not to be uncovered. Sexual perversions are proscribed. The Ten Commandments are to be followed, as are the Judaic taboos on unclean foods. Pagan superstitions, signs, charms, and magic are to be abandoned. Judges are to refuse bribes and be righteous and impartial in judgment. Acts of kindness are to be shown toward neighbors and strangers.

Guided by the directives of this national script, the Amhara monarchs went forth to conquer other peoples and the clergy went forth to convert and reform them. Modeled on the drama of the kings of Israel, the script gave Old Testament themes a particularly prominent place. Hubbard has determined that there are five times as many Old Testament quotations and allusions in the *Kibre Negest* as New Testament ones. The names of the outstanding emperors of the period —Amde Siyon (Pillar of Zion), Dawit I (David), Yishaq (Isaac), and Zera Ya'iqob (Seed of Jacob)—reflected an identification with ancient Israel. Authors of royal chronicles described kingly virtues in Old Testament terms: Amde Siyon, for example, was portrayed as "gentle and humble like Moses and David." After long controversy, the Ethiopians under Zera Ya'iqob persuaded representatives of the Alexandrian Patriarchate to authorize their observance of the Jewish Sabbath in the Christian church. Long after all other Christians had rejected the Judaic concept of the covenant,[10] it was resurrected on the highland-plateau fastnesses of the Amhara. Theirs was the divinely ordained mission of a uniquely chosen people.

The Tigrean Contribution

If the principal beneficiaries of this covenant were the kings of Amhara, the fact remains that those who drafted its terms were Tigreans. If the story of the *Kibre Negest* has long dominated the fastnesses of Christian Ethiopia, it must also be noted that only in the northern part of Tigrinya-speaking territory does one find a cluster of places celebrated in local lore for having been associated with the legend of Makeda and Solomon. Near Adwa there is a place called Hinzat which is reputed to have been the location of Makeda's royal headquarters. On the outskirts of Aksum is a large reservior, Mai Shum, where Makeda is said to have taken her baths. Farther north, on the Asmera Plateau, is a river named Mai Bela—"Fetch some water!"—where Makeda is believed to have stopped on her way back from Jerusalem and to have issued that order as she began the labor that issued in the birth of Menilek. A coffeehouse in Asmera now bears the name Mai Bela as well. The actual birthplace of Menilek is locally identified as a large piece of gneiss rock near the village of Adi Shemagali northwest of Asmera. Just west of Aksum are two large slabs of finished granite which are said to mark the site of Makeda's tomb. In the same region the ruins of an Aksumite building at the foot of Mount Zohodo are considered to be the tomb of Menilek I himself. Finally, the Old Church of Saint Mary in Aksum is believed to this day to contain the original Ark of the Covenant brought by Menilek I and Azariah from Jerusalem, locked within seven caskets inside the sanctuary.

Another set of local traditions in northern Tigray, moreover, relates to a comparably important primordial experience, the advent of the "Nine Saints." These were a group of Syrian missionaries who laid the foundations for the doctrinal and liturgical traditions of Ethiopian Monophysite Christianity. Settling in the Aksum Plateau toward the end of the fifth century, probably as refugees from the anti-Monophysite persecutions in the Byzantine Empire after the Council of Chalcedon, they established a number of monasteries and translated the Bible and other religious works into Ethiopic. Local lore in northern Tigray still celebrates the advent of these saints, with legends about the places visited by Abba Pentellewon and Abba Liqanos flourishing around Aksum and those concerning the activities of Abba Gerima and Abba Aregawi current in Adwa. Residents of Adwa even cherish the belief that Abba Gerima is alive in their vicinity today.

The ancient homeland of the Tigrean people thus possesses a particularly intimate relationship with the two central symbolic complexes that undergird the traditional Ethiopian political order: Solomonic genealogy and Monophysite Christian authority. Both of these complexes, as I have remarked elsewhere,[11] derive a peculiar force because they stem from outside the Ethiopian system. The legitimacy of the Ethiopian monarchy has traditionally been based on (1) the king's affiliation with a genealogy believed to descend from King Solomon of Jerusalem and (2) his anointment by an archbishop sent by the Monophysite patriarch at Alexandria. These traditions are reaffirimed in the 1955 Constitution of Ethiopia, which stipulates that the emperor must be a descendant of the line of Solomon and Sheba and profess the Monophysite faith, and states that "by virtue of His Imperial Blood, as well as by the anointing which He has received, the person of the Emperor is sacred, His dignity is inviolable, and His power indisputable" (art. 2).

If the ultimate origin of these two long-lived legitimating principles lies outside the Ethiopian system, clearly their geographic point of entry has been the Aksum Plateau. To think that the political relevance of Aksum terminated with the downfall of the Aksumite dynasty is to overlook a fundamental feature of the evolution of the Ethiopian political system. It can be argued, rather, that it was precisely because Tigray lost political power that it was able to play a distinctive role in the evolution of a national society in Greater Ethiopia.

I began this chapter by suggesting that ancient Aksum can be viewed as a "seedbed" society. In *Societies: Evolutionary and Comparative Perspectives,* Talcott Parsons discusses some general characteristics of seedbed societies—those which are agents of cultural innovations that become very significant to societies of a different time and place. One of the points Parsons makes about seedbed societies is that before their cultural products could affect later distant societies they had to experience a loss of political independence and to transfer primary prestige to personalities who were not political powers but specialists in maintaining and developing distinctive cultural systems. This is exactly what occurred in northern Tigray. By the time Aksum's kings were overthrown, a stratum of monks had been securely established who were heirs to the prestige formerly associated with the Aksumite polity. They could more easily diffuse their ideas among peoples farther south who had had little or no contact with the Aksumite imperium, and the Amhara kings could more readily accept their moral authority and ideological formulations because Tigray was no longer a serious political competitor.

What parochial thrust the *Kibre Negest* had, then, was chiefly an effort to uphold the special place of Aksumite traditions in Ethiopian culture. In a colophon appended to some manuscript copies of the epic, Yishaq observed that the *Kibre Negest* was not translated into Ethiopic during the Zagwe Dynasty because those Agew-speaking Christians, "not being Israelites," would appear in its light to be illegitimate rulers. The subsequent usurpation by Yikunno Amlak and his descendants was therefore not only a victory for the Semitic-speaking Amhara; it was as much a vindication of the centrality of Aksumite traditions concerning Makeda and Solomon as a source of cultural legitimation for the monarchy. Tigreans and Amhara leaned on one another in a particularly effective way at that juncture, as they have done intermittently ever since.

Whatever the utility of the metaphor of Aksum as a seedbed society, the significance of Aksum as a source of legitimating imagery throughout the six centuries of Amhara rule after 1270 cannot be denied. Not only did the clergy of Aksum produce the script of the *Kibre Negest,* but the city itself became romanticized and revered throughout the Amhara kingdom. In writings often appended to the *Kibre Negest* Aksum was described as "royal throne of the kings of Zion, mother of all lands, pride of the entire universe, jewel of kings. . . . She was the second Jerusalem. Because of her grandeur and her immense glory, all the kings are called Kings of Aksum, and the archbishops who came from Egypt are called archbishops of Aksum."[12] It was to the Church of Saint Mary of Zion in Aksum, the holiest place in Ethiopian Christendom, that the crowns of former emperors were customarily sent for preservation. In spite of the fact that the Amhara royal headquarters were usually located far from Tigray, Amhara elite steadfastly believed that the proper place for the coronation of kings was Aksum. Although we have evidence in only four cases—Zera Ya'iqob, Sertsa Dingil, Susneyos, and Iyasu I—of Amhara monarchs actually making the journey to Aksum for the ceremony, the symbolic importance of the idea is shown by the frequency and lavish care with which descriptions of the proper rites of coronation at Aksum appear in court chronicles and other Ethiopic writings over many centuries.[13]

During the last two centuries the Tigreans have also made direct political contributions of major importance in the effort to create a national society in Greater Ethiopia, a matter to which some attention will be paid in chapter 10. In this chapter, however, I have been concerned to document their primary historical role, which has been the indirect one of providing some of the core symbolism that served to fashion, inspire, and legitimate the project of creating an Amhara imperium.

8

The Amhara System

The symbolism of the *Kibre Negest* represents a set of ideal patterns —models *for* action—that have been efficacious at the national level of Amhara society. The foregoing account of those models must now be integrated into a model *of* the Amhara system, one that deals both with local levels of action and with their relations with the national levels.

In this chapter and the next I shall describe briefly the basic associational units of traditional Amhara and Oromo life and then analyze some principal structural features of the two sociocultural systems. For detailed descriptions of those societies the reader is advised to consult the ethnographic sources listed in the bibliography.

Household, Seignory, and Parish

The basic unit of Amhara social life is the household, or *beteseb*—literally, a "house of people." Amhara households are oriented to subsistence production and are largely self-sufficient. They are situated in relatively isolated homesteads dispersed over a mountainous terrain. Homesteads range from units of one or two wattle and daub or stone huts containing a single nuclear family to hamlets of a dozen or more structures containing a few related families with their servants and retainers.

The household is less a family grouping than a unit of political economy—an oikos, as Wolfgang Weissleder has aptly termed it. The Amhara household has two distinguishing characteristics: its members are expected to carry out specific tasks allocated according to sex and other criteria, and they are all under the authority of a single senior male. Men are assigned such tasks as plowing, sowing, harvesting, threshing, cattle and grain trading, slaughtering, herding, driving pack animals, building houses, and cutting wood. Women are repsonsible for cooking, brewing beer, buying and selling spices, making butter, carding and spinning, cutting hops, and carrying water and wood.

Male and female tasks are further divided according to the degrees of status honor attached to them and are assigned to different household members according to age and other status criteria. The membership of a typical household includes the head, his spouse, perhaps an aging parent of either, and as many of the head's and his wife's children, collateral kinsmen, poor dependent retainers, and servants (formerly slaves) as are useful in exploiting the economic resources at the head's disposal. That the Amhara household is organized more by economic than kinship considerations is shown by Allan Hoben's study of a sample of Gojjam households. Hoben demonstrated that household size corresponds more closely to the size of landholding than to the number of living offspring claimed by the head.[1] As the fortunes of a household wax and wane, and as individuals see their life chances better served in one place than in another, the roster of members in a household may change. What remains constant is the organization of tasks to be performed and the authority structure.

Households are linked to one another and to the central institutions of Amhara society chiefly along three separate axes—economic, political, and religious. The division of Amhara terrain into climatic zones which support different agricultural products means that some trade is essential for meeting all the consumption requirements of any household. Weekly markets provide opportunities for highland dwellers to trade surplus wheat, barley, lentils, or sheep for teff, onions, garlic, red pepper, or goats from the lowland regions. Such markets are also the only place where householders can obtain such items as pottery, spears, plowshares, and leather goods, the work of caste specialists with whom social intercourse is ordinarily avoided. Other needs are satisfied by trading for imports from more distant parts of Ethiopia or beyond—salt bars, coffee, sugar, foreign fabrics, and currency. Occasionally surpluses of farm products are bought up by traders for transporting to national market centers.

Traditionally, however, most farm surpluses have found their way not into the open market but into channels defined by political authorities and ecclesiastical requirements. The center of political authority at the local level is a "lord," the holder of what has been called a seignory. This is a domain ranging in size from a few dozen to several hundred households, ruled by an appointee of a provincial governor. The rights of such seignory-holders are known in Amharic as *gult*. *Gult* rights traditionally included the collection of tribute from each of the households in the seignory—often, as Hoben estimates, one fifth to one fourth of their crops—and the appropriation of a certain number of days of labor for work in the lord's own fields or any other project he might designate. The lord used the tribute thus received primarily to support his own extended household, which included as many armed retainers as he could afford to maintain. He in turn paid tribute to his overlord for support of the latter's household, and so on up to the imperial court.

Seignories differed with respect to the terms of tenure and specific types of tribute expected. The terms used to designate seignory-holders also varied; in Gojjam they are called *gulte-gezh* (*gult* governor); in parts of Begemdir *feresenya* (horseman, knight); in northern Shoa *melkenya* (from the same root as *amlak,* "God"). Local lords were recruited from widely differing backgrounds. They could be sons of noblemen who had inherited their fathers' personal followings; self-made military leaders for whom the seignory was a reward for loyal services or a bribe to ensure pacification; minor court officials; abbots of monasteries; or personal agents of the provincial ruler. *Gult* rights have also been held by monasteries. Despite these and other variations, the position and functions of the local lordship were basically similar from region to region. The lordship entailed responsibility for adjudicating disputes over land and other matters, commanding the local militia, organizing local work projects, and representing higher political authorities whenever called upon.

In addition to the claims imposed by its local lord each household has obligations to a local church. The social unit which defines these churchly obligations has been called a parish. Amhara parishes range in size from around five dozen to five hundred households. In many regions the parish is coterminous with the local seignory. In others there may be two, three, or several seignories within the same parish.

The focal point of parish life is the sacred ark, or *tabot.* Kept within the innermost sanctuary of the church building, the sacred ark may be attended only by ordained priests or deacons. The ark is named after one of the saints or angels of the Ethiopian Christian religion. The proper name of a parish is made up of the local place name followed by the name of its sacred ark.

Each household in a parish is obliged to contribute a certain amount of grain each year for the communions, perhaps to maintain a parish church-school teacher, and to supply labor and materials as needed for the construction and repair of church buildings. Parishioners must also baptize their children and bury their dead at the local church. The main support for church functions comes from persons with special kinds of landholdings which entail specific church-related contributions in lieu of tribute to the secular lord. These support the principal activity of the parish church, performance of the masses. Mass must be celebrated several times each month, on Sundays and on a number of monthly and annual holidays. Since each mass requires the services of two priests and three deacons, mobilizing resources to fulfill this solemn ritual requirement is no simple matter. It is accomplished by a set of encumbrances on church-entailed land such that the holders of that land must provide a fixed number of priest- or deacon-services, either directly if clergymen or else by paying in kind or cash for someone else to serve the mass.

Household, seignory, and parish compose the basic ecological units of the traditional Amhara social system. Except for those who opt to live outside the system, following a marginal style of life as beggars, outlaws, wandering minstrels, or pious hermits, virtually all freeborn Amhara possess the rights and obligations of membership in some household, seignory, and parish. The norms of these three units provide most of the institutionalized structure of Amhara social relations at the local level.

Kinship and descent make up one other institutional complex which has importance for Amhara life, even though kinship does not form the basis for any ecological unit or other persisting corporate structures among the Amhara. Not only do kinsmen frequently reside in different seignories or parishes, they also tend to be in chronic competition with one another for land and political favors. Kin relations are salient, however, in a few important areas: selection of marriage partners, blood feuds, and land tenure.

The Amhara rule of exogamy stipulates that marriage partners must not be closer than "seven houses"; that is, spouses must not have a common great-great-great-grandparent. A basic knowledge of the family's genealogy is thus essential. Amhara custom also enjoins relatives to avenge the murder of a kinsman, though this is usually observed only by fairly close kin. What is most important for the Amhara, however, is that kin relations determine the distribution of rights to the use of land. Rights to plow plots of land and potential rights to additional plots are obtainable in traditional Amhara areas only through inheritance. Since the Amhara descent system is ambilineal, these rights are inherited bilaterally—by sons and daughters equally, and through both parents. Since most Amhara are constantly searching for ways to increase the size of their landholdings, they make frequent reference to these inherited land-use rights, or *rist,* in a context of deciding which cluster of kinsmen to ally themselves with temporarily against another cluster of kinsmen in order to maintain or activate *rist* rights held by self, spouse, or children.

Social relations among the Amhara are also organized through a number of routinized forms that are independent of the inexorable institutional claims of kinship, household, seignory, and parish. Like the weekly market, these associations are voluntary and are pursued for very specific purposes. They include the daily "coffee klatch" (*tirtib*), attended in one another's homes by varying constellations of neighbors, friends, and kinsmen; the monthly religious feasting association (*mahiber*) held in honor of a particular saint or angel; and occasional arrangements for reciprocal help in connection with plowing, harvesting, house-building, preparing wedding feasts, and trading. Finally, there are a number of widely utilized forms of voluntary dyadic personal relationships, including those of the godparent-child, adoptive parent-child, friendship, guarantor-guarantee, confessor-confessee, and the like. The more general category of patron-client relationship is of particular importance for the operation of the Amhara social system and will be considered below.

The Nation as Community

To specify the main structural characteristics of the Amhara system is to determine the principal ways in which members of diverse households, seignories, and parishes are linked together. As was indicated in chapter 6, this can be done at three levels: by characterizing the boundaries of the system as a whole, by analyzing the relations between the whole and its parts, and by identifying the characteristic ways in which parts are related to other parts. I shall consider each of these levels of analysis in turn.

To begin with: What are the boundaries of the community in which Amhara have traditionally identified themselves as members?

The horizons of most Amhara are narrowly circumscribed. Most of their interests and energies are directed to the local units described in the preceding section. Yet none of these complexes forms a corporate entity with which they are deeply identified and to which they remain steadfastly loyal. They look beyond their household to others which may offer greater economic opportunities or less restrictive regimes. They look beyond their seignory to others where they can mobilize rights to additional land. They look beyond their parish to another whose sacred ark may promise greater personal benefits or to which they are indebted for previous favors and oaths.

The regional community is much more salient as a source of identity and an object for loyalty. Similarities in use of language, custom, reciprocal stereotypes, and some sense of common historical destinies bind together the people of Gojjam in contrast with those of Shoa, those of Begemdir in contrast with Tigray. These regional boundaries are fluid, however; not only have the territorial definitions of these regions changed considerably over the generations, but at times subregional differences—as between Menz and Ifat in Shoa, or between Shire and Adwa in Tigray—are more salient than regional ones.

Despite the pervasiveness of regionalism among Amhara-Tigreans, however, some sense of a truly national consciousness seems to have been present at least since the fourteenth century. This manifests itself through references to a national ethnic community; through the agency of a national monarch; and above all through the organization and ministrations of a national church.

In their home territory Amhara rarely express a strong sense of belonging to the community of all Amhara. They identify themselves either on a regional basis—Gojjami versus Gondare—or else by means of the supraethnic term *Habesha.* In both Amharic and Tigrinya, *Habesha* is a general term for a native Ethiopian. Although modern-educated Ethiopians tend to object to the use of the English counterpart of this term, Abyssinian, they commonly use the term *Habesha* among themselves in the traditional meaning as referring, in its more limited sense, to all Amhara and Tigreans or else, in its more extended sense, to all those who are subjects of the Ethiopian monarchy.

The monarchy itself of course was a constant reminder of a supra-regional and multiethnic community, the community of subjects to the King of Kings of Ethiopia. The *Kibre Negest* not only resolved the conflicts among the Cushitic and diverse Semitic components of Tigrean identity, it also charted a mission for a *national* community. The royal chronicles repeat this emphasis by extolling the "Kingdom of Ethiopia." Each seignory was traditionally linked to this national kingdom because the lord's appointment depended on regional governors whose legitimacy in turn derived from the monarch.

Each parish, similarly, was linked to the national community in that all local priests and deacons had to be ordained by a national bishop, the *abun.* Although the *abun* did not exert central control over his appointees as the monarch did over his appointees, the fact that the ritual system of the entire society ultimately depended on him was doubtless understood throughout the parishes. In addition, the high culture of Ethiopian Christianity was transmitted by an uncoordinated but *nationally* distributed set of monastic centers. It was widely known that the best schools for the study of liturgical chants were in Begemdir and Tigray provinces; for the study of religious verse composition one went to Gojjam or Lasta; for religious dance and the study of the holy texts, the chief center of instruction was at Gonder. In their own writings and other expressions, the clergy did much to keep alive a sense of the reality of Ethiopian nationhood. Thus traditional accounts of the life of the celebrated medieval Saint Tekle Haymanot depict him as moving readily from one part of the land to another—from Shoa to Damot to Amhara to Tigray and back—and he is not identified as a Shoan, or an Amhara, but as *hawarya ze-ityoppya,* an apostle of Ethiopia; upon his death "there was much lamentation and crying, and the report of his death was heard *in all the country of Ethiopia*" (emphasis mine).[2]

In short, both through the ultimately national sources of legitimacy which affected their local routines and through the national symbolism provided by king and religion, the Amhara belonged to a national community and always kept some sense, however dim at times, of being a part of that more inclusive collectivity.[3]

Functional Specialization

With respect to internal structure, the Amhara system is divided into four distinct institutional spheres. Each of these consists of a clearly defined cluster of status-roles organized to pursue a specific set of activities.

The kinship sphere consists of bilaterally traced descendants of diverse apical ancestors. The descent groups thus formed maintain and activate *rist* rights, rights to the use of land plots historically granted to their ancestors. The economic sphere consists of independently organized households, under the authority of a head. The members of each household carry out assigned activities related to producing, trading, preparing, and consuming food and to the construction and repair of homesteads. The political sphere consists of lords appointed by and reporting to regional and provincial governors who are in turn appointed by and responsible to the monarch. They mobilize armies, resolve secular disputes, and collect taxes.[4] The religious sphere consists of parish churches with their priests, deacons, and lay religious officers; monasteries; and the archbishop or *abun.* They fulfill the ritual requirements of the system and provide ministrations at the time of christening, death, and church weddings.

Two features of the Amhara institutional order are particularly worthy of comment. One is the relatively limited role that kinship plays in this system. The major economic, political, and cultural functions are not carried out by groups organized on the basis of kin relationships, nor is kinship a determining factor in recruitment to the roles which do serve these functions. Political appointments are made on the basis of a man's military abilities, demonstrated or presumed loyalty, local power base, or tactical utility. Ecclesiastical appointments are made on the basis of training in centers removed from family settings. Even the head of a household is likely to prefer a competent and devoted servant to a lazy or disobedient son.

Of particular interest for the questions raised in this book is the extent to which the political and religious orders are separate from one another. They have separate sources of legitimacy, distinct bases of power and influence, contrasting patterns of internal organization, and specialized societal functions.

The legitimacy of members of the priesthood derives from their being ordained by the *abun.* In turn his authority derived, from the middle of the fourth century up to the middle of the twentieth, from his being appointed by the Coptic patriarch at Alexandria. The power of individual clergymen depends on their ability to provide or withhold ritual favors, to pronounce excommunication, and to offer or withhold meaningful counsel. Their influence is based on such factors as ritual purity, doctrinal knowledge, ability to perform miracles, and capacity to provide moral guidance.

The legitimacy of secular rulers ultimately depends on appointment by the monarch and, in some regions, on being descended from local dynasties. The legitimate authority of the emperor in turn derives, as we have seen, from his claim to descent from the Solomonid line. The power of secular rulers depends on military strength and the capacity to provide followers with food, equipment, and rewards of *gult* or other benefices. Their influence rests on their reputations for maintaining security and resolving disputes shrewdly.

The internal structures of the ecclesiastical and political domains show equally sharp contrasts. The former manifests a high degree of local autonomy and internal differentiation, the latter a pyramiding centralization and virtually no internal differentiation. The chief authority in religious matters has traditionally been the abbot of a regional monastery. He passed judgment on doctrinal matters and disputes involving church regulations and had the authority to consecrate local sacred arks. There was no national hierarchy of ecclesiastical offices to which he was subordinate. It was therefore possible for monasteries in different districts to develop in quite different directions, a situation which favored the outbreak of controversies on doctrinal issues, such as appeared with the Michaelite, Eustatian, and Stephanite "heresies" of the fourteenth and fifteenth centuries, and the schisms among followers of the Unionist, Unctionist, and Triple Birth doctrines in the eighteenth and nineteenth centuries. There was also considerable diversity in the roles played by clergy. One can identify four markedly distinct roles available in this area: priests, monks, *debtera* (chorister-scribes), and high ecclesiastical officials, each of which was recruited in a different manner and was honored for different reasons.[5]

By contrast, there was one basic role for the secular ruler. He was at once governor, judge, military leader, and courtier. This was true at all levels of the political hierarchy. The main difference between the monarch and the local lord was the degree of deference each claimed. All local lords, moreover, were linked eventually to the monarch through chains of command in which each level was isomorphic with the next.

The two "estates" of course had a good deal to do with one another, and each tried to influence decisions made in the other's realm. Secular rulers tried to determine the course of theological disputes. This was particularly true of certain emperors, like Zera Ya'iqob (1434–68), Yohannes I, "the Pious" (1667–82), and Yohannes IV (1871–89), who intervened decisively to settle doctrinal controversies. Secular rulers also were responsible for appointing all high ecclesiastical officials other than the *abun*. The ecclesiastical officials, in turn, tried to influence secular policies and appointments, and the monastic clergy repeatedly attempted to reform the morals of secular rulers.

On occasion, to be sure, some bold individual or group of clerics insisted on a purity of separation between the two spheres. This position was stressed by Saint Istifanos, a rebellious monk of the fifteenth century who founded a "heretical" order. While expounding his theological views at a provincial court one day Istifanos was interdicted by an opponent in the name of the king. Istifanos refused to acknowledge the interdiction, on grounds that the name of a temporal king had no relevance to doctrinal discussions. Later, when sumoned before Emperor Zera Ya'iqob, Istifanos consistently abstained from offering comments on cases being tried in the royal court. "It is forbidden," he argued, "for us to participate in the judgments of the world. And I did not come here for this but because you summoned me for matters of religion and of the spirit. It is for rulers of this world to judge according to the Pentateuch and the Book of the Kings."[6]

Although Istifanos expressed an extreme position on the question, his views reflected the reality of functional specialization in Christian Ethiopia. However much contact religious and political officeholders might have, they related to one another from structurally separated positions, positions essentially devoted to performing distinct functions. In the words of a well-known proverb, "If he is not a monk, even the king cannot give orders to a monastery." As a result of this differentiation, secular officials could devote themselves to political expansion unencumbered by ritual responsibilities, while churchmen could cultivate their cultural traditions and propagate the faith unencumbered by political responsibilities. The polity could prosper to some extent even in times of ecclesiastical disarray and religious demoralization, and the church could pursue its mission when the state dissolved into a field of internecine conflicts. As we shall see, this degree of functional specialization stands in marked contrast with that permitted by the institutional order of the Oromo.

Hierarchical Interaction

In addition to defining the *boundaries* of a social system and the extent and type of *differentiation* among its parts, one must determine *how its parts are related to one another* in order to have a working sense of its general structural characteristics. Although persons and roles are related in many ways in any society, each social system has typical ways of structuring interpersonal and intercollective relations into patterns which are sanctioned by custom and which its members are motivated to reproduce in a variety of situations.

A useful scheme for conceptualizing such patterns can be generated by considering the two main dimensions along which individuals relate to one another, vertical distance and horizontal distance. The first variable separates people by gradations of authority, power, and prestige. Where such gradations are accentuated to the degree that expectations of deference and compliance dominate the interaction, one speaks of *hierarchical* patterning. Where the significance of vertical gradations is minimized so that they do not entail great amounts of deference and are balanced by antiauthoritarian orientations, one speaks of *egalitarian* patterning. In the former pattern, incumbents of various roles relate to one another as superordinates and subordinates; in the latter case, as comrades, partners, or associates.

The variable of horizontal distance concerns the degree of affective closeness and common identification felt among different actors. Where this is very high, we speak of *solidaristic* association. Where it is low, and individuals relate to one another mainly on a utilitarian and competitive basis, we speak of *individualistic* association. The reports of all observers of Amhara society confirm the generalization that its social relationships are organized to an overwhelming degree on the basis of *hierarchical* patterns and *individualistic* association.

Carefully delineated status hierarchies are readily observable within every household, seignory, and church. Relationships among members of these groups are determined first and foremost by their gradations of honor and authority. The household is less a family unit than it is a vertically ordered set of status-roles. The head of the household is addressed by all others with the honorific term *getoch,* "masters," or *getay,* "my master." All others in the household know their place with respect to one another and are expected to show the appropriate degree of deference. Siblings are ranked on the basis of age and sex. The master's children are not necessarily shown more deference than are other dependent relatives or servants, particularly if the latter are older or have other special status claims.

The same pattern appears on a grand scale in the court of the local lord. With many positions to distribute, the seignory-holder can establish elaborate hierarchies. As Arnauld d'Abbadie observed more than a century ago,

> A lord of even mediocre importance names his seneschal, his provost, his guards, a foreman of domestics, a chief baker, a butler, a squire, and various captains and pages; then he sets up a hierarchy often in ridiculous disproportion to his position; his inferiors do the same, and there is no one down to the well-to-do peasant who does not institute certain offices and analogous grades in his home.[7]

Secular officeholders above the local lord have in turn been ranked according to the amount of land they control and the type of honorific title they have been awarded. The chief axis of social relations at the imperial court, finally, has been a scrupulously detailed and periodically revised status hierarchy based above all on royal favor.

Similar hierarchies exist in the ecclesiastical order, though of course they rest on different criteria. At the parish level the criterion is ritual purity. Four gradations of ritual purity determine where parishioners stand inside and outside the church building when the mass is performed. At monasteries the criterion is ascetic piety and the relative importance of various titles held by monastic officials and teachers. The religious teacher is shown as much deference and compliance by his students as is the local lord by his clients. In the theological sphere, moreover, the Amhara's relationship with God is mediated by a hierarchy of saints and angels.

The pervasive tendency of the Amhara to order their relationships in the form of hierarchies manifests itself behaviorally in two characteristic patterns. One is the frequent use of an elaborate set of gestures which express different degrees of deference: bowing to various levels, draping the cape in various ways, kissing various parts of the body, and using different terms of address and grammatical forms. The other is expressing a willingness to comply readily with the demands of any superior and withholding any direct criticism of his ideas or actions. Disagreement with a superordinate can be expressed, but only in indirect ways.

Undergirding the hierarchical patterns of Amhara social relations are a set of ideas and values expressed through proverbs, folklore, and holy writings. The *Kibre Negest* stresses that one should show appropriate deference both to kings and to clergy. Biblical passages are occasionally cited to make the same point. But such didactic formulations merely confirm the obvious. The ethos of Amhara culture is saturated with a sense of the rightness of respecting superordinates and complying with their commands. Allan Hoben summarizes the matter succinctly: "It is a fundamental postulate of Amhara culture . . . that *social order, which is good, can be created and maintained only through hierarchical, legitimate control deriving ultimately from God.*"[8]

Individualistic Association

Two other postulates underlie what may be called the competitive individualism of Amhara social relations. One, deriving from the Cushitic layer of this culture, exalts the value of masculinity as demonstrated by displays of outstanding aggressive prowess. The other, of Semitic origin, stresses man's frailty and the sinfulness of human nature. The idea that other people are not to be trusted, combined with the idealization of aggressive masculinity, supports and expresses an orientation to social relations in which individual interests are vigorously pursued at the expense of possible collective interests.

Since most other members of the society are one's actual or potential competitors or enemies, interpersonal relations are handled with extreme discretion. The main device in this regard is to keep others at a distance. This separation is accomplished, first of all, by the residential pattern. Homesteads are usually built at a respectable distance from one another. When Amhara meet, moreover, they are expected to act in a restrained manner. They maintain distance through highly stylized patterns of communication, scrupulously adhering to a rigid code of etiquette. Their conversation is guarded; long silences are common, as are uncommunicative facial expressions. Privacy is respected; staring at a person or at his possessions is frowned upon. Ambiguous expressions serve to conceal more than they reveal about one's thoughts and desires.

As was noted above, Amhara feel little sense of loyalty to such units as household, descent group, parish, or seignory. They have a very pragmatic, unsentimental, and unritualized orientation to such collectivities. Insofar as their individual purposes are served by complying with their norms, they will comply. If greater opportunities are to be found in some other household, or by serving some other lord, or saint, they will switch. In any event, the allegiance—ephemeral or long-lasting—is not owed to a corporate group but on an unmistakably *personal* basis to the *authoritative head* of the group in question.

The last point may be put in other words by saying that the *dyadic* tie of the *patron-client relationship is the fundamental type of relational bond of the Amhara social system.* The essential ingredients of such bonds are the needs of a client and the present or prospective capacity of a potential patron to fulfill them. A man's power in this system is based on the number of persons who are dependent on him, whom he can mobilize in time of need on the basis of favors granted or promised. It is in his interest to keep his dependents from becoming too abundantly satisfied (*tigabeñña*), lest they no longer feel the need to follow him. He thus may make a point of keeping clients aware of their mutually competitive position.

Although the distance and hostility among peers is often moderated by personal ties with close kinsmen or friends, the basic pattern of association in Amhara society is one of relating to peers by either competition, formal politeness, or mutually advantageous specific arrangements, and to subordinates and superordinates through firm bonds of patronship or more superficial expressions of deference, compliance, and respect. These properties define the basic Amhara relational pattern as one of hierarchic individualism.

System Stability and Historical Change

The structural features of the Amhara system which we have identified —inclusiveness in a multiethnic community under a common monarch and a supratribal religion; organization of local action through the role-complexes of the household, ambilineal descent groups, seignory, and parish; specialization of political and religious functions through the separate hierarchies of a segmentary state and a national church; and the patterning of social interaction in the form of hierarchical and individualistic relationships—appear to have characterized the Amhara system since the fourteenth century. Although there have been many changes in the details of Amhara life since then, these basic structural features have shown great durability. Despite considerable local variations, the central traditions and institutions have been maintained continuously. Demographic vicissitudes, fluctuations in the amount of territory under Amhara rule, and shifting economic conditions have entailed little serious structural change.

For all the repressiveness and constraints of the system, it does not appear to have imposed excessive demands on its members. The time spent on litigation over land-use rights and the number of religiously prescribed holidays have removed much labor power from agricultural production, but never so much as to threaten a minimal supply of subsistence commodities in an agriculturally advantaged land. Heavy fasting requirements have contributed to malnutrition and have made Amhara vulnerable to attack by enemies during the Lenten months, but they have persisted. Neither these nor other stresses have prompted a basic reorganization of the Amhara social system until recent times.

Even today the patterns described obtain, but they have been affected by three significant changes emanating from the national center in the decades since World War II.[9] The control exerted by households over younger members has been loosened by the development of a secular school system which now has branches in many rural districts. These schools offer an alternate route for growing up to children of ambitious families or to defiant children of conservative families. The control exerted by the local lord has been diminished by the development of a centralized national bureaucracy. Functions which previously were performed by the local lord are to a growing extent carried out by agents of the ministries of Interior, Finance, Defense, and Justice. Finally, the independence of the ritual head of the church from the monarch, based on the importation of the former from Egypt, was brought to an end, in 1950, when an Ethiopian became *abun* for the first time. In 1958 an agreement was signed with the Alexandrian Patriarchate enabling the Ethiopian archbishop henceforward not to be appointed by the Coptic patriarch but to be elected by the fourteen Ethiopian provincial bishops, subject to the approval of the emperor; and in 1971 Abuna Tewoflos became first Ethiopian *abun* to be installed on the basis of those new procedures.

That the system may soon require additional structural change is a possibility which will be discussed in the concluding chapter. The point to be stressed here, however, is that the combination of a strong center with great toleration for local variation and individualistic strivings has made the traditional Amhara system very flexible and, for that reason, extraordinarily durable.

9

The Oromo System

The Oromo are in many ways the antithesis of the Amhara. Not only did the two people confront one another for centuries as great historical antagonists, but the traditions they brought to the encounter contrast radically. Where the Amhara system is hierarchical, the Oromo is egalitarian. Where the Amhara is individualistic, the Oromo is solidaristic. Where religious and political functions are segregated in Amhara institutions, for the Oromo they are fused. Where the Amhara historical project is to build an empire, that of the Oromo is to maintain a parochial tradition. The historical consequences of these and related contrasts will be assessed after we have examined the Oromo system itself.

Because so many Galla have become acculturated to other Ethiopian traditions, it is necessary to base a reconstruction of the traditional Oromo system upon an examination of the Galla groups which have changed least since the sixteenth century: the Borana and Guji tribes of Sidamo Province. They live in and around what was the heartland of Oromo culture in the sixteenth century, an area containing shrines which until recently were visited by Galla pilgrims from distant areas. The Borana in particular retain the social institutions and style of life which apparently characterized the Oromo at the time of their great invasions. My analysis of Oromo society will therefore draw primarily upon Asmarom Legesse's recent pioneering monograph on the Borana Galla, supplemented by personal communications from John Hinnant based on recent fieldwork among the Guji, Eike Haberland's *Galla Süd-Äthiopiens,* and other ethnographic literature. In what follows I shall use the term "Oromo" to refer to what may plausibly be construed as core patterns of the traditional culture; the term "Galla" when referring to patterns observed among a number of present-day Oromo groups; and specific tribal names, like Mecha or Guji, when referring to patterns which appear to be distinctive of or have been reported only for a particular tribe.

Olla, LINEAGE, AND CLASS

The Oromo household is normally a small, nuclear family unit. Unlike the Amhara household it rarely contains members who are not spouses or immediate kin. It generally consists of the wife and her unmarried children, supplemented on occasion by a dependent kinsman of the wife or her husband.

The Oromo are polygynous, the number of wives in a family depending on a man's wealth. They also practice the levirate: when a man dies, his wives are inherited by his oldest living brother. The husband moves about among the houses of his various wives. Usually he has a favorite wife with whom he spends most of his time.

Relations among co-wives are typically strained; so each wife normally lives in a separate house with her own children. Other factors also contribute to the small size of the Oromo household: sons are often sent to distant regions to graze herds of cattle, and tension among brothers often motivates them to move out and establish their own households as soon as they can.[1]

The Oromo family is much more stable than the Amhara family. While many if not most Amhara marriages end in divorce, the Oromo have no laws or procedures that permit divorce.[2] In Amhara families, relations between spouses and between parents and children are relatively tense and oriented to the expression of deference, whereas relations in Oromo families are relatively spontaneous, emotionally expressive, and good-humored. Another factor that contributes to the stability of Oromo marriages is that, again in sharp contrast to Amhara custom, extramarital sexual relationships are not only enjoyed by virtually all adult males and married females, but are considered entirely proper as well.

With respect to the performance of diverse societal functions, however, the Oromo family serves no more than the Amhara family as a vehicle for major activities. Its sphere is restricted to the performance of a small number of subsistence functions allocated on the basis of sex. Women are responsible for most activities within the home, men for those outside. Women have the exclusive right to build huts, a condition which makes Oromo men particularly dependent upon having a wife.[3] Women fetch water from wells, prepare and distribute food, and make milk containers and leather garments. Men are responsible for building kraals and fences, carving wooden utensils, watering and milking cattle, and providing defense. Men also participate in discussions outside the home to decide about the performance of rituals.

Beyond this, most Oromo activities are carried out by other kinds of groups: *olla,* lineages, and classes. The *olla* is a residential grouping whose members carry out a number of activities on a cooperative basis. Once a site for the *olla* is chosen and the prospective residents agreed upon—in Borana land such camps can be set up anywhere, since the land belongs to all Borana—they erect a thornbush fence around the cluster of individual dwellings. They build cattle kraals together, and jointly take their cattle to pasture and to the wells for water. The Guji also carry out various agricultural activities cooperatively.

Among present-day Borana and Guji, *olla* are of variable size and duration. The Borana *olla* has been defined as a "band" although, strictly speaking, the Borana are not nomads. Unlike the Beja, Afar, and Somali, they do not use pack animals or carry their homes with them from place to place. They are what might be called serially sedentary, moving from one semipermanent camp to another. The Borana band consists of between five and twenty households which assemble to live together for the duration of a season or, at most, a year. When the time comes to move to new pastures, their camp is left behind and its members go in different directions to join other kinsmen or friends in setting up new camps. The Guji *olla* has been defined as a "neighborhood." Since the Guji combine pastoralism with agriculture, their *olla* are maintained for longer periods. They are also somewhat larger; the Guji *olla* consists of all households which can hear a message shouted from one's doorway. But Guji neighborhoods are not permanent units either, and the Guji, too, have moved about a good deal in response to famines, population pressures, and Sidamo expansion.

Neither the Borana nor the Guji regard these territorial residential units as significant bases of social organization. The Oromo locate themselves above all with respect to patrilineal descent group affiliation. Asked where he comes from, an Amhara will give the place name of his parish; an Oromo will name his lineage (or a place name that is often a clan name). Actually, he will present a set of descent group names which identify his position within the kinship structure of the whole tribe.

At the most general level, he will name one of two exogamous tribal halves, or moieties. In the sixteenth century these were apparently known as Borana and Barettuma, the two great divisions of the Oromo named by Bahrey. Among the Borana today they are named Gona and

Sabbo; among the southern Guji, Darimu and Kontoma.[4] He will then list four or five other names which identify his submoiety, clan, major lineage, minor lineage, and perhaps minimal lineage. These are descent group categories of decreasing genealogical depth, the last of which, the *warra,* extends about four or five generations back.

Lineage groups not only serve to locate Oromo with respect to one another, they take action as corporate bodies. They are agents of moral control over their members. Clansmen meet to discuss offenses and determine punishments when a clan member has failed to divide his inheritance properly or has committed an offense within his extended family. They also meet with the family of a potential bride of a lineage member for negotiations and divination. Lineages are responsible for digging, maintaining, and regulating the use of wells, a major focus of attention in Oromo life. They perform certain indispensable rituals, from birth and marriage rites, for which minimal lineages are responsible, to tribal ceremonies carried out by the most senior men of the lineage system, the *qallu.*

Each Borana moiety is headed by a *qallu,* whose position is inherited within a specified minor lineage of a particular clan but whose authority is believed to be of divine origin. Some other important traditional statuses are assigned on the basis of lineage affiliation: the first wife of a *qallu,* for example, must be a member of a particular lineage. The *qallu* and other lineage leaders at the clan level are also responsible for selecting the Oromo "political" leaders who serve terms as members of a central law- and policy-making body, the *gada* council.

The *gada* council is the apex of a system of status-roles which crosscut those connected with the lineage structure. The status-roles of the *gada* system are defined by two kinds of social classes, one based on generational position and one based based on age. The former, which may be referred to by the term "*gada* classes" or the Oromo term "*luba,*" consist of all the sons, of whatever age, born to the fathers of another specified class. The latter, known in Gallinya as *hariyya,* and properly referred to as age sets, consist of all the males born within a specified eight-year period. Much of the confusion concerning the operation of the *gada* system in previous literature has stemmed from a failure to distinguish *gada* classes from age sets, a difficulty which has now been resolved, thanks to the work of Legesse.

The details of the operation of the *gada* system—how the various classes are constituted, and their respective functions and interrelations—are enormously complicated. Indeed, the *gada* system represents one of the most complex systems of social organization ever devised by the human imagination. For present purposes I shall limit myself to identifying the three most important structural features of the system: the schedule of *gada* grades; the constitution of *gada* classes; and the role of age sets.

The schedule of gada *grades.* Each *gada* class, or *luba,* proceeds over time through a cycle of eleven named grades. The duration of each grade is eight years, except for the fifth and seventh grades, which last for thirteen and three years respectively. The transition from one grade to another is normally marked by a specific ceremony. Each grade is marked by a particular set of characteristics.

1. Boys in the first grade are dressed, addressed, and otherwise treated like girls. Their hair is worn long and adorned with leather strips and cowrie shells. They receive special love and attention, and are regarded as intermediaries between man and God. Their mothers are entitled to special honorific treatment.

2. When a class enters the second grade its members are given proper male names for the first time, and they are given a boy's haircut, shaved down the middle. In this grade they are made responsible for looking after calves and horses. They also spend time singing songs of love, war, and mischief.

3. The principal activity associated with the third grade is to take family herds into untamed river valleys for long periods. Toward the end of the third grade, class members carry on collective activities such as singing, feasting, roaming, and electing class leaders.

4. At the beginning of the fourth grade the *luba* class is ritually constituted as such. Six men are invested as senior councillors of the class. During this grade the class must undertake a prescribed war party.

5. The fifth grade extends for thirteen years. Entrance to this grade entitles class members to marry. No Oromo may get married before that point. They may still not beget children, however. There are two additional prerequisites for fatherhood. One is to go on a major killing expedition (a requirement that today is usually fulfilled by cattle-raiding expeditions instead of outright warfare). The other is to take part in a long, complicated ceremony which occurs during the eighth year of this grade. In connection with this ceremony participants use a special ritual argot, observe a number of taboos, sing at a shrine, pray under a special tree, distribute sacred branches, shave their hair, cele-

brate a mock remarriage with their wives, and feast. Oromo were traditionally expected to abandon any children born before this fatherhood ceremony. After the ceremony they may raise sons, but not yet daughters.

6. The sixth grade of the *gada* cycle is called the *gada* grade. It extends from the forty-fifth to the fifty-third year of the cycle. When a *luba* class enters this grade it becomes the new ruling class of the tribe. Its leaders, a council of six carefully selected men, become the center of political and ritual leadership for the duration of the eight-year term. They enter office as the outgoing class leaves, through a ceremony known as the "exchange of scepters." During the third year of this period occurs the circumcision ceremony in which Oromo men attain full adult status. After this point they may raise daughters as well as sons. The major activities of the *luba* class leadership during the *gada* grade are to preside over the deliberative assemblies at which Oromo laws are reconsidered and to move about the country according to a prescribed calendar, performing a number of different ceremonies at various sacred shrines.

7–10. The next four grades of the *gada* cycle are not differentiated by distinctive activties. The twenty-seven-year period they encompass is known by a single name, *yuba.* During this period Oromo men are expected to act as elder statesmen. Outstanding members of the four *yuba* grades take part in an octennial "assembly of the multitudes." Some of them carry on a certain amount of politicking on behalf of their sons who have political ambitions. Others may be called on to serve as ritual experts.

11. At the eightieth year of the *gada* cycle a class moves into a period of quasi-monastic withdrawal. In the eleventh grade men may not carry arms or kill any living creature. They are expected to use a special ritual argot. Considered sources of blessing and refuge, they are shown special consideration by others. At the end of this grade the class "exchanges incense" with the incoming class of retired men, then fades into a status that lies outside the *gada* system altogether.

Constitution of gada *classes.* The assignment of membership in a *luba* is regulated by two carefully observed principles. One is that no person can enter the *gada* cycle until his father's class has carried out the fatherhood ceremony during the fortieth year of the cycle. Children born before this event have traditionally been abandoned, though the more recent practice has been to send them away to other tribes or have them adopted by families with legitimate fathers. The other principle is that a boy enters that *luba* which is forty years, or five grades, behind that of his father. If, for example, a man is in the eighth grade, all his sons will belong to that class currently in the third grade, while the man's father will belong to a class situated in what would be equivalent to a thirteenth grade.

It is clear, then, that the defining feature of a *gada* class is not age, but generational position. *Gada* is not an age-grading system; it is a generation-grading one. The calibration of generational positions through the *gada* cycle becomes particularly evident at two points. When a man goes through the fatherhood ceremony at the fortieth year of the cycle, his own father is at that very time retiring to the "monastic" grade in the eightieth year of the cycle. Similarly, when a man achieves complete adult status through a circumcision ceremony in the forty-eighth year of the cycle, his father withdraws from the *gada* cycle completely, and his sons for the first time become full-fledged members of the system when they are initiated and given proper boys' names as they enter the second grade. This cross-generational linking between classes in contrasting positions of the *gada* cycle is a matter of great interest to the Oromo. The group of classes consisting of grandfather's class, father's, son's, son's son's, and so on is given a special name, the *gogessa.* The *gogessa,* or "patriclass" as Legesse defines it, plays a significant part in the more general organization of traditional Oromo life, which I shall discuss below.

The role of age sets. Although the corporate units of the *gada* system are social classes based on generational position, the Oromo also have a type of grouping based on age. Known as *hariyya,* these age sets are formed by boys in their late teens. They wander from camp to camp recruiting other age mates to join them in singing and dancing excursions. The main activity of the age sets is to form regiments which, led by those members of the age set who are at the same time members of the appropriate *luba,* carry out raiding and military expeditions. The Borana formula for this interrelationship is that "the *luba* [generational class] decides, the *hariyya* [age set] executes."

All traditional Oromo males, then, belong to three crosscutting organizational complexes: a set of segmentarily expanding lineage groups; a generational class linked with paternal and filial classes but opposed to them with respect to position of authority; and a group consisting of all their age peers.[5]

The Agnatic Community

Struck by the numbers and virility of the Galla whom he encountered as Louis-Philippe's envoy to the court of King Sahle Sellassie of Shoa in 1840, Charles Rochet d'Héricourt had visions of a triumphant future for this attractive people. "Led by an enterprising chief," he prophesied, "this great nation—for one can call it that—could make itself the mistress over all Africa."[6]

The question is whether one can indeed speak of a "Galla nation," as Rochet d'Héricourt and several others after him have done. If by nation one means a sizable group of people who have some sense of belonging to a single societal community by virtue of sharing important past experiences and a common historic destiny, then the Galla do not constitute a nation, nor have they since their appearance as significant actors in the arena of Greater Ethiopia during the sixteenth century. The Galla expansion was not a concerted action of a single invading force, as was the *jihad* under Grañ, but a series of invasions carried out by different tribes which had already separated or were in the process of separating from one another. Arsi traditions place the breakup of the Oromo into separate tribes in the first decade of the sixteenth century. Bahrey (1593) writes that although the Galla formerly had followed the practice of setting off to war together, they subsequently quarreled among themselves and separated into a number of distinct tribes and confederacies.

Each of the major tribal groups the Galla formed created a distinct identity and developed a keen sense of alienation from other Galla groups. Borana, Guji, Arsi, Ittu, Mecha, and others have myths of origin which provide a common past for themselves, but no living myth for the Galla people as a whole apart from a general creation myth that represents the origin of mankind. The Borana consider themselves the *angafa,* the firstborn and thus most highly placed of all the Galla; yet they have no traditions concerning the emigration of other Galla groups, nor do the Guji. Both groups have little awareness of other Galla tribes beyond their immediate neighbors. It was not for lack of an enterprising chief that the Galla nation did not emerge—there have been many enterprising chiefs in modern Galla history—but for want of a definition of their community as one that comprises all members of the Oromo people.

Rather, the Galla conception of an inclusive collectivity has been based either on a sense of common descent from an eponymous tribal ancestor or of inclusion in a narrowly defined tribal unit. Galla typically refer to themselves as Borana, Guji, Arsi, Mecha, and so on, rather than as Galla or Oromo. These tribal communities, and none higher, claim their loyalty. Each such community has maintained its own ritual and political leaders, men who have traditionally had nothing to do with one another. Indeed, within *one* branch of the *northern* Guji —the Alabdu—there are two subdivisions, the Hallo and Woysitsu, each of which has its own *gada* system and its own *gada* leaders. In contrast with the Amhara-Tigreans who, despite a chronic proclivity toward internecine warfare, were to some extent restrained by a sense of guilt about killing "fellow Christian" compatriots, Oromo culture contains no ideas which declare it improper for members of one Galla tribe to wage war on another. The Galla's most esteemed adversaries in war have in fact been other Gallinya-speaking communities.

There exists, moreover, a sense in which Oromo tradition identified a subtribal group—the *gogessa,* or patriclass—as the vehicle of a significant shared past and historical destiny. The Borana believe that historical destiny, represented by the concept of *dachi,* which Legesse defines as "the mystical influence of history on the present course of events," is transmitted either from specific ancestors to their descendants or from *a whole ancestral gada class to one of its successor classes.* The experience of a particular ancestral *gada* class—calculated, through an epicyclical historical calendar, as one that was in power thirty-five *gada* periods, or 280 years, earlier—is believed to have a determining influence, a *dachi,* upon the fate of its latterday successor. The class currently in power is obliged to avoid the chief misfortunes which befell its ancestors or to repeat the outstanding successes. At the same time it is setting a precedent which will affect its patriclass descendants thirty-six *gada* generations in the future. The Oromo's sense of historical destiny thus has been tied to a particular social class, when not to a tribe; but never to a national community of all Galla, let alone a multiethnic Ethiopian community.

Functional Redundancy

Structural differentiation appears as extensive in the Oromo as in the Amhara system. It includes a segmentary organization of lineage groups; five patriclasses, each playing several kinds of grade-appropriate roles; age sets; and specialized positions like the *qallu,* the moiety ritual leader; *abba gada,* senior figure in the *gada* system; *abba dula,* the war leader; *abba bokku,* the ritual expert of the *gada* class; and a number of other positions involved in the *gada* council such as senior councillors, junior councillors, and auxiliaries.

In spite of this profusion of separate *structures,* the Oromo system exhibits a low degree of *functional* specialization. Although differentiated roles and institutional sectors exist, they tend to be associated with similar and overlapping activities, a condition which Asmarom Legesse has aptly described as functional redundancy. A number of different positions are carefully discriminated within the *gada* council, but occupants of these various positions carry out identical activities. The *qallu* is supposed to select the *gada* leaders, but both the *abba gada* in power and the age sets play a role in determining that decision. War parties are recruited on the basis of both age set and *gada* class affiliation. Religious rituals are performed both by lineage leaders and by the *gada* leaders. In the Amhara system, by contrast, official rituals can be performed *only* by ordained priests; and in large households and the courts of noblemen, persons assigned to carry out specific functions jealously defend their exclusive rights to do so and resist efforts to impose other kinds of tasks upon them.

The most significant aspect of Oromo functional redundancy concerned the relations between the offices of *qallu* and *abba gada.* Each represents the apex of the two great cross-cutting institutional complexes of Oromo society, the lineage system and the generational class system. The office of the *qallu* is filled on an ascriptive basis: it goes to the firstborn son of the previous *qallu.* The office of *abba gada* is filled on the basis of active competition among a number of candidates, selection among whom is based on personal merit, including the accumulated merits of their ancestors, and political pressures. The position of *qallu* is held for life; that of the *abba gada* changes every eight years. Occupants of the two offices are kept apart, except for an octennial ceremony in which the *abba gada* leads a pilgrimage to pay homage to the *qallu.* Yet both offices are responsible for performing both religious and political functions. The *qallu* together with the council of his lineage has the task of electing the new *abba gada;* the *abba gada* and his council make decisions about tribal activities and elect a group of junior councillors for the incoming regime. The *qallu* and the *abba gada* alike spend a great amount of time officiating at religious ceremonies.

Chapter Nine

Egalitarian Interaction

Observers of the Galla have been impressed by their egalitarianism quite as observers of the Amhara have been struck by their preoccupation with gradations of power, authority, and honor. This is not to say that differentials of power and rank do not exist in Oromo society; they exist and are important. Some lineages have more power and prestige than others. The position of the *qallu* is an exalted one. Classes in the *raba* (fifth) and *gada* grades have more prestige and authority than others, and senior councillors of the *gada* grade have more power than anyone else in the society. Married men have considerably more prestige than bachelors; killers more than cowards; fertile women more than the barren; wealthy men more than the poor; fathers more than sons.

Nevertheless, the Oromo characteristically are disposed to minimize the significance of such vertical differentials. If authority is delegated to some, it is balanced by a countervailing authority held by others. Where prestigious positions are held, their incumbents are likely as not to be regarded ambivalently, and treated with humor if not ridicule.

This general tendency to reduce the effects of status differentials is equally observable in the Galla family, the *gada* system, and the residential community. Although the Galla father is clearly a patriarchal figure, his position is attenuated by a good-humored, bantering relation with wife and children. The special status accorded the firstborn son, the *angafa,* serves immediately to qualify the special position of the father. In many Galla tribes parents are referred to as "father of . . ." and "mother of . . ." the *angafa,* rather than by their own names.

By keeping adjacent generations, with their manifold natural rivalries, at a distance from one another, the *gada* system has the effect of protecting the filial generation from excessive control by the paternal one (as well as the latter from the intrusions of the former). As the paternal *luba* class comes to power, their sons receive their own identity by being initiated and given names. As the paternal class goes through the grades of semiretirement, the filial class becomes more independent and better organized. By the time the filial generation is ready to assume power, the paternal class proceeds to a grade of full retirement.

The circulation of elites entailed by the *gada* cycle, such that no ruling class is in power for more than eight years, represents another way in which the Oromo system operates to check authority. The point is graphically presented in a traditional ceremony of the Tulema Galla in which, after several years in office, the leader of the ruling class climbed a platform of stones to proclaim the laws as usual but was shouted down and ceremonially pushed from the platform—a reminder that his term of rule would soon be over.[7] In the constitution of the Borana ruling council, moreover, great care is taken to assure a balanced representation of councillors from the two moieties. Still another antihierarchical aspect of the *gada* system is that younger men, who on the basis of age should defer to older men, often occupy more prestigious grades than their elders.

In the local community, men with high status are never deferred to with obsequious gestures or automatic compliance, nor are they entitled to order about anyone other than children and wives. P. T. W. Baxter observed among the Borana that even a young stockless client has to be respectfully requested to assist with herding or watering, and is never ordered to do so. Among the Mecha of western Shoa, similarly, Herbert Lewis found that prominent landowners or local leaders are never more than first among equals. The word *qite,* Lewis writes,

> which means a meeting to settle a dispute or discuss problems of community interest, is an extension of the word for "equal." This stresses the ideal that when they come together, all the members of the group are equal. In fact, some men have more influence and esteem than others; they speak more, they direct the flow of the discussion, and their words count more heavily than those of others present. But the ideal does reflect important aspects of the reality: each member of the community is invited to and expected to take part in community affairs; each man can participate as an equal limited only by his own abilities.[8]

The egalitarian ethos extends to gestures which ridicule people of high status in the same breath that they are being shown honor. A telling instance of this appears in a Galla folk song recorded by Enrico Cerulli. The song was recited at a *butta* ceremony, during which it was customary for Galla braves to recite their record of heroic victories and receive the appropriate decorations. The decorations were awarded by a respected elder of the tribe who placed some feathers of a red vulturelike bird in his hair for the occasion. The warrior began by boasting of his easiest victories and by degrees enumerated the more difficult. Some of the easier victories described in the song translated by Cerulli were reported to the elder as follows:

> O thou with the vulture's feathers, I have killed a great baboon
> who was emitting farts in his den!
> A great baboon, who looks like you, I have killed!
>
> O thou of the vulture's feathers, I have killed a porcupine
> wicked like thee
> who was injuring the budding plants!
> A porcupine who resembles thee have I killed![9]

When he reached the noble animals and human enemies, the warrior then shifted his simile and likened the fearsome victims to himself. An open, directly disrespectful expression of this nature would be unthinkable in Amhara culture.

The chief exception to Galla egalitarianism concerns the *qallu,* whose status is especially elevated because he represents the divine spirit. Even here, however, Lewis notes that Shoan Galla may shout disapproval of a suggestion or judgment directly at a *qallu,* and Legesse reports that the Borana show ambivalence toward the *qallu,* often laughing at them for being like women since the *qallu* may not bear arms or defend themselves against wild animals. During important public events, moreover, the Borana *qallu* make an effort not to stand out conspicuously. For the Oromo, no position of superiority puts a man beyond control or criticism from his fellows. The god of the Galla, Waqa, has been described as a figure of great mildness, forebearance, and patience, toward whom they show less fear than the Amhara toward the Christian god.[10]

Solidaristic Association

Whereas the Amhara associate with one another for the most part as competitors or short-term partners for specific purposes, the Galla associate mainly on the basis of membership in solidary groups. They are oriented not to the pursuit of individual interests through contractual relations, but to the pursuit of corporate interests through cooperative endeavors. Galla pursue individual interests as well, but the goods they seek are typically not obtained at the expense of their neighbors—as is the case in the Amhara competition over land and for honorific appointments—and the satisfaction of success is often linked with the greater glory of their lineage. Any Oromo male can qualify for honorific decorations and an appreciative wife by killing enemies and wild beasts. His achievement does not diminish his fellows' chance to make similar achievements, and it is celebrated not merely for his personal glory but for the credit it brings the groups to which he belongs. In addition to the boasting songs of individual warriors, the Galla have a genre of boasting songs known as *farsa* which celebrate the deeds of famous ancestors. The *farsa* are sung to glorify Oromo solidary groups—clans, lineages, age sets, or *gogessa.* Although the Amhara are prolific with individual boasting songs, they have no genre for collective boasting comparable to the *farsa.*

Lineages not only have collective interests in honorific achievements, they have corporate material interests as well. These include the securing of water resources—the excavation and defense of access to wells—and the control of positions in the *gada* council. They also have interests in maintaining traditions of rights to perform particular sets of rituals which are appropriated on a lineage, not an individual, basis.

Not only are corporate identities especially salient for the Oromo, and material and ideal interests defined by corporate affiliations, but most activities are carried out on a highly cooperative basis. Settlements are constructed and cattle are grazed and watered by members of the *olla* groups working in concert. Among the agricultural Guji, sowing and harvesting similarly are carried out on a communal, cooperative basis. Comparable collaborative patterns appear in Oromo military expeditions. The Oromo formed age regiments, or *chibra,* which collectively undertook to collect supplies for the campaign, elect leaders, recruit scouts, and distribute booty. These *chibra* served as solidary fighting units and followed a carefully organized battlefield strategy. The efficacy of massed collective action in waging war is celebrated by a Galla proverb, *Gudda, salpa, fardi gondan dessa;* "Large and small animals—even horses flee from troops of ants."[11] In another Galla saying—*Lafeko lafeketi, lafeketi lafeko;* "my bones are your bones and your bones are my bones"[12]—a sentiment is expressed concerning close friendships which, again, is far more solidaristic than the way Amhara tend to conceive of intimate relationships.

System Instability and Historical Change

Apart from the tendency to subdivide into rather narrowly conceived tribal groupings and to form easily entered residential communities with members associating on a cooperative basis, few structural features of the Oromo system had not undergone some kind of transformation by the twentieth century. I shall discuss first the changes undergone by the most conservative of the Oromo tribes, the Borana, and then indicate the main directions of change experienced by the other groups.

The principal changes in Borana social structure evident from a reconstruction of Borana social history during the last few centuries concern the organization of the *gada* system. In all probability the *luba* classes of the *gada* system were originally age classes as well as generational classes. The norms appropriate to each grade through which a *luba* class passes are quite evidently appropriate to a corresponding phase of the life cycle. Because of the two basic rules governing recruitment into those classes, however—the rule of a forty-year interval between paternal and filial classes and the rule that no sons could be born before a man reached the fortieth year of the cycle—there was a cumulative tendency for the population to be distributed into classes occupying increasingly advanced grades in the *gada* cycle. A man in the "ideal" age position, that is, forty years old when he experienced the fatherhood ceremony, could have a son when he was fifty-seven who would enter the *gada* cycle as an infant in grade three. That son at age fifty-seven might have a son who then would enter the cycle in grade five, and so on. Over time, this pattern would occur with sufficient frequency that the lower grades acquired fewer and fewer members while the higher grades acquired disproportionately more. The effects of this process of "senectation" were twofold. On the one hand, too many infants were born into the warrior and ruling grades, so their classes could not properly carry out their functions; on the other hand, there were too many politically "unemployed" men in the semiretired and retired grades. As Asmarom Legesse reconstructs it, the Borana made two structural modifications to deal with these problems. They created a separate category of age-homogeneous groups, the *hariyya,* to provide an adequate supply of young warriors. And they created additional roles for members of the semiretired grades, enabling some of them to become ritual experts and junior councillors, so that their experience could be utilized and the highly populated classes of the semiretired grades could secure direct political representation. Legesse has found that this process of extending the scope of activity and membership for *yuba* grade members continues to the present day; whereas the senior council, comprised of members of the ruling *gada* grade, has consisted of six members throughout the period for which reliable data were available, the junior council, consisting of representatives from the "older" *yuba* grades, increased by one over each of the last four *gada* periods, that is, from six to ten members.

In addition to the strain introduced by the process of senectation, another strain endemic in the traditional *gada* system stems from the rule of infanticide for children born to men who have not gone through the fatherhood ceremony. If, as William Graham Sumner observed in a famous aphorism, the mores can make anything right, it is also true, as Robert E. Park subsequently noted, that the mores have a harder time making some things right than others. Particularly among a people so oriented toward achieving fertility and so warm in their personal relations, the injunction to abandon children born out of schedule never could have been easy to follow. The strain thus experienced did not motivate the Borana to abandon the forty-year rule. They have solved the problem either by sending illegitimate children to other places or by facilitating their adoption by legitimate fathers. Among some other tribes who retained the *gada* system, however, resistance to the infanticide rule did engender a structural change. The rule was simply dropped, with the result that children could enter the system at any time. This change took place among the Guji and the Arsi, with the result that those tribes came to have a disproportionate number of members in the lower grades of the cycle (as well as, in some cases, a disproportionate number in the upper end of the cycle).

By making the modifications noted above, the Borana have been able to maintain the basic institutions of the traditional *gada* system despite the demographic changes and the strains on human nature. All the other Galla tribes, however, have abandoned one or more central features of the system or have eliminated it entirely. One can identify four general directions of transformation of the Oromo system away from the "classical" pattern oriented around the *gada* cycle.

1. *Restriction of the gada system to the performance of purely ritual functions.* The Amhara conquest of the independent Galla tribes in the nineteenth century was followed by efforts to subordinate their political systems to that of the Imperial Ethiopian Government. In some instances *gada* ceremonies were suppressed and in most cases political authority was bestowed upon rulers recruited on a different basis from that of the traditional *gada* leaders. In those tribes which nonetheless continued to adhere to the basic schedule of events associated with the *gada* cycle, *gada* activities no longer included military and legislative actions but were restricted to the observance of religious

ceremonies. This type of transformation is exhibited by the Guji and the Arsi.

2. *Expansion of the political role of the war leaders.* Galla tribes which migrated farther from the sixteenth-century homeland abandoned virtually all of the customs associated with the *gada* cycle. In part this was due to the distance from the homeland, since many activities associated with the *gada* cycle were tied to sacred shrines in the Borana and Guji regions, and the Oromo system lacked mechanisms for providing social controls at great distances. The need for a continuing paramilitary organization was felt in areas where conflict with Amhara and other people was chronic. In such circumstances successful leaders of military expeditions, known as *abba dula,* transformed what had been a temporary role of war captain into a permanent role of political leadership, often called *moti.* This subversion of traditional principles was favored not only by the distance from the traditional culture base but also by the senectation process: large numbers of Galla men came to be located in the retired grades where, lacking status within the *gada* system proper, they had relatively little stake in the survival of the system. Conversion to Islam completed the process of disaffection from the traditional basis of support for the *gada* system. When all these factors coalesced, as they did in the north among the Yejju and Wello Galla and in the southwest among the tribes of the Gibe region, the tribes established kingdoms under local dynasties.

3. *Expansion of the role of the* qallu. Among the Mecha Galla of western Shoa, and perhaps elsewhere, the eclipse of the position of powerful landowning war leaders due to the extension of the authority of the Ethiopian government was accompanied by an expansion of the functions of the *qallu.* Instead of remaining a sacrosanct office tied to the lineage system and responsible for the performance of a limited number of rituals, the position of *qallu* among the Mecha came to provide a center for the organization of nearly all local ceremonial, social, and parapolitical activity. The *qallu* preside over large annual ceremonial assemblies and over biweekly gatherings where people speak to divine spirits, carry on litigation, resolve disputes, name children, and do a good deal of singing and dancing. Such *qallu* have become wealthy landowners and recipients of substantial gifts of livestock, money, and other goods, which they use to maintain their elaborate households and dispense to their many followers. One Mecha *qallu*

was described in the mid-1960s as having nine ritual centers dotted over a fifty-mile area and at least thirty thousand followers.[13]

4. *Complete assimilation.* Where *gada* rites and the roles of *abba dula, moti,* and *qallu* have all been forgotten, Galla tribes have lost the core distinctive ingredients of their traditional sociocultural system. This appears to have happened among those Ittu tribes who fused with the Somali, those of the Tulema tribes who fused with the Shoan Amhara, and others.

The traditional Oromo system was a brittle assemblage of complex social forms tied to a rigid calendar of prescribed activities. Under the pressure of demographic changes, extension to distant territories, resistance to the infanticide rule, the attraction of other cultures and, most recently, the constraints imposed by the Ethiopian state, it broke down in a variety of ways. The demise of the *gada* system is remembered as a terribly disruptive experience by many Galla:

> When gada was destroyed, they left gada. The bull refused to mount the cow, men no longer respected justice. . . . There were no longer any real elders, and few children were born. The cows gave birth to deformed calves. Pregnant women gave birth to their children at the wrong time. They bore children at the wrong time. Lambs were born without forelegs and without tails. . . . When the gada customs were destroyed, everything else was also destroyed. When gada no longer existed, there was no justice. The crops that were cultivated no longer grew. And the oxen refused to fatten. The man who had formerly respected truth and justice abandoned them.[14]

In its classical form, however, the *gada* system had served to galvanize one of the most massive ethnic movements in African history. Both its successes and its breakdown have been momentous factors in the evolution of Ethiopian society.

10

Comparisons and Explanations

Summarizing the analyses of the previous chapters, the principal differences between the traditional Amhara and Oromo sociocultural systems may be formulated as follows.

Among the Amhara interests are structured chiefly on an individual basis. There are no fixed corporate groups with which Amhara normally identify so strongly as to derive from them a definition of material and honorific interests. Horizontal relationships thus tend to take the form of utilitarian exchange or competition. Among the Oromo interests are structured to a large extent on a collective basis. Patrilineal descent groups and *gada* classes define shared economic interests, political ambitions, status honor, and rights to perform certain rituals—not exclusively, but to a significant degree. Horizontal relations tend to be based on a community of sentiment or else on group antagonism.

Among the Amhara controls are structured through a finely graded hierarchy of statuses in which those in superordinate positions are entitled to unquestioning deference and public compliance. In Oromo society, controls are exerted by authority figures who are constantly kept in check by formal and informal processes which reflect a distrust of hierarchy and a concern for the expression of group consensus.

These first two sets of differences may be combined by characterizing the Amhara relational pattern as one of *hierarchical individualism* and the Oromo pattern as one of *egalitarian collectivism.*

With respect to the institutional orders of the two systems, in the Amhara system functional differentiation has proceeded to the point where an esoteric religious cultural system is maintained by a set of roles that are clearly separated from a set of political roles. The two role-complexes interact a good deal but draw on distinct traditions and derive legitimacy from different sources.

In the Oromo system, by contrast, it is scarcely possible to identify distinct "religious" and "political" roles. The two major role-complexes, that of the patrilineal descent system culminating in the office of *qallu* and that of the generation-grading system culminating in the *abba gada,* overlap in their functions, draw on a single tradition, and derive their legitimacy from a common source. The *qallu* selects the *abba gada* and his colleagues, and the latter spend much of their time, like the *qallu,* in fulfilling ritual obligations. Both sets of leaders, moreover, are chosen in part on the basis of affiliation with a particular patrilineage.

The difference in question may be characterized as involving the *degree of autonomy of the political and cultural spheres.*

With respect to the societal scripts of the two systems, the Amhara script defines the inclusive community as a multiethnic entity. It does this through references to a supratribal people, the *Habesha,* or Ethiopians; by upholding the transcendent authority of a monarch of Ethiopia, under which all Ethiopians are subjects; and by supporting a church which in outlook and organization operates on a multiethnic and national basis. The Oromo script, on the other hand, defines the inclusive community as a subethnic entity, the tribe; within that, it stresses loyalty to the crossgenerational patriclass, or *gogessa.* Where the *gada* system has broken down, loyalty has been expected not toward a broader Galla nation, but toward one's clan or, at most, one's local tribe.

Related to these contrasting definitions of the two societal communities are the expectations regarding future action—what may be called the "historical project" contained in the societal scripts. The Amhara historical project is to carry out the divine mission set forth in the *Kibre Negest,* a project of imperial expansion. The Oromo historical project is to carry out the charter implied in the cycle of *gada* classes: for each *gada* class in power to live up to the successes or redeem the failures of its ancestral class that lived 280 years before and to set a precedent, through wise administration and careful performance of rituals, for its successors in the future.

Finally, we may note that the basic structural features of the Amhara system remained relatively stable despite the historical vicissitudes of the last seven centuries, whereas the Oromo system broke down in several directions within a century or two of the Oromo expansions. Even among the Borana, where it remained relatively intact, the system underwent significant structural modifications.

The questions posed in chapter 6 may now be addressed. Four of the most problematic episodes in the Ethiopian experience were identified,

Table 3
Selected Structural Features of the Traditional Amhara and Oromo Systems

Feature	Amhara System	Oromo System
Interactional pattern	Hierarchical individualism	Egalitarian collectivism
Institutional differentiation	Autonomous political and cultural spheres	No autonomous political and cultural spheres
Societal script:		
Communal identity	Multiethnic	Subethnic
Historical project	Imperial expansion	Cyclical class performance
System Stability	High	Low

and for the purpose of explaining them sociologically I defined the historical actions in question as a set of dependent variables. These points are reproduced in table 4.

Table 4
Selected Historical Explananda

Historical Episode	Dependent Variable
Amhara expansion, 14th–15th centuries	I. Capacity for political domination
Oromo victories, 16th–17th centuries	II. Military effectiveness
Amhara resurgence, 19th century	III. Regenerative capacity
Oromo integration, 18th–20th centuries	IV. Capacity for extraethnic affiliation

In this chapter I shall offer a structural explanation of those differences in historical performance. I shall argue that they are associated empirically and can be shown by theoretical analysis to be connected with a set of causal factors that are in turn the product of the general structural features which have been identified. These factors and analyses will be presented in the course of dealing with the four explanatory questions that have been posed. The total complex of causal relationships to be posited here will be presented in schematic form at the end of the chapter.

The Question of Amhara Expansion

Power motivation. Most students of personality hold that the way people relate to outsiders is determined in good part by response patterns established through significant learning experiences they have with insiders. The point usually refers to the effect which socialization experiences within the family have on personal relationships outside the family. It can be extended, however, to the more general proposition that the way people learn to relate to one another within their society shapes the manner in which they are disposed to relate to members of other societies.

If this assumption is valid, we must look at how the Amhara and Oromo conduct social relations within their own societies to understand why they related as they did to other peoples in Ethiopia. Once this is done it quickly becomes apparent that the Amhara success in imperial expansion is connected at the motivational level with a passion to rule.

A disposition to command others is thoroughly ingrained in Amhara character. An Amharic proverb celebrates the point by proclaiming *Amara yazzal inji aytazzezim*—"the Amhara is to rule, not to be ruled." This disposition is clearly the product of a social order in which the dominant interactional pattern is that of hierarchical individualism. The pervasiveness of hierarchical relationships within Amhara society generates desires to escape from the liabilities of subordinate positions and to acquire the manifold benefits of superordinate positions. The statement commonly made by Amhara boys—"I want to grow up and have children so I can order them around as I have been ordered"—expresses a motif to be found at all levels of Amhara society.

The individualistic cast of Amhara social relations reinforces the passion to rule by providing conditions which make it relatively easy to acquire new increments of authority. Uninhibited by ascriptive liabilities on individual advancement or by collective responsibilities and constraints which would dampen personal ambition, any freeborn Amhara has been able to rise where opportunities permitted and at times even to create those opportunities. His deepest wish has been to acquire sufficient authority and status to lord it over his fellows.

The Galla, by contrast, reveal little passion to acquire power. The pattern of egalitarian collectivism in their social relations helps to account for this lack of power motivation. The egalitarian emphasis in Galla interaction means that there is little pressure to escape from subordinate positions and not much to be gained from seeking superordinate ones. The constraints of lineages and residential communities hold in check persons who are inclined to acquire too much power. Whereas a man who sought to advance by exploiting his kinsmen and neighbors would be quickly whittled down to size by the Galla, an Amhara of that sort would, despite a mild flurry of moralistic gossip, be admired for his fortitude and cunning and could become a culture hero.

The Amhara imperial expansion, then, can be seen as the externalization of an overarching passion to rule, generated by the common interactional patterns within Amhara society. This passion was not found among the Oromo, who consequently made no effort to establish dominion over other peoples—except for Galla who became acculturated to the Amhara pattern.

Political capacity. It was the formal structure of specialized political roles that enabled the Amhara to channel their motivation to dominate into historically efficacious actions. The role complex consisting of the emperor, regional and local lords, and their staffs of retainers comprised a hierarchically organized set of relationships which made it possible for the Amhara to create and make use of a considerable amount of political power.

Through a regulated flow of honors, facilities, benefits, and rights downward from the emperor and his chief appointees, the Amhara produced a resource base which made it possible for those in top positions in the system to mobilize its members to pursue authoritatively defined collective goals. Political activity, moreover, was carried out on a continuous basis. Rulers were constantly tending to arrangements that would secure them the most effective followings, and they were always available to devote attention to formulating and promulgating policies for the system. Amhara society thus had a continuously active center to set and implement goals related to territorial expansion and the administration of dominated areas.

Although the political system of the Oromo was highly effective as a means of resolving intratribal tensions, it was not organized to produce and use great amounts of political power. The Oromo system provided no specialized political roles, nor any extensive vertical hierarchy of statuses that could generate power for the system. Military and political energies were mobilized only at particular times and places and scarcely constituted a generalized capacity available for the system as a whole. Major policy decisions were made infrequently, at the assemblies of the multitudes every eight years.

Cultural exportability. The Solomonid monarchs sought to impose cultural as well as political hegemony over their subject peoples. This effort mainly took the form of raising the level of adherence to the canons of Orthodox Christianity among nominal Christians and of converting the heathens.

The Amhara missionizing process was made possible by the availability of an autonomously institutionalized set of cultural agents. The Amhara clergy had the task of maintaining a specialized body of religious culture, a task they could fulfill in any place. What is more, the content of that religious culture was not bound to the needs of any particular local community; it could have meaning anywhere. Conversely, converts from any ethnic background could study at Orthodox religious centers and become qualified representatives of the Amhara faith.

The Oromo ritual leaders, by contrast, were tied to their societal home base. Their role was not to maintain an independently established religious tradition but to minister to the ritual needs of a particular tribe. The content of their religious activities had meaning only within the context of a local Galla societal community. Outsiders could not qualify for positions of special ritual significance, for these were tied to specific lineages. The Oromo religious culture could therefore not be exported to other peoples. Amhara armies were preceded, accompanied, and followed by monks and priests who facilitated the imperial expansion by planting the roots of Amhara Christian culture.

Historical project. The substance of Amhara Christian culture supported political expansion no less than the fact that this culture was exportable. It offered Solomonid monarchs and their followers a script in which imperial expansion figured as a kind of manifest destiny. As we have seen, the *Kibre Negest* codified beliefs that not only assured the Tigreans and their Amhara successors of superiority over the Jews, toward whom they had feelings of rivalry, but also gave them a mandate to carry on, as the new chosen people, a policy of spreading the true faith of the Lord of Hosts. What is more, the covenant they appropriated was not the Mosaic covenant, whose terms pledge a people to adhere faithfully to a code of moral laws under pain of a scourge of curses, but the covenant of Abraham, Noah, and King David—a covenant which God gratuitously bestows upon his favored ones, promising unilateral support without exacting reciprocal obligations. Such a conception would surely boost the morale of the Solomonid rulers and energize their quest for dominion.

The concept of a single, powerful heavenly deity tied to a transcendent ethical imperative is common to all the Semitic religions. They vary in the content of that imperative and its relation to political authority. Judaism, Islam, and Catholic Christianity competed with Ethiopian Orthodox Christianity for the souls of Ethiopians, but the last was unquestionably the most adaptive for the purpose of building an Ethiopian state. Judaism is ill suited to be a royal ideology: it must reject transcendent earthly authority and be tied only to the fortunes of a Jewish nation. Both Islam and Western Christianity, for different reasons and in different ways, can legitimate monarchic rule; but as universalistic religions there are no grounds on which either could certify one state as intrinsically superior to all others. In contrast, Ethiopian Orthodox Christianity encompassed the belief system of the *Kibre Negest,* which could secure for Ethiopia the status of being chosen without being bound by the stipulation of Jewish ethnicity, and which could utilize the authority of Christian belief to legitimate loyalty to one particular nation under a divinely endowed dynasty. The Amhara thus had a religious system, conversion to which also meant inclusion in a supratribal polity under an emperor.

The historical project implicit in Oromo culture was in no way comparable to this. Such sense of destiny as the Oromo experienced under the traditional *gada* system was directed to the successful administration of an intratribal grouping, the patriclass, during the term when that class came to office at forty-year intervals. The future was expansive only in the sense of accumulating credits for that parochial collectivity. The Amhara future was expansive in a way that directly facilitated imperial growth. The Amhara scenario was to convert the heathen and to establish Solomonid rule over the greatest possible area of Greater Ethiopia.

The Question of the Oromo Victories

Although the Amhara were far more successful than the Oromo or any other Ethiopian group in establishing an extended sphere of political authority, the Oromo were consistently more successful than the Amhara in military encounters for a period of nearly two centuries after their invasions began. Although Emperor Sertsa Dingil sought to account for this difference by observing that the Galla, in contrast to the Amhara, go into battle determined to conquer or die, the difference in question is not simply a reflection of the different emphases which Amhara and Galla culture place on military courage. In point of fact, both cultures lay tremendous stress on the virtues of aggressive masculinity. In both societies boys are trained to be fearless fighters. Men who slay dangerous wild beasts or fearsome human enemies are lavishly honored. Special boasting chants, called *fukera* and *shillela* in Amharic and *fakar* and *gerarsa* in Gallinya, are declaimed to shame cowards and incite the brave. Amhara verses often resemble Galla verses of this sort.

Amhara	
Shellelew shellelew	War cries, war cries!
Mindenew shellelew	Of what use is boasting and challenging
Baddisu gorade	Unless you decorate your new sword
Demun telamesew	With his blood!

Galla	
Sala buttan dakkutti sala	The sword's edge on the apron is shameful
Chirriqun durba sala	To spit on a girl is shameful
Sala lama batani	After bringing two edges [of a spear]
Lama bachifatani	After ordering two [edges of a spear] to be brought
Dirarra diessun sala	The flight from men [enemies] is shameful.*

Amhara:	
Wend lijj teweldo	If a male child is born
Kalhone indabbatu	Who is not like his father
Setut amelmelo	Give him a spinning stick
Yiftil indennatu	Let him spin like his mother!

Galla	
Motin ilma wa sadi	The kings of the children are three:
Tokko jagna dalata	One is born valiant
Tokko gamna dalata	One is born wise
Tokko arja dalata	One is born generous
Isen bira charancharetti lugna	Except these, the other useless cowards
Golfan ma tap ingone	Why are they not cut down by fever?

As might be expected, moreover, warriors of both peoples created barbed lines to ridicule the character of the other:

Amhara	
Atamenut ye-gallan gofere	Pay no heed to the warrior headdress of a Galla
Inkwan be-wejigra	Let alone a rifle, he flees at the sound of
Yisheshal be-werre	a rumor.

*The "apron" referred to is a shepherd's garment. The verse means that just as it is shameful to assail peaceful shepherds or to insult a girl, so it is shameful to flee when one hears arms.

Galla

Kan abba butta nqallu	Whose father does not make the *butta* sacrifice
Gana hati rako nqabdu	Whose mother has not received the *rako* sacrifice
Kanafa jesani	After killing warriors such as these
Dada dibbachun sala	It is against custom to anoint oneself with butter.[1]

Galla custom forbids men to anoint themselves with butter after killing ignoble beasts—those which cry out when they are wounded. In the last verse the singer compares Amhara to animals because they have none of the signs that distinguish men from beasts. A similar piece of Galla boasting was recorded more than three centuries earlier by Bahrey:

> Those who have killed neither man nor animal do not shave their heads. . . . In the time of the government of Mul'ata they ate the buffalo and said, "Since we eat it, it is like an ox, and we ought not to shave our heads when we kill it." One party said an outrageous thing when they declared, "Let us not shave our heads when we kill the inhabitants of Shoa and Amhara, for they are but oxen which speak, and cannot fight."[2]

Amhara and Oromo cultures alike, then, laid stress on military courage. Amhara as well as Galla warriors were motivated by fierce desires to slaughter their enemies. Where they differed was in the *extent to which those motivations were activated.* This difference is one that reflects variations in their dominant interaction patterns.

The Amhara pattern of hierarchical individualism had the effect of making the motivation of individual soldiers contingent on the particular reward structure of a given campaign. Amhara troops fought for personal gain from booty and to be acknowledged and rewarded by their superiors. The presence of the king or lord on the battlefield typically made a great difference in how bravely Amhara soldiers were inclined to fight. If the relevant lord was killed, or if there was no chance of his learning about a soldier's bravery, the latter was likely to feel that there was not much point in fighting. If their lord was defeated in battle, Amhara soldiers often shifted allegiances and went over to another side. If the gains possible from any battle situation seemed too small, they felt no moral compulsion to continue the fight.

In the Oromo case, by contrast, several factors made the activation of their military ethic less contingent on the particularities of the battle situation. For one thing, killing a man was intrinsically an important accomplishment for any Galla male who wanted to live a self-respecting life. It enhanced his chances of securing a wife or wives, and not to be married at the appropriate time was considered quite shameful. It gave him the self-esteem associated with wearing the victorious warrior's hairstyle: he could shave his head and wear some plaited strands, the usage referred to but only partially understood by Bahrey.

This personal motive was reinforced by the fact that military expeditions were truly corporate undertakings. The Galla went to battle in organized divisions called *chibra.* These *chibra* collected supplies for the campaign, elected regimental leaders, recruited scouts, distributed booty, and served as actual fighting units in battle. For the Galla, support, control, and morale were thus provided by their comrades, whereas Amhara fought as individual soldiers, expected to provide their own supplies and capture their own booty, and to participate only as ordered by their authoritative superior.

The ritual killing expedition associated with the *butta* ceremony, moreover, placed the collective requirement to go to war every eight years in a context of transcendent historical meaning. The *gada* class which undertook the expedition fought not only for itself but also to live up to the reputation of its ancestral classes and to accumulate merits for its *gogessa* in perpetuity.

The Oromo warrior therefore needed no lord to inspire and reward his particular exploits in battle. In his desire to appear a fully competent male in the eyes of his home community, to contribute to the corporate success of his fighting division, and to play his part in the drama of Oromo history he had a set of motivations for battle that were continuously operative and not contingent on the circumstances of the particular battle.

In sum, it was their democratic collectivism and their historical project, the very factors which made the Oromo unsuited for extending political dominion over others, that gave them a special short-term advantage over the Amhara in waging aggressive warfare.

The Question of Amhara-Tigrean Resurgence

The long succession of Oromo military victories destroyed the medieval unity of the Amhara empire. Oromo incursions cut off the imperial center from previously controlled territories in the south and established Galla enclaves in the north which separated the regions of Shoa, Lasta, and Tigray from one another. The Yejju Galla dynasty then subverted the imperial center itself by reducing the Gonderine emperors to a state of weakness.

In spite of their advantaged position the Galla never spawned a movement for Oromo nationalism. No one arose to unite the dispersed Galla peoples behind a single standard and to assert Galla leadership on behalf of a new Ethiopian empire. The structural reasons for this failure have already been indicated. The Galla were neither oriented toward political domination nor guided by a conception of a panethnic, let alone multiethnic, community. They quickly broke down into tribes and subtribes that spent as much time warring among themselves as against other peoples, if not more. Indeed, a large part of the increased slave trade in the first half of the nineteenth century consisted of Galla captives being sold by other Galla.

In the early decades of the century the Solomonid empire grew increasingly fragmented. The large northern provinces of Shoa, Wello, Gojjam, and Tigray became divided into dozens of autonomous chiefdoms which engaged in what seemed like a constant war of all against all. This strife was compounded by divisions among the clergy, whose differences on subtle points of theological doctrine escalated into bitterly fought sectarian disputes. Yet the regenerative capacity of the Amhara system was such that this state of affairs was reversed: emperors Tewodros, Yohannes, and Menilek gained effective followings and reunited the empire.

Part of the explanation for this resurgence must certainly lie in the fact that the Amhara carried in their heads a picture of the world in which a divinely charged Solomonid monarch of Ethiopia played a crucial role, even though no such monarch had been on the scene for generations. The vision projected by the *Kibre Negest* and fortified by legends concerning centuries of Solomonid royalty had not died, it had merely gone underground. The Amhara reacted to the disorganization of the empire in the first decades of the nineteenth century by experiencing a revival of this vision—a "return of the repressed."

This yearning became most openly expressed in connection with the naming of the two great Amhara emperors of the century, Tewodros and Menilek. The bestowal of names is a symbolic act of the greatest significance in Ethiopia, as Tekle-Tsadik Mekouria has abundantly documented in his monograph on Ethiopian proper names.[3] In naming a newborn child or a new king, the close relatives or the royal entourage typically give considerable thought to the matter. In so doing they are often mindful of a Ge'ez proverb, *simu yimerho haba gibru*—"one's name leads to one's deeds."

The visionary Kasa chose the royal name of Tewodros (Theodore) in response to beliefs about the name which had been agitating his countrymen for decades. Sven Rubenson interprets the episode as follows:

> Kasa needed to define his mission to himself and to his countrymen: he needed to identify himself with something or someone in the traditions of his people that would set him apart from his own past as one among the warring *mesafint* [princes] as well as from his predecessors, the powerless representatives of the House of David and Solomon at Gondar. Kasa did all this in one single word. He declared that he was Tewodros, the King who was to come in the latter days and rule the world in righteousness, peace and prosperity for forty years.[4]

Prophetic beliefs about a saving monarch named Tewodros derived from two sources in the medieval Amhara experience. One was the brief, obscure reign of Emperor Tewodros I, who ruled from 1411 to 1414. For some reason this reign was especially memorable for the Amhara. Half a century before Kasa was born, Bruce reported the popularity of ideas about Tewodros I: "There must have been something very brilliant that happened under this prince, for though the reign is so short, it is before all others the most favourite epoch in Abyssinia. It is even confidently believed that [Tewodros] is to rise again and reign in Abyssinia for a thousand years."[5]

In addition to oral traditions about the fifteenth-century emperor, there was an apocryphal writing which lent considerable authority to the idea of a messianic Tewodros. This was the *Fikkere Iyesus,* the Interpretation of Jesus, a work that probably originated as an ancient Jewish apocalyptic tract and underwent a Christianizing process in the course of being translated into Ge'ez. Considered a holy book by the Falashas and the Ethiopian Christians alike, the *Fikkere Iyesus* attributes to Jesus the prophecy that after a long period of earthly corruption followed by harsh divine punishment, there would come from the Orient a king named Tewodros who would reign forty years in an era of peace, joy, and piety.

The chaotic conditions of highland Ethiopia in the early nineteenth century quickened hopes that the promised messianic ruler would appear. Candidates were not wanting. Impostors in various parts of the country claimed to be the expected Tewodros. In 1831 an abortive attempt was made to enthrone a man not of the royal family who proclaimed himself the expected Tewodros. The wide support that made it possible for Tewodros II to go as far as he did in reunifying the empire in the 1850s was a response not merely to Kasa's military abilities but also to the image he projected of himself as Tewodros and the yearnings of the Amhara and Tigrean people for the reign of an extraordinary Solomonid monarch.

While the myth of Tewodros was animating pretenders and followers in the northern provinces, that of the *Kibre Negest* was inspiring the Shoans. Sahle Sellassie, king of Shoa from 1813 to 1847, had wanted to take the throne name of Menilek. He was dissuaded by a monk who prophesied that the name would bring him great misfortune, but who instructed him to bestow the name upon the son of his firstborn son, Haile Melekot. Thus named, Sahle Sellassie's grandson would become the conqueror of all Ethiopia and the greatest of the kings. In 1844 an illegitimate grandson was born and given the name of Sahle Maryam. When Haile Melekot legitimized his offspring by marrying the boy's mother, Sahle Sellassie was overjoyed. Following the monk's counsel he renamed the infant with the legendary and auspicious name of Menilek.

During the period of acute national disorganization, then, significant elements of the Amhara populace yearned for a Tewodros and a Menilek—for monarchs who would fulfill the annunciations of the fourteenth and fifteenth centuries. This was a striking instance of the tenacity with which Amhara and Tigreans have adhered to their cultural traditions. That was not their only option. The kind of disruption they experienced in the eighteenth and nineteenth centuries could have led to demoralization and conversion to new beliefs, which was in fact the response of the Galla.

Disruption of the traditional Oromo order came not from dismemberment due to the penetration of alien elements, but from the overextension of population into distant lands and the internal processes of dislocation of members of the *gada* system. The central beliefs of the Oromo were severely challenged by the migration of Galla tribes away from their traditional ritual centers and by the senectation which produced numbers of men who had no proper status within the *gada* system. The Galla response was largely not to revive the old beliefs but to modify or abandon them. Waqa was forsaken for Allah and Egziabher; the *muda* ceremony was replaced by Ramadan or Fasiqa

(Easter); and *gada* democracy was replaced in some areas by centralized chiefdoms and even full-blown monarchies.

For all their conflicting regional ambitions and Christological differences, Amhara and Tigreans remained bound to the faith of their fathers. Despite the cruelties and excesses which disfigured the last years of his reign, Tewodros II had demonstrated that the old idea of an Ethiopian empire united under a Christian Solomonid monarch was still viable. After his death the leading political contenders—Wagshum Gobeze of Amhara, Kasa of Tigray, and Menilek of Shoa—could each have withdrawn and lived successfully as lords of their respective provinces. Not one of them chose to do this. Each aspired to reunite the empire in his own version of the age-old vision.

If there is one feature of the Amhara system that above all others accounts for the durability of its traditional beliefs and values, it is the institutionalization of a set of roles with special responsibility for perpetuating the central oral and written traditions of Amhara culture. Whatever the distresses of other parts of the system, priests and monks had support, facilities, and protection that enabled them to keep alive the central ideas of their tradition. At times this survival literally depended on inaccessible mountaintop and island monasteries that were safe from the usual ravages of war and brigandage. It was these cultural specialists who kept alive such beliefs as the Solomonid legend as recorded in the *Kibre Negest* and the prophecy of Tewodros in the *Fikkere Iyesus* and transmitted them from generation to generation.

I referred in chapter 7 to the particularly close connection between the people of Tigray and those hallowed traditions. It was principally because of this intimate relationship to the sacred center of Ethiopian national culture that, despite centuries of subordination to Amhara kings and governors and a tradition of antagonism to the Amhara, the Tigrean elite maintained some continuing loyalty to the idea of an Ethiopian national community. The deterioration of the Amhara monarchy during the latter Gonderine period provided opportunities for Tigreans to give more active political expression to this loyalty. As the empire began to fall apart after the 1750s, it was the Ras of Tigray, Mikael Sehul, a descendant of the Solomonid line through Dawit II, who as a formidable power behind the throne served for decades as the primary proponent of the Ethiopian national cause. His efforts were ultimately in vain and the Ethiopians descended into that period of internecine warfare which, again drawing on Old Testament themes as inspiration for their political imagery, they came to refer to as the Era of the Judges. During this period the rulers of Tigray, like those of the other major provinces, were in actuality independent sovereigns.

This state of affairs favored the resurgence of Tigrean political ambitions, though it was not until the ascendance of Dejazmatch Sebagadis that the numerous competing regions of Tigray were brought together in an independent autonomous province. In 1831 Sebagadis was defeated and killed by the ruler of Lasta, who in turn was subjugated by Tewodros II. So it was not until the demise of Tewodros in 1868 that Tigrean dynastic aspirations could come to the fore. They found a perfect embodiment in the man who became Emperor Yohannes IV in 1871.

Yohannes had impeccable credentials for being the one to return the throne to Tigray after an interregnum of a thousand years. Through genealogical connections on both his mother's and his father's sides he was related to a number of earlier Solomonid emperors. A devout Orthodox Christian, he promoted the strength of the church by the unprecedented procedure of importing four bishops from Egypt rather than the traditional lone *abun*. Thoroughly devoted to the ancient traditions respecting the Ethiopian monarchy, he was the first emperor in two centuries to hold the prescribed coronation ceremony in Aksum, and he recovered from England the royal copy of the *Kibre Negest* which the British expedition against Tewodros had taken away.

It is clear that Yohannes was not a parochial Tigrean ruler. Amharic, not Tigrinya, was made the official language at his court. Galla notables were given important roles in his kingdom. If Yohannes is often remembered for his policy of pressuring Muslim leaders in Wello to convert to Christianity—a policy grounded on desperately important national political reasons—he should also be remembered for having many Muslims in his entourage and assigning Muslims to positions in his court, as he is fondly remembered by some of the Muslims of northern Tigray today. That he was not such a religious fanatic as he has often been portrayed is shown by his willingness to propose an alliance with the Sudanese Mahdists against England.

It was the ambition and the genius of Yohannes, rather, to reunite the diverse provinces of Greater Ethiopia on a practical and enduring basis. We now have, thanks to the painstaking analysis of previously unexamined documents and oral traditions by Zewde Gabre-Sellassie, an informed account of how he did this. Through consistent adherence to the ideal of a united and independent Ethiopia and a prudent policy of strengthening the hands of traditional regional rulers and entrusting them with responsibility, Yohannes succeeded in bringing together a large number of regions of Greater Ethiopia without antagonizing the populace as had his predecessor. At Yohannes's death the reunified empire remained intact. The materials assembled by Gabre-Sellassie provide substantial support for his conclusion that "But for the achievements of Yohannes, Menilek and his successors might never have succeeded in maintaining Ethiopia's independence in an Africa almost entirely colonized."[6]

The resurgence of the Ethiopian polity in the nineteenth century was thus essentially a joint Amhara-Tigrean effort, just as, in a different way, had been the establishment of the Solomonid state in the fourteenth century. Tigreans have continued to make important contributions to the national polity after the death of Yohannes, despite the tensions created by the transposition of the throne back to the south and the formation of an Italian colony in Eritrea in 1890. The collaboration of Tigreans was of course crucial in the concerted effort to combat the Italian forces in 1896. More recently, in spite of political differences which have subsequently become more troublesome, Tigreans in Eritrea were moved by sentiments rooted in the ancient symbolism of the *Kibre Negest* to express strong support for the Federation of Eritrea and Ethiopia in 1952. Today, many Ethiopians from Tigray Province and highland Eritrea play important parts in the administration of the Ethiopian government.

The Question of Oromo Affiliation

The Oromo had no stratum of cultural specialists. This lack helps to explain the relative fragility of Oromo traditional culture when its bearers were removed from the controls of a local community operating on a customary basis. But the inability of the traditional Oromo system to regenerate itself after much stress and disruption does not in itself explain the notably successful adaptations of the Galla to other Ethiopian cultures and the degree of their integration with other ethnic groups.

To understand the phenomenon of Oromo affiliation it may help to call attention to certain more general features of Galla behavior. To an unusual degree the Galla appear to be oriented toward associating with others on a friendly basis. A recent survey of interethnic attitudes among Ethiopian college students supports this general impression. Of the three ethnic groups represented in significant numbers in this survey—Amhara, Galla, and Tigrean—the Galla were liked by more respondents and disliked by fewer than were the other two, largely because non-Galla respondents perceived Galla as sociable, not exclusive, and not domineering. These traits were not mentioned in positive out-group descriptions of the Amhara and Tigreans.[7]

A comparable contrast can be drawn from the observations of scholars who have spent time in rural communities of Galla and Amhara. Herbert Lewis has observed that "Shoa Galla communities are open communities, easy for newcomers to join, composed of people who are, in the first place, cooperating neighbors. . . . New settlers are accepted if they are willing to participate in community affairs. . . . Members of other ethnic groups, such as Amharas, are accepted if they are cooperative."[8] Precisely the opposite condition seemed to me to characterize the Amhara of northern Shoa and my impression has been confirmed by others. Amhara live in closed communities, hard for newcomers to join. New settlers are regarded with suspicion and, if they belong to other ethnic groups, find it extremely difficult to gain acceptance. Again, Lewis has spoken of similar openness toward newcomers among the Galla of Jimma Province, and John Hinnant has reported the ease with which members of other ethnic groups, like the Sidamo, Derasa, and Borana Galla, are incorporated into Guji Galla society through the fiction of adoptive patrilineal affiliation.

The Galla's ability to make friends with outsiders and to incorporate them or affiliate with them readily in local communities has been reported for so many times and places that I am inclined to regard it as a characteristic aspect of their mode of relating to outsiders. To explain such a trait, as I suggested earlier, one must look at how Galla are brought up to relate to insiders.

In a social system where interactions tend to follow a pattern of egalitarian collectivism, one would expect to find socialization practices which produce a disposition to be friendly toward others. From the agreement of lineage members concerning how a firstborn son disposes of his father's estate to the agreement of *gada* councillors when a new law is to be promulgated, important decisions in the traditional Oromo system are made not by domineering authorities but through the respectful interchange of views among men whose inequalities of status are not stressed. From the synchronized movements of work parties drawing water from deep wells to the joint grounding of new residential camps or neighborhoods to the collective manage-

Chart 3
System Structures and Group Action Capabilities

Structural Feature	Amhara System		Oromo System	
Dominant Interaction Pattern	Hierarchical individualism		Egalitarian collectivism	
Power motivation	*High*	→ I	*Low*	—X→ I
Activation of military motivation	*Contingent*	—X→ II	*Continuous*	→ II
Affiliation motivation	*Low*	→ III	*High*	→ IV
Existence of Autonomous Political Sphere	Present		Absent	
Political power	*High*	→ I, II, III	*Low*	—X→ I, III
Political activity	*Continuous*		*Intermittent*	
Existence of Autonomous Cultural Specialists	Present		Absent	
Cultural exportability	*High*	→ I	*Low*	—X→ I
Cultural durability	*High*	→ III	*Low*	—X→ III; → IV
Societal Script				
Scope of community	*Multiethnic*	→ I	*Subethnic*	—X→ I
Historical project	*Imperial expansion*	→ I	*Cyclical class performance*	→ II
System Stability	*High*	→ III	*Low*	—X→ III

Relationship between Variables:
(heavy arrow) → = structurally determines
→ = promotes
—X→ = inhibits

Group Action Capabilities:
I = capacity to dominate
II = military effectiveness
III = regenerative capacity
IV = capacity to affiliate

ment of supplies and operations as a band of Oromo brothers goes to war, important activities in Oromo society are carried out not by individualistic competition and bartering but on a highly cooperative basis. These patterns have required individual Galla of the same *olla, gada* class, or age set to relate to one another in a friendly, collaborative manner.

When the Oromo went forth from their homeland they had to find ways of relating to the peoples near whom they settled once the antagonisms of battle were temporarily or permanently set aside. Their own script contained no mandate to establish a dominion over others. On the contrary, since they had no corps of cultural specialists their own traditions proved relatively fragile and left them open to a variety of new cultural influences. A pronounced need to affiliate with others made them particularly ready both to share their culture with others and to adopt the cultures of others. These factors help to explain the Galla's capacity to join both with Amhara-Tigreans at the national level and with diverse alien groups in various local regions.

Where Oromo culture was fragile, Amhara culture was durable. Where the Oromo were inclined to associate with one another as equals, the Amhara were disposed to rule. The variables which led the Galla to cooperation, acculturation, and interethnic affiliation led the Amhara to a resurgence of traditional political and religious culture and the establishment of a hierarchical order throughout Greater Ethiopia.

11

Social Evolution in Ethiopia

As the twentieth century opened, Greater Ethiopia appeared as a resolutely independent empire in the early stages of becoming a multiethnic national society. The internal basis for this feat of survival was a sequence of six major developments:

1. the settlement of a vast ecological area by peoples of kindred traditions engaged in a loose network of interrelationships
2. the creation of the germs of a national culture in the Tigrean seedbed
3. the expansion of a durable supratribal political center under the kings of Amhara
4. the formation, through the spread of Christianity and Islam and the Galla migrations, of vast corridors of ethnic intercourse
5. the resurgence of the Amhara-Tigrean imperial idea in the nineteenth century
6. the integration of the Galla with other ethnic groups and with the national center.

In outlining this sequence of developments I have spoken as though the achievements of the Amhara and the Galla, and the contrasting structural characteristics which made them possible, were matters of historical accident. At this point I wish to suggest that additional light can be thrown on the contrast between the two systems, as on the Ethiopian experience as a whole, by applying the perspective of evolutionary theory.

In doing this I repudiate at once certain ideas which have often been associated with the concept of social evolution and which have given that concept a bad name among critical scholars: that human evolution follows one fixed set of stages, that it is irreversible, and that more highly evolved forms are in essence morally superior to less evolved ones. One can reject all these ideas and still acknowledge certain realities that make an evolutionary perspective useful, if not indispensable. One is the reality of *emergent novelty:* over time human groups have created social and cultural forms which previously did not exist. Another is *functional specialization:* new forms have been retained because they better satisfied certain needs. A third is the reality of *societal integration:* the new forms have increased the scope of human association, relating larger numbers of persons within societal systems.

Social evolution can accordingly be defined as the process by which different human populations and the species as a whole gain greater control over their physical and human environments by creating and transmitting novel adaptive forms and stabilizing expanded levels of social organization. The evolutionary process differs from the totality of human history in that history contains numerous cases of adaptive failures and regressions and is for the most part taken up with working out human destinies within a given evolutionary level rather than with shifts from one level to another.

To consider the development of Ethiopian society within an evolutionary perspective is thus to identify the major transformations in adaptive capacity of the constituent peoples of Ethiopia and to link these changes with the main formative episodes in Ethiopian history just outlined. In this chapter I shall speak of five such transformations, distinguished according to the extent and types of functional specialization involved.

Holistic Specialization

The first broad category of evolutionary changes to be considered encompasses the long-term process of creating a number of distinct cultural traditions in Greater Ethiopia. In this process, Ethiopia's physical environment gave its peoples two signal advantages. The maze of mountains and the barrier of coastal deserts enabled them to live in protective isolation, relatively free from the massive invasions which repeatedly obliterated historic societies in the African plainlands. The diversity of ecological zones, moreover, provided an opportunity to develop many different kinds of adaptation. Together these conditions made it possible for Ethiopians to utilize multiple cultural differences as sources of ecological complementarity and as alternative points of departure for further evolutionary developments.

Thanks to these favorable conditions, Ethiopian prehistory was taken up with the creation of numerous specialized modes of subsistence in the various ecological niches afforded by the highland plateaus, lowlands, and waterways. Hunting and fishing cultures, pastoral nomadism, seminomadic pastoralism, slash-and-burn cultivation, horticulture, plow cultivation, and specialized crafts were all elaborated and stabilized. The general pattern of this first evolutionary transformation was one of *increasing heterogeneity among a number of homogeneous cultures of small scale.*

It seems appropriate to apply to this development the concept which Marshall Sahlins and others have adopted from evolutionary biology, that of adaptive radiation—the outward spread of a generalized group, followed by a progressive differentiation of species as adaptive modifications make the various populations more efficient in particular modes of life. It would be in conformity with our linguistic and ethnographic knowledge to conceive that four generalized groups —belonging to the Ethio-Semitic, Cushitic, Omotic, and East Sudanic language families—spread over Ethiopia to differentiate into separate small-scale societies with distinctive languages, religions, social organizations, and technologies.

The changes brought about by this process of adaptive radiation represent a modality of general evolution which I propose to call holistic specialization: holistic because the patterns evolved are shared more or less equally by all members of each differentiated society; and specialization because the patterns involve a certain amount of skill and training, are appropriate to a particular habitat or ecological niche, and provide the basis for exchanges with other groups.

These four characteristics of holistically specialized societies indicate that groups adapted in this evolutionary modality will exhibit certain common structural features, whatever the content of their specialized patterns. Because of their internal cultural homogeneity, such groups will not contain sharply differentiated social strata. No social category will be allotted a preponderance of knowledge, virtue, wealth, or power; differences of this sort are distributed according to the differential abilities and fortunes of individuals and their families. The division of labor is organized almost exclusively on the basis of sex-role differences.

The existence of generally practiced special skills important for the adaptation of the group means that individuality will be assessed and praised in terms of outstanding performance of those general skills. Because the cultural patterns are specialized with respect to adjustment to a particular kind of habitat, the mechanisms of pattern maintenance in such societies will be highly conservative. Religion will be oriented to supporting the existing system of adaptation by placating deities and spirits, expressing communal harmony, and securing the correct operation of the forces of nature. The presence of other kinds of cultures in a larger ecological setting means that members of such societies tend to develop a keen sense of their own identity and how they differ from neighboring peoples, but they also develop ways of procuring from those others whatever special goods and services they can profitably get by exchange.

The Majangir, recently studied by Jack Stauder, are one of the very few peoples in Greater Ethiopia who still exist in the modality of holistic specialization. Majang culture is largely oriented to the exigencies of shifting cultivation in a rain-forest area of southwestern Ethiopia: an ecological niche, Stauder notes, in that this rain-forest area is well suited to the Majang slash-and-burn cultivation but not suited to the cultures of their immediate neighbors the Anyuak, who rely on savannah rivers for fishing and transportation, and the Mecha Galla, whose animals are vulnerable to the tsetse flies which thrive in the altitudes where most Majangir live.

The homogeneous character of Majang society has been captured in Stauder's report:

> All Majangir share the same, materially simple, culture. They all gain their livelihood in the same manner. They all possess more or less the same skills and same kinds of property. Their homes, their ways of dressing, are always similar. Their conversations, their ideas and views of the world, tend also to be similar, to conform to the same pattern. So does their behaviour.[1]

In Majang society there are neither chieftains, nor slaves, nor artisans. The division of labor is almost exclusively sex linked: men clear fields, brew honey wine, and weave baskets; women cultivate fields, brew grain beer, and make pots. The only other axis of specialized activity is that of individual ritual experts, whose actions are oriented to relieving tensions and maintaining the status quo; they serve to propitiate dangerous spirits, cure illness, mediate disputes, and manipulate the natural elements. Toward neighboring tribes the Majangir's posture is cautious and defensive. In the past peoples like the Galla and the Sheku raided their communities for slaves, but also provided them their necessary knives, axes, and spears in exchange for quantities of the Majangir's bountiful supply of honey.

Mutualistic Specialization

A new modality of adaptation is achieved when a small society no longer relies solely on intermittent contact with outside groups to obtain goods and services which it cannot provide for itself, but moves to secure them on a regular basis by finding a place for the suppliers within its own home territory. This is the condition represented by tribes which have incorporated caste groups.

Thanks to the suggestive analyses of scholars like Herbert Lewis and C. R. Hallpike, the nearly omnipresent caste groups in Greater Ethiopia need no longer be regarded as fortuitous remnants of aboriginal populations who were simply subjugated by dominant Ethiopian stocks. Although the question of their precise origins is complex and yet to be elucidated, it is clear that in many instances the members of caste groups are highly skilled craft specialists who have migrated and settled among one or another host tribe for the sake of finding a regular source of demand for their products. It is not impossible that in some instances they include members of the host tribe who have taken up the occupational specialty in question and become assimilated to the caste group. Whatever the manner of recruitment, the caste groups in Ethiopia are in their host societies but not of them.

Why this is so should be clear from what has already been presented on the nature of holistically specialized societies. Specialized occupational activities that are basic to a group's adaptation and shared by the entire community cannot be a matter of moral indifference, as we have understood since Emile Durkheim's monograph on the division of social labor. Since I am assuming that the Ethiopian caste groups do not represent specialization on the basis of internal social differentiation, the only kind of specialization to which Durkheim deemed his concept of the division of labor applicable, I shall follow Durkheim's usage by using the term he proposed for the exchange of specialized services between different groups: mutualism.[2] Mutualistic specialization, the kind of adaptation involving the incorporation of occupational specialists as a semialien caste group within a society, can be understood as representing a compromise between a society's desire for certain products which it is structurally incapable of producing and its feeling that the very activity of making those products is in some sense morally reprehensible.

The difference between holistically specialized societies and those adapted on the basis of mutualistic specialization is small but significant. The incorporation of caste groups confers two clear adaptive advantages. First and most evidently, they ensure a regular supply of the resources at their disposal: cured leather, forged iron tools, pots, woven cloth. Yet the most conspicuous thing about the caste groups is not that they are indispensable, but that they are despised. This suggests that they provide moral as well as economic services to the society.

By constituting a moral enemy from within, caste groups provide a constant reminder of the significance of the host group's norms and a boost to its morale. If the caste group is despised for eating unclean foods, that reinforces the host culture's norms about eating and its related religious sentiments and sense of collective uprightness. Among the Konso, one of the few Ethiopian societies where caste groups have been closely examined, groups of blacksmiths, weavers, potters, and tanners known collectively as Hauda are reviled for being mercenary and hard bargainers. This stereotype has the effect of reinforcing the Konso's basic values of generosity, loyalty, and social harmony. In his analysis of the Hauda C. R. Hallpike concludes with a line that parallels the present argument. The pejorative stereotypes which a group like the Konso hold concerning their craftsmen, he writes, "serve not only to reinforce that group's sense of its own identity, but also its sense of superior rectitude."[3]

Being at the moral edge of society, moreover, especially qualifies caste group members to provide links with supernatural agencies. Among a number of Ethiopian peoples, including the Borana Galla and the Gurage, caste group members play distinctive and indispensable ritual roles such as performing ritually prescribed circumcisions and serving as functionaries in religious ceremonies.

With respect to the adaptive capacities of the constituent societies of Greater Ethiopia, then, the incorporation of caste groups has provided both greater flexibility of economic and ritual resources and a firmer sense of group identity. With respect to the intersocietal system of Greater Ethiopia, moreover, caste groups have added a new kind of connecting link. The similarities among caste groups in diverse Ethiopian societies has often been noted. This condition not only has made the constituent societies more similar, but also, together with other kinds of evidence concerning the actual migration of craft specialists from one area to another, may be taken to indicate a general pattern of caste group circulation among different Ethiopian societies.[4]

Internal Specialization: The Formation of Elites

A third kind of evolutionary modality appears when new specializations are stabilized not by the society as a whole, nor through the inclusion of outside groups, but by differentiation among the fully accredited members of a society. Without digressing into the vexed question of the steps involved in this development, one can identify a first order of internal specialization as comprising the formation of a ruling elite and its division into strata of religious and political authorities in varying degrees of separateness from one another. A hallmark of this process is the adoption of what has been termed craft literacy, the use of written language for religious, magical, and administrative purposes by a restricted group of literati.

In Ethiopia, this type of evolutionary advance was first made in ancient Aksum. The requisite cultural specialization—script, minted coinage, and the apparatus of a royal state—were developed in the course of interchanges with Sabaean and Hellenistic societies. Use of the ox-drawn plow, adopted we know not when or whence, supported the establishment of elites by contributing agricultural surpluses, as did revenues from the considerable commerce through the Red Sea ports.

Although Aksum waned with the closing off of sea trade, the symbolism of royal authority and craft literacy were retained, preserved under the Zagwe dynasty, and consolidated once and for all by the Amhara. The Amhara synthesis differed from that of Aksum in certain adaptations to the conditions of life in the Ethiopian interior. A permanent urban capital was replaced by a mobile royal headquarters, an army of tents which accompanied the kings of Amhara as they moved about their domains. Minted coinage was replaced by a simpler currency of gold, salt bars, and iron pieces. In its formation of a ruling elite, however, Amhara society represented a direct continuation and indeed a perfection of that creation of a first order of specialized strata which had begun at Aksum.

Many features of the Amhara sociocultural system described in previous chapters appear in this perspective not as accidental attributes, nor as aspects of a particular culture that happens to have chosen a certain way of life, but as mutually implicated elements of a specific evolutionary modality. The first order of internal specialization differs from all types of holistic specialization in several determinate ways.

The presence of craft literacy is one key feature of this contrast. Writing makes possible the activity of a stratum which can elaborate and transmit an esoteric tradition. The literati thereby become not only different but also more independent from other members of the society, and their cultural tradition becomes independent from any concrete social nexus. This provides the adaptive advantages of durability and exportability.

The formation of a specialized stratum of political authorities enables rulers to formulate explicit policies for their societies on a continuing basis and to mobilize resources to implement them. This condition gave the Amhara the incentive and the means to expand their territory, build up their strength, and extend their cultural domain. The existence of a specialized religious stratum, moreover, meant that political leaders were not obligated to perform all the major ritual and moral services required by the society. This freed them to perform the purely political activities more efficiently.

If specialized strata are to devote their time to religious and political activities, they must be sustained by economic activities of other members of the society and be accepted as authoritative spokesmen. This requires the elaboration of symbolism to legitimate their privileged status. For the Amhara, this symbolism was provided by the clergy and was crystallized, as was argued in chapter 7, in the form of a national epic, the *Kibre Negest.* To legitimate a ruling elite on religious grounds, moreover, requires some departure from the kind of cultural system in which man, god, and nature are intimately intertwined and which stresses simple propitiation and harmonious balance. It requires some conception of a differentiated transcendent order which can serve as an authoritative basis for legitimating superordinate social strata.

The Amhara conception provided this and more. Adopting the Semitic concept of a transcendent deity endowed with moral authority standing over the inhabitants of this world, the Amhara were oriented to try to transform the world rather than to stress simple adjustment and harmony. This orientation did not entail, as in Western Europe, a thrust toward mastery of the physical environment. It did, however, justify an extension of religious authority into new jurisdictions and efforts to reform the beliefs and morals of those made subject to the Christian monarch. The core concept of Oriental Semitic culture—"the idea of universal kingship under the aegis of the god whose people prevails over the others," as Sabatino Moscati has formulated it[5]—

formed the structurally congruent symbolic code for this expansive thrust.

A written tradition, the apparatus of royalty, and a body of symbolism legitimating a superordinate stratum are the cultural inventions which enable religious and political functions to be performed in a more continuous, concentrated, and efficient manner than is possible in a holistically specialized society. For this order of functional specialization to operate effectively, moreover, the religious and political spheres must have access to relevant human as well as physical resources. The interactional pattern of hierarchical individualism is particularly appropriate to this order of internal specialization. Domination by superordinate strata entails a pervasive hierarchical organization, and the need for specialized talent entails a degree of mobility favored by individualistic relations. In the Amhara system such mobility was achieved by making a favorable impression on dignitaries or patrons within the ecclesiastical and the political-military hierarchies. This process of selection drew specialized talent to both spheres and enabled outstanding religious and political leaders to surface.

Recruitment into these spheres on the basis of demonstrated ability, rather than by virtue of membership in ascriptive sodalities such as descent groups, generational classes, and local communities, in turn requires value-orientations that are somewhat more universalistic than those found in holistically specialized societies. For such values it is essential that the societal community be conceived in a less parochial manner. The societal community of the Amhara was accordingly defined in supratribal terms—that of all Christian Ethiopia rather than as a particular ethnic, tribal, or regional group.

The main structural features of the Amhara system—the relative autonomy of the religious and political spheres, the pattern of hierarchical individualism, and the script for a national community with a mission to expand political and religious influence—are thus coherent parts of a determinate evolutionary modality. The crystallization of this order during the millennium from Ezana to Zera Ya'iqob had widespread repercussions among the constituent societies of Greater Ethiopia. As Morton Fried has observed, when a pristine state appears in a given area of the world it tends to convert its environing societies into parts or counterparts of itself. The rise of the Amhara state stimulated the growth of many rival kingdoms in Ethiopia (as did, one may conjecture, the Aksumite state before it). The Falasha kingdom in the north, Muslim states in the southeast, and pagan kingdoms in the southwest appear to have developed more specialized political-military strata, in some cases at least, in a deliberate attempt to bolster themselves by imitating the adaptive advantages of the Amhara system. Other groups became assimilated to Amhara culture. To the extent that environing societies in Greater Ethiopia became transformed into parts or counterparts of the Amhara state, there was a net reduction of cultural heterogeneity. The stage was set for the possible extension of the Amhara type of adaptation as the dominant modality in the entire area.

An equilibrium based on limited economic interdependencies among peoples with specialized cultures adapted to different ecological niches was increasingly affected by an equilibrium based on balances of power among a number of small states. The only way Amhara society could have reached a point of decisive competitive superiority in this situation would have been to achieve a breakthrough to a new evolutionary modality, one based on a second order of internal specialization. In the terms of political sociology, it would have had to shift from the form of a patrimonial empire to the form of a bureaucratic empire.[6] The centralization of power and the mobilization of resources possible under a bureaucratized system would have enabled the Amhara rulers to continue to extend their domain and to maintain a more effective administrative apparatus in the areas ruled.

This shift did not occur. The patrimonial system represented an extremely successful adaptation to the internal conditions of Amhara society. Highly successful adaptations are not wont to change and are typically not the basis for further evolutionary advance. S. N. Eisenstadt's comparative analysis of the conditions which have given rise to historical bureaucratic empires suggests why the patrimonial system was so stabilized in Amhara society. A necessary condition for the emergence of bureaucratized empires, Eisenstadt found, was the presence of a number of differentiated social strata producing and competing for generalized resources. Historically this condition has been found only in cities. The success of the Amhara kingdom, however, was based on the peripatetic court. The Ethiopian highlands were such that the kings had to move around the country continually in order to make the royal authority felt throughout the realm. The later establishment of a permanent capital in the city of Gonder in the seventeenth century is generally believed to have been a principal cause of the downfall of the Gonderine throne. The initial success of the Amhara empire thus seems to have been tied to conditions which precluded its becoming more successful in later centuries. The achievement of a second order of internal specialization would have to await the regime of Haile Sellassie I in the twentieth century.

Amhara political power peaked in the fifteenth century. Since conditions did not permit the development of a bureaucratic empire, the Amhara system could only oscillate between periods of centralized patrimonial control and periods of increased feudalization. Outlying areas could establish firmly fortified enclaves highly resistant to further Amhara expansion, as did the Kefa and the Konso peoples, or even launch serious attacks on the Amhara kingdom which, in the case of Adal, could be terribly costly if not totally devastating.

Despecialization and New Evolutionary Potential

If the above analysis is valid, then the significance of the Galla invasions will have to be reconsidered. They no longer can be viewed merely as a destructive onslaught of barbarian hordes. Even if the Galla invasions promoted the feudalization of the Amhara empire, that process had already begun and would probably have continued in any case, given the limited resources available to ensure centralized control in the patrimonial system. With respect to the evolution of Ethiopian society, however, the Galla invasions had the following positive consequences:

1. The establishment of a massive Galla presence in the Ethiopian heartland provided a permanent buffer between the Amhara state in the interior and both the pagan kingdoms of the southwest and the Turkish-dominated coast on the east. This buffer may have helped the Amhara state to preserve its evolutionary gains by saving it from offensive or defensive reactions that would have overextended its resources and capacities.

2. As was mentioned earlier, the Galla presence provided an interaction chain between the Amhara and numerous other Ethiopian peoples. This created communication links and new kinds of interdependencies that would promote the transformation of Ethiopia from an intersocietal to a single societal system.

3. The Galla contributed new resources for a political and military center in Ethiopian society. They stimulated the Amhara to move beyond the limited ethnic hegemony of the early Solomonid period toward a truly multi-ethnic national elite.

In various ways, then, the Galla contributed to the evolutionary advance of Ethiopian society as a whole even though their own evolutionary modality was less advanced than that of the Amhara. Indeed, one can argue that the Galla could play the particular role they did precisely because they themselves were not yet so internally differentiated. Had they evolved to the point of having autonomous cultural and political spheres they might well have become an evenly matched competitor to the Amhara, forming a traditional state with equivalent staying power, and an unresolved struggle might have persisted right up to the twentieth century. It was probably fortunate for the long-term viability of Ethiopian society that Oromo expansion took a quite different form.

The form taken by the Oromo expansion is a variant of adaptive radiation. A population with a common type of adaptation expanded into a variety of new habitats and in each place assumed a type of adaptation more appropriate to the ecological situation at hand. Instead of evolving the new modes of adaptation from scratch, however, they selectively adopted the cultures of peoples they found already settled in those diverse regions. In some cases the adaptation was to an evolutionary modality very like their traditional culture, in others to internally specialized societies with more universalistic religions. What is striking is the diversity of their adaptations.

This phenomenon is illuminated by another idea from modern evolutionary theory, one that Elman Service calls the Law of Evolutionary Potential. The law states that the more specialized and adapted a form in a given evolutionary stage, the smaller is its potential for passing to the next stage—or, I would add, for shifting to another kind of adaptation in the same stage. I have alluded to this principle by observing that the Amhara found it hard to shift to a second order of internal differentiation because they were so thoroughly and successfully adapted in the first order.

At first glance the Galla experience seems to contradict this principle, for the adaptational pyrotechnics involved were launched from a traditional base, centering on the organizational complex of the *gada* system, in itself a highly specialized mode of adaptation. The Oromo talent for assuming new kinds and levels of adaptation can be illumined by this principle, however, if two additional considerations are kept in mind.

One is the process of senectation in the *gada* system, a process which produced large numbers of Galla men who were ineligible to participate in the *gada* cycle because they were born at a time when their class would already have completed the cycle. They thus constituted a kind of social proletariat, a population not fully integrated into the major institutionalized complex of Oromo society and available for integration into new kinds of systems when the opportunity appeared.

The other point is that Oromo culture lent itself particularly well to a process of simplification: although Galla beliefs and rituals were closely tied to traditional Oromo forms of social organization, the Oromo orientational system as a whole *was not intimately linked to a particular ecological basis.* In this respect Oromo culture contrasts markedly with the cultures of most other peoples in Greater Ethiopia. Among the Gurage, for example, cultivation of the ensete plant is a core activity tied to all aspects of Gurage life. It is important in the Gurage economy both as a staple food crop and as a source of materials for clothing and housing. It has social implications as a center around which are organized a number of communal activities, including annual planting and harvesting ceremonies. It provides the basis for the accumulation of wealth, the primary criterion for political leadership. Ensete also permeates the ritual systems of Gurage culture: it is served in connection with all ceremonies which honor Gurage deities, and specific parts of the ensete plant are employed in rituals connected with birth, puberty rites, marriage, and death.[7]

Comparable kinds of specialization around particular ecological themes are apparent elsewhere in Ethiopia. The economy, social organization, and ritual system of the Majangir are intimately tied to their slash-and-burn style of rain-forest agriculture and related "swidden" cycles of shifting cultivation. Those of the Afar are just as closely tied to the nomadic herding of goats and camels in a parched region of desert, lava streams, volcanoes, and salt depressions. That is why, Trimingham notes, the Afar "is such a fine 'specimen' if viewed in his life in his own deserts and a demoralized and useless individual if seen outside them."[8] The Konso have made a similarly specialized adaptation to their stony highlands in the far south. They long ago perfected the art of using stone to make terraces for farms cultivated by communal work parties and to build walls that protect their fields against floodwater and cattle. Stone walls are also erected around their distinctively organized towns. Stone is used for grinding corn, for sharpening knives, to make anvils, for throwing at enemies and birds, for building houses, and for constructing dams. Basalt columns are erected as phallic emblems of great cultural importance. "Stone is as much a part of Konso life as soil," writes Hallpike. "Their use of stone gives a clarity and defintion to their towns and homesteads which is extremely striking to the observer; it conveys a sense of harmony, order, and industry, and is in these respects a true expression of their values."[9]

Oromo culture, by contrast, was not so firmly tied to a particular ecological setting. Before their invasions the Oromo appear to have employed a very simple agricultural technology unencumbered by social and ritual complexities. At the time of their invasions they were primarily, if not exclusively, pastoralists. It is likely that cattle were then, as they are now for the Guji, Arsi, and Borana, a major focus for thought and sentiment.[10] But this did not represent the overwhelming preoccupation with cattle in social and religious activities and the related commitment to a pastoral life-style which are exhibited by such Nilotic peoples as the Nuer. Large numbers of the Oromo were able to relinquish some of the specialized orientations associated with their cattle complex and move to other habitats with differing physical resources and technological imperatives without experiencing the thoroughgoing disruption of customary life that such moves probably would have entailed for peoples such as the Gurage, Majangir, Afar, or Konso.

The Galla migrants, in other words, were readily able to give up what was only a moderately specialized adaption to their homeland, remain vigorously themselves, and proceed to take on a variety of new specialized adaptations. Consequently they became the only ethnic group to have substantial numbers pursuing each of the four main types of livelihood practiced in Greater Ethiopia—pastoral nomadism, hoe cultivation of tubers, plow cultivation of grains, and trade. They became the only ethnic group to have simultaneously adopted radically contrasting political forms; alongside their classical democratic ruling assemblies some Galla groups formed independent despotic kingdoms, whereas others became fully integrated into the imperial system of ranks and offices under the Amhara monarchs. They became the only ethnic group to become fully integrated into both the Ethiopian Orthodox Christian community and the Ethiopian Muslim community, while a substantial number of members continued to adhere to the traditional Galla pagan religion.[11] In sum, if the Amhara reached the most advanced level of general social evolution in premodern Ethiopia, the Galla manifested the highest degree of potential for further evolutionary adaptations.

Internal Specialization: The Creation of Free-floating Resources

For the sake of completeness a fifth evolutionary modality should be mentioned here, even though its historical period lies outside the time span of this volume. This is the transition from patrimonial to bureaucratic empire, a process that has been analyzed with brilliance in the work of Max Weber and S. N. Eisenstadt. One central feature of this process is the creation of resources—manpower, wealth, political support, and cultural orientations—that are not embedded within or committed beforehand to any primary ascriptive group, such as descent groups, generational classes, or local communities, or to particularistic relationships, such as patron-client nexuses. In the patrimonial form of empire, resources are to some extent disengaged from primary ascriptive groups but remain the personal prerogative of various authoritative figures. Administrative officers cannot pursue their tasks efficiently because they are regarded as the private servants of the king or provincial rulers, and the king cannot pursue broader political objectives at will because the resources he needs are subject to the control of other traditional rulers with their own special interests and motivations.

As Eisenstadt has argued, the transition to an order of internal specialization which contains generalized resources available to the wider community requires both an ambitious monarch who is determined to strengthen the societal center and a plurality of social strata with interests other than those of traditional primary ascriptive groups. We cannot deny that Amhara society would have benefited from such a breakthrough once the primary expansion of the fourteenth and fifteenth centuries had been accomplished, but no ruler with the ambition of creating a centralized bureaucratic empire appeared at the time. The first Amhara ruler with such ambitions was Tewodros II in the 1850s, and the tragedy of his reign was that he was ready for such a transformation when his society was not. His successors, Yohannes IV and Menilek II, chose to perfect the traditional patrimonial system rather than to embark on vain efforts at structural change.

Only during the reign of Haile Sellassie I, and primarily after the Liberation in 1941, did this effort prove both desirable and possible. Haile Sellassie successfully steered the precarious course of all rulers who have forged or maintained bureaucratic empires by creating a variety of free-floating resources relatively unconstricted by traditional restraints and yet maintaining a firm control over these new resources and over the persons and groups who produce them.

By promoting entrepreneurial activity on a limited scale Haile Sellassie encouraged this formation of free-floating economic resources, while subjecting the enterprises in question to heavy regulation and controls. By creating a large national army and police force, he mobilized military resources that are independent of regional lords and placed them under his direct command. He encouraged the formation of social strata independent of the feudal nobility by appropriating the right to confer all titles and honors, insulating power holders in various spheres from one another and freeing subordinate rural strata from excessive dependence on and control by traditional elites. He reduced the legal autonomy of traditional groups by promulgating a national constitution and new civil and criminal codes, at the same time controlling the new legal institutions by maintaining special legal offices in the central administration, limiting the scope of action of members of the legal profession, and subjecting them to close royal supervision. He founded new academies, schools, and religious institutions, but maintained close control over their activities and cultural expressions. Finally, he generated a great amount of new political resources by establishing an extensive centralized bureaucracy and a bicameral parliament, using the media to promote new kinds of political consciousness identified with the throne and its policies, providing new opportunities for advancement through the framework of the centralized political institutions, and stimulating new kinds of political expression through the exercise of quadrennial elections for parliamentary deputies—in all instances maintaining a fairly close control over the new political loyalties and ambitions thus generated.[12]

These changes have significantly enhanced Ethiopia's adaptive capacities in several respects. They have reduced intertribal warfare and wanton banditry[13] and strengthened Ethiopia against attack from outside. They have enabled Ethiopia to compete for economic and cultural resources in the world community. They have made it possible to deliver some health care and emergency relief to previously isolated parts of the empire. They have produced new knowledge about Ethiopia's physical resources and development potential. And all these changes were accomplished without major destructive conflict between the traditional groups and the newer strata who have been the producers of these free-floating resources.

THE PRESENT EVOLUTIONARY SITUATION

The ink was barely dry on the script for Ethiopia's transformation from a patrimonial to a bureaucratic empire when some Ethiopians began to agitate for yet another transformation, to the type of evolutionary modality Talcott Parsons has referred to as the "system of modern societies." The key features of the modern system have been said to include (1) the exercise of considerable autonomy by the producers of free-floating resources, (2) considerable differentiation of the forms of political activity, (3) the distribution of civil, political, social, and educational rights among the ruled, and (4) the institutionalization of formal channels of competition for authoritative political positions. Although the movement toward a modern system in Ethiopia still remained in an incipient stage in 1973, it had grown with unprecedented speed during the prior decade owing to the exposure of thousands of Ethiopians to modern forms of education and to gains in rapid communication within the international community.

At this time the peoples of Greater Ethiopia remain anchored in the five types of evolutionary modality previously described. Those who have been integrated into the bureaucratic empire are only a very small percentage of the total population. Since the apparatus of a centralized bureaucracy has existed for so short a time in Ethiopia, most elements of Amhara-Tigrean society remain embedded in the attitudes and relationships characteristic of the archaic, patrimonial form of that society.

A relatively high degree of evolutionary potential continues to be manifested by the Galla. Although most Galla have long since been stabilized in specific local modes of adaptation, others have entered spheres where free-floating resources are produced: large numbers of Galla have entered the national security forces, the small industrial labor force, and the fields of trade, transportation, and education. They have been joined by marginal or ambitious members of other traditional societies who have left their homes for the attractions of towns and modern schooling. It is possible that in this transition the Galla have an easier time than traditional Amhara, who are weighted down by the cultural baggage of a society deeply wedded to the patrimonial life-style.

There remain, moreover, substantial numbers of Ethiopians who are likely to resist further encroachments of the dominant Amhara-

Tigrean cultural complex in either its archaic, its bureaucratic, or its modernizing forms. Peoples such as the Majangir, the Konso, the rural Gurage, and the Afar have perfected specialized modes of adaptation to their local habitats and, apart from the need to produce public revenues in areas where taxes can be collected reliably, have no compelling impetus to change.

The survival of such enclaves of more or less holistically specialized traditional cultures has seemed threatening to those spokesmen for evolutionary advance who act as ideologists of modernity. These ideologists frequently assert that such traditional cultures must be forcibly upset so that their peoples too can be swept into the vortex of general evolution.

Such a prospect is neither plausible nor desirable. It is not plausible because the conditions which have enabled these peoples to survive so successfully in their local habitats for so long will continue to be operative for some time to come, protecting them against outside stimuli and motivating them to defend their traditional ways with passion. It is not desirable for several reasons. One is that the traditional cultures of these peoples provide extremely effective ways of exploiting their environmental resources, ways that have been tried, tested, and sustained for a long period and in most cases have proved highly satisfactory. Another is that it can hardly be regarded as humane to wreak violence on a people in the name of some alien concept of salvation: wanton, deliberate cultural genocide is no less a crime than extinction of a species.

One can conceive, moreover, of a wholly new order of adaptation within Greater Ethiopia based on the stabilization of relationships among peoples exhibiting radically different kinds of evolutionary modalities, an order based on what I should like to call the Principle of Evolutionary Complementarity. The principle is that societies at very different stages of general evolutionary advance, like individuals at different stages of internal differentiation and personal growth, can and frequently do perform important complementary services for one another. This point has generally been overlooked because those who are sensitized to such relationships tend to think of them only in terms of the language of exploitation. Yet although such relationships may be exploitative—at either end or both ends of the relationship—they are not inherently so.

I know of no existing efforts to conceptualize the properties of a national society based on a set of complementary relationships among constituent peoples living in quite disparate evolutionary modalities. Such an outcome is more conceivable today than it would have been a decade or two ago because of a growing consciousness of two phenomena. One is the increased appreciation of the part that ascriptive sodalities can play even in the most modern kinds of social systems.[14] The other is the increased appreciation of the qualities of expressiveness, security, communality, and egalitarianism found in societies with less internal specialization, an appreciation recently evinced by those members of the avant-garde in American culture who have worked to recover and revitalize some of the customs, symbols, and experiences of the American Indians and nonliterate black Africans.[15]

Social evolution in Greater Ethiopia, then, may be moving in a previously unheralded direction—not toward a nationwide community of individual specialists producing free-floating resources and participating equally in a single set of national political and educational institutions, but toward a radically pluralistic community. An internally specialized central sector may provide security and relief from natural disasters for the entire population while a number of groups with little internal differentiation provide specialized agricultural products and crafts as well as living examples of kinds of human experience and values which may give deep satisfaction to modernized Ethiopians.

The Evolution of Ethiopian Society

I hope this chapter has demonstrated the utility of supplementing the prevailing scholarly images of Ethiopia with one derived from the perspective of modern evolutionary theory. I will now review the major strands of the argument of this book in order to articulate some of the implications of that scholarly image.

One part of the argument goes backward through a succession of types of scientific explanation. In answering the question of how Ethiopia survived as an independent state until the 1930s, we found that a series of determinate formative historical episodes led up to that achievement (genetic explanation). Those historical episodes represented characteristic group action capabilities of the major collective actors, the Amhara, Tigrean, and Oromo peoples (reductive explanation). Those respective action capabilities are in turn explained by reference to selected structural features of the traditional sociocultural systems of the Amhara, Tigreans, and Oromo (structural explanation). The present chapter suggests how those structural features can be related to characteristic modalities of adaptation in the process of general evolution (telic explanation).

The other part of the argument goes forward in an effort to reconstruct the main lines of the evolution of Ethiopian society. It begins with the assumption that a small number of ethnic stocks settled in the Ethiopian plateau in prehistoric times. Through a series of adaptive radiations, these peoples spread out into the diverse ecological zones of Greater Ethiopia and produced a variety of holistically specialized cultures. Many of these were so successful in exploiting the resources of their respective habitats that they have been able to maintain a specific dominance in their locales and to resist the incursion of more widely dominant types.

The differentiated peoples of Greater Ethiopia in time established various lines of communication and interdependence through trade, migration, and other processes. Through continued interaction and the coalescence of culture traits, Greater Ethiopia became to some extent a cultural as well as an ecological community. The incorporation of occupational specialists in the form of caste groups provided an additional basis for interchange as well as enhancing the adaptive capacities of the constituent societies.

Aksum and its successor states provided a basis for the development of a political community. There emerged from the Aksumite seedbed and the Amhara consolidation a society at a higher level of general evolutionary adaptation whose formation of specialized strata enabled it to spread at the expense of other types. Its expansion continues today as increasing numbers of Ethiopians from other traditions attach themselves to the national center or assimilate the Amharic language and other aspects of Amhara culture.

However, stabilization of Amhara society at the level of a first order of internal specialization, in the form of a patrimonial empire, seriously limited the extent to which Amhara kings could keep up the process of expansion or even administer the regions nominally under their control. Other societies in the area increased their strength, checking and at times damaging the Amhara position, while the Amhara system failed to evolve further from the fifteenth through the nineteenth century.

From the sixteenth century onward, there appeared a new pattern which greatly affected the whole evolutionary situation of Greater Ethiopia. The Oromo had neither a highly specialized local adaptation nor a functionally specialized internal structure, but exhibited considerable capacity for cultural despecialization and adaptation—a particularly high degree of evolutionary potential. The values and organization of their traditional order facilitated both their movement into new areas through military incursions and their ability to merge with other ethnic groups in new regions of settlement. The Oromo expansion eventually had the effect of reinvigorating the widely spread Amhara pattern, challenging it both from within as Galla became absorbed into the national elite and from without as a constant spur for the Amhara to reassert and extend themselves.

The Amhara military success in the nineteenth century was mainly due to their control of the traffic in firearms. They proved politically successful largely because their societal community was defined as a nation rather than as a tribal or subtribal entity. If the Amhara elite was fairly exclusive during the centuries of initial expansion, it clearly broadened its ethnic base in the succeeding periods: both Galla and Tigreans came to play important roles in court politics and royal military campaigns after the seventeenth century. On this broadened base, emperors Yohannes IV and Menilek II revitalized and expanded the empire by perfecting the patrimonial system. Under Haile Sellassie I, a new evolutionary level was attained with the formation of a bureaucratic empire involving a second order of internal specialization.

Appendix

Roster of the Peoples of Ethiopia

Ethnic Group	Location	Language	Language Family	Religion	Economy
I. *North Eritrean*					
Beni Amer	Eritrea	Bedawie (also, Tigre)	N.C.	M	Pastoral
Bet Mala	"	Bedawie (also, Tigre)	"	"	"
Ad Sawra	"	Tigre	N. E-S.	"	"
Ad Sheikh	"	"	"	"	"
Ad Mu'allim	"	"	"	"	"
Aflenda	"	"	"	"	"
Bet Asgede:					
Ad Tekles	"	"	"	X → M	Plow
Ad Timaryam	"	"	"	"	Pastoral
Habab	"	"	"	"	"
Bet Juk	"	"	"	"	Plow
Marya	"	"	"	"	Pastoral
Mensa	"	"	"	"	Plow
Meshalit	"	"	"	"	Mixed
Sabdarat	"	"	"	M	Mixed

Abbreviations for language families:

C.C.	Central Cushitic
E.C.	East Cushitic
E.S.	East Sudanic
K.	Koman
N.C.	North Cushitic
N.E-S.	North Ethio-Semitic
N.O.	North Omotic
S.E-S.	South Ethio-Semitic
S.O.	South Omotic

Abbreviations for religions:

J	Jewish
M	Muslim
P	Pagan
X	Orthodox Christian
Prot.	Protestant
Cath.	Catholic
→	replaced by

II. *Agew*					
Awi (=Southern Agew)	Gojjam	Awngi	C.C.	P	Plow
Beta Israel (=Falasha)	Begemdir	Kwarinya (also, Amharic and Tigrinya)	"	J	Crafts
Bilin (=Bogos)	Eritrea	Bilin	"	X → M	Plow
Central Agew	Wello, Begemdir	Khamir, Khamtanga	"	X	"
Kimant (=Qemant)	Begemdir	Kimant	"	P	"
Kunfel	Begemdir	Awngi	"	X	Plow/hunting
III. *Ambara-Tigrean*					
Amhara	Wello, Begemdir, Gojjam, Shoa, Harerge	Amharic	S. E-S.	X	Plow
Jabarti	Wello, Begemdir, Tigray, Eritrea, Shoa	Amharic, Tigrinya		M	Trade, crafts
Tigrawi (=Tigreans, Tigrinya)	Tigray, Eritrea	Tigrinya	N. E-S.	X	Plow
IV. *Core Islamic*					
Afar (=Danakil)	Harerge, Wello, Tigray, Eritrea	Afar	E.C.	M	Pastoral, mining
Argobba	Harerge, Shoa	Argobba	S. E-S.	"	Plow
Harari (=Adere)	Harerge	Harari	S. E-S.	"	Trade, plow
Saho	Tigray, Eritrea	Saho	E.C.	"	Pastoral
Somali	Harerge, Bale, Sidamo	Somali	E.C.	"	Pastoral

Appendix (Cont.)
Roster of the Peoples of Ethiopia

Ethnic Group	Location	Language	Language Family	Religion	Economy
V. *Galla* (=*Oromo*)					
Arsi	Arusi, Bale	Arsi Gallinya	E.C.	M/P/X	Pastoral
Borana	Sidamo	Borana Gallinya	"	P	Pastoral
Eastern Galla:					
Annya	Harerge	Eastern Gallinya	"	M	Plow
Ittu	"	"	"	P	Plow
Qottu (Ala, Babille, Jarso, Nole, and Oborra)	"	" (also, Somali)	"	M	Mixed
Gibe cluster:					
Gera	Kefa	Mecha Gallinya	"	M	Plow
Gomma	"	"	"	"	"
Guma	Illubabor	"	"	"	"
Jimma	Kefa	"	"	"	"
Limmu Inarya	"	"	"	"	"
Guji	Sidamo	Guji Gallinya	"	P	Mixed
Kereyu	Shoa, Arusi	Afar, Gallinya	"	M/P	Pastoral
Leqa	Wellega	Mecha Gallinya	"	X/Prot.	Plow
Mecha	Shoa, Wellega	Mecha Gallinya	"	X	Plow
Raya (=Azebo)	Tigray	Raya Gallinya	"	M	Pastoral
Soddu	Shoa	Tulema Gallinya (also, Amharic, N. Gurage)	"	X	Hoe: ensete
Tulema	Shoa	Tulema Gallinya, Amharic	"	X	Plow

Wello	Wello	Wello Gallinya, Amharic	”	M	Plow
Yejju	Wello	Wello Gallinya, Amharic	”	M	Mixed
VI. *Lacustrine*					
A. *Gurage Group*					
Aklil	Shoa	West Gurage	S. E-S.	P/X	Hoe: ensete, grains
Aymellel	”	Soddo	”	X	”
Chaha	”	West Gurage	”	P/Cath.	”
Gafat	Gojjam	Gafat, Amharic	”	X	Plow
Geto	Shoa	West Gurage	”	P	Hoe: ensete, grains
Gogot	”	”	”	M	”
Indegen	”	”	”	P	”
Innemor	”	”	”	”	”
Inneqor	”	East Gurage	”	M	”
Izha	”	West Gurage	”	P/X	”
Mesqan	”	West Gurage	”	X	”
Muher	”	Muher	”	X	”
Silti	”	East Gurage	”	M	”
Urbareg	”	”	”	M	”
Weleni	”	”	”	M	”
Zway	Arusi	”	”	X	Fishing
B. *Sidamo Group*					
Alaba	Sidamo	Alaba	E.C.	M	Hoe: ensete, grains
Burji (=Bembela)	”	Burji	”	P	”
Derasa	”	Derasa	”	P	”
Hadiyya	Shoa	Hadiyya	”	M	”
Kembata	”	Kembata	”	X	”
Qabenna	”	Qabenna	”	M	”
Sidamo	Sidamo	Sidamo	”	P	”
Timbaro	Shoa	Timbaro	”	M	”

Appendix (Cont.)
Roster of the Peoples of Ethiopia

Ethnic Group	Location	Language	Language Family	Religion	Economy
C. *Konso Group*					
Arbore	Gemu-Gofa	Arbore	E.C.	P	Pastoral
Bussa	"	Bussa	"	"	Hoe: ensete, grains
Dasenech (=Geleba)	"	Dasenech	"	"	Mixed
Gawwada	"	Gawwada	"	"	Hoe: ensete, grains
Gidole (=Gardulla)	"	Gidole	"	"	"
Gobeze	"	Gobeze	"	"	"
Konso	"	Konso	"	"	"
Tsamako	"	Tsamai	"	"	Hoe: grains
Werize	"	Werize	"	"	Hoe: ensete, grains
VII. *Omotic*					
A. *Kefa-Janjero Group*					
Anfillo	Wellega	S. Mao	N.O.	P	Hoe: grains, ensete
Bosha (=Garo)	Kefa	Garo	"	M	"
Gonga	Gojjam	Shinasha	"	P	"
Janjero	Kefa	Janjero	"	P	"
Kefa	Kefa	Kefa	"	X	"
Mocha	Illubabor	Mocha	"	P	"
B. *Gimira-Maji Group*					
Bencho	Kefa	Gimira	"	P	"
Dorsha	"	Maji	"	"	"
Maji	"	Maji	"	"	"
Mere	"	Gimira	"	"	"
Nao	"	Nao	"	"	"
Sheko	"	Sheko	"	"	"
She	"	Gimira	"	"	"

C. *Ometo Group*[1]

Amarro (=Badittu)	Gemu-Gofa	Koyra	N.O.	P	Hoe: grains, ensete
Basketo	”	Basketo	”	”	”
Borodda	”	Welamo	”	”	”
Chara	Kefa	Chara	”	”	”
Dita	Gemu-Gofa	Welamo	”	”	”
Doko	”	Doko	”	”	”
Dollo	”	Dollo	”	”	”
Dorze	”	Dorze	”	”	”/weaving
Gamu	”	Welamo	”	”	Hoe: grains, ensete
Gatami	Sidamo	Kachama	”	”	Hippo-hunting/fishing
Gidicho	”	Gidicho	”	”	Plow
Gofa	Gemu-Gofa	Welamo	”	”	Hoe: grains, ensete
Konta	Kefa	Kullo	”	”	”
Koysha	”	Kullo	”	”	”
Kucha	Gemu-Gofa	Kullo	”	”	”
Kullo (=Dewaro)	Kefa	Kullo	”	”	”
Male	Gemu-Gofa	Male	”	”	Plow
Ochollo	”	Welamo	”	”	Hoe: grains, ensete
Oyda	”	Oyda	”	”	”
Welamo	”	Welamo	”	”	”
Zala	”	Welamo	”	”	”
Zayse	”	Zayse	”	”	”

[1] The Ometo group comprises the most complicated and least known group of tribes in Ethiopia. In addition to the peoples listed here, there are some three dozen small societies, known as *dere,* in the highlands of eastern Gemu-Gofa. Judith Olmstead has kindly provided a provisional list of these additional *dere:* Anduro, Balta, Bonke, Chaisa, Chencha, Dara, Dogile, Doqame, Ele, Ezo, Gatse, Gambile, Gamo Anko, Ganta, Gerets, Gumaye, Goza, Haniqa, Hurumo, Manana, Marzo, Malo, Otolo, Shama, Shara, Sharaqe, Shela, Schochare, Ufa, Umo, Wobara, Woiza, Wusamo, Zada, and Zegets.

Appendix (Cont.)
Roster of the Peoples of Ethiopia

Ethnic Group	Location	Language	Language Family	Religion	Economy
D. *Ari-Banna Group*					
Baka	Gemu-Gofa	Ari	S.O.	P	Hoe: grains, ensete
Bio	”	”	”	”	”
Dime	”	Dime	”	”	”
Shangama	”	Ari	”	”	”
Sido	”	”	”	”	”
Ubamer	”	”	”	”	”
Banna	”	Banna	”	”	Hoe: grains
Beshada	”	”	”	”	”
Hamer (=Amar Kokke)	”	”	”	”	”
Karo	”	Karo	”	”	”
VIII. *Sudanic*					
Berta	Wellega	Fadisho, Gamila, Indu, Wetawit	Berta	M	Hoe: grains
Anyuak	Illubabor	Anyuak	E.S.	P	Fishing/hoe: grains
Bume (=Inyanyatom)	Kefa	Turkana	”	P	Hoe: grains
Gumuz	Begemdir, Gojjam	Gumuz	K.	P	”
Koma	Wellega	Koma	K.	”	”
Kunama	Eritrea	Kunama	Kunama	M/P/Cath. Prot.	Hoe: grains
Majangir	Illubabor, Kefa	Mesengo	E.S.	P	Slash-and-burn; hunting
Mao	Wellega	N. Mao	K.	”	Hoe: grains
Meban	Illubabor	Mabaan	E.S.	”	”

Mekan:					
Golda (=Tishena)	Kefa	Me'en	E.S.	P	Hoe: grains
Bodi	Gemu-Gofa	Me'en	"	"	Pastoral
Nara (=Barya)	Eritrea	Nara	"	M	Hoe: grains
Nuer	Illubabor	Nuer	"	P	Pastoral
Suri	Kefa	Suri	"	"	Hoe: grains/hunting
Surma:					
Kai (=Tid)	Kefa	Surma	"	"	Pastoral/hoe: grains
Mursi	Gemu-Gofa	"	"	"	"
Tirma	Kefa	"	"	"	"
Zilmamu	"	Zilmamu	"	"	Hoe: grains

IX. *Caste Groups* (listed by ethnic category of host group)

Ethnic Host	Caste Group	Occupational Specialty
Agew of Lasta	Tebib	Smiths
(II) Felasha	Faqi	Tanners
Kimant	Arabinya	Tanners
(III) Amhara	Faqi	Tanners
	Gafat	Smiths, potters
	Teyb	Smiths, potters
	Weyto	Hippo hunters
Tigrean	Tebib	Smiths
(IV) Argobba	Faqin	Tanners
	Qetqech	Smiths
Somali	Midgan	Hunters, tanners
	Tumal	Smiths
	Yibir	Hunters, tanners
(V) Borana	Watta	Hunters
Eastern	Tumtu	Smiths (m.), potters (f.)
Galla	Watta	Hunters; also, tanners, potters

Appendix (Cont.)
Roster of the Peoples of Ethiopia

Ethnic Host	Caste Group	Occupational Specialty
Jimma Galla	Faqi	Tanners
	Fuga	Potters
	Gagurtu	Beekeepers
	Semmano	Weavers
	Tumtu	Smiths
	Watta	Hunters, foragers
Leqa	Faqi	Tanners
	Tumtu	Smiths, potters, weavers
Mecha	Watta	Hunters
(VI) Gurage	Fuga	Woodworkers, hunters
	Gezha	Tanners
	Nefwra	Smiths
Sidamo	Adicho	Potters
	Awacho	Tanners
	Tunicho	Smiths
Burji	Faqi	Tanners
	Tumtu	Smiths
Konso	Hauda	Smiths, weavers, potters, tanners
Tsamako	Oritto	Smiths
(VII) Janjero	Fuga	Hunters, potters, tanners
	Yirfo	Smiths
Kefa	Manjo	Hunters, royal guards
	Manno	Potters, tanners
	Qemmo	Smiths
Bencho, She	Kwayeju	Hunters
Maji	Geimi	Smiths

		Kwegu	Hunters
	Sheko	Bando	Hunters
	Amarro	Mana	Tanners, weavers, potters
		Wagache	Smiths
	Chara	Dima	Smiths
		Mana	Tanners
	Dorze	Degala	Tanners
		Mana	Potters
	Gofa	Mana	Tanners
	Konta	Mana	Potters
	Male	Gito	Hunters, smiths
	Welamo	Degala	Tanners
		Mana	Potters
		Wogache	Smiths
	Zala	Mana	Potters
		Qachoa	Tanners
		Wogache	Smiths
	Ari	Gittamana	Smiths
	Shangama	Mana	Smiths
	Dime	Bacha	Hunters
		Gitsu	Smiths
		Kaisa	Ritual functionaries
		Manna	Tanners
	Baka	Manni	Potters
(VIII)	Bodi	Kwegu	Hunters

Notes

Chapter 1

1. Trans. Robert Fitzgerald (New York: Anchor Books, 1963), p. 2.

2. *The Histories,* trans. Aubrey de Selincourt (Baltimore: Penguin Books, 1965), p. 184.

3. Trans. David Grene, in *The Complete Greek Tragedies* (Chicago: University of Chicago Press, 1959), 1: 340.

4. Trans. Francis G. Allinson, in the Loeb *Menander: The Principal Fragments,* p. 481.

5. *Corpus Christianorium Series Latina* 39, p. 980.

6. Cited in Harold G. Marcus, *The Modern History of Ethiopia and the Horn of Africa: A Select and Annotated Bibliography* (Stanford: Hoover Institution Press, 1972), entry no. 23.

7. *Abyssinia and Its People* (London, 1868), p. 13. The term Abyssinian has hitherto been derived by scholars from the name of a South Arabian tribe which emigrated to the Ethiopian highlands, but more recent scholarship has questioned this origin. In any case, South Arabian inscriptions do use the word Habeshat to refer to Aksumite Ethiopia, and later Arab writers consistently use *habasha* for Ethiopian. European equivalents of the term come to be used with increasing frequency from the thirteenth century on.

8. *Historical Library,* bk. 3, chap. 1.

9. Cited in Frank M. Snowden, Jr., *Blacks in Antiquity* (Cambridge, Mass.: Harvard University Press, 1970), p. 148.

10. Herodotus, *Histories,* p. 182. Herodotus also describes the Ethiopians collectively as the "tallest, handsomest, and most just of men."

11. Jeremiah 38: 7–13.

12. *Rasselas, Prince of Abissinia,* chap. 8.

13. Cited in J. Spencer Trimingham, *Islam in Ethiopia* (London: Frank Cass, 1965), p. 44.

14. Cited in Snowden, *Blacks in Antiquity,* p. 211.

15. Enrico Cerulli, *Etiopi in Palestina* (Rome, 1943) 1: 81 f., 116.

16. *Royal and Historical Letters during the Reign of Henry the Fourth, King of England and France, and Lord of Ireland,* vol. I, *1399–1404,* ed. F. C. Hingeston (London, 1860), p. 421.

17. *Orlando Furioso,* canto 33.

18. Harold Marcus, "The Black Men Who Turned White: European Attitudes towards Ethiopians, 1850–1900," *Archiv Orientalni* 39 (1971): 155–66.

19. *Historical Library,* bk. 3, chap. 8.

20. *Geography,* chap. 17.

21. Psalms 72:9. Septuagint and Vulgate versions of this passage use the term *Aethiopes.* The Hebrew original, however, does not use Kush, the word normally translated in Greek as Ethiopia, but rather *tsiyim. Tsiyim* actually means navies; it might conceivably mean wildernesses. This latter meaning underlies the King James and other English translations of verse 9, which read, "They that dwell in the wilderness shall bow before him." The Greek and Latin translators apparently equated living in the wildneress with being Ethiopian.

22. *"Extremos et teterrimos hominum." Corpus Christianorium Series Latina* 39, p. 980.

23. *Some Records of Ethiopia, 1593–1646,* ed. C. F. Beckingham and G. W. B. Huntingford (London: Hakluyt, 1954), chap. 13. More impatient with the Ethiopians' deviations from Roman Catholic practices, Almeida's less generous contemporary Alphonzo Mendez regarded them as a group of benighted infidels.

24. Those who purveyed this pejorative image were chiefly from England, Germany, and Italy. It is striking that the principal French commentators on Ethiopia in the nineteenth century—Edmund Combes and Maurice Tamisier, Charles Rochet d'Héricourt, Antoine and Arnauld d'Abbadie, Paul Soleillet, Martial de Salviac, Prince Henri d'Orleans, Hughes le Roux—were generally appreciative and tended if anything to idealize Ethiopians.

25. W. Cornwallis Harris, *The Highlands of Aethiopia,* 2d ed. (London, 1844), 2: 165, 361, 138, and 162.

26. *A Visit to Abyssinia* (London, 1881), p. vii.

27. Cited in Harold Marcus, *The Life and Times of Menilek II* (Oxford: Clarendon Press, 1974), chap. 6.

28. *Sport and Travel: Abyssinia and East Africa* (London, 1906), pp. 67–73.

29. *Historical Library,* bk. 3, chap. 1.

30. *Some Records of Ethiopia,* p. 8, n. 1.

31. See B. G. M. Sundkler, *Bantu Prophets in South Africa* (London: International African Institute, 1961), chap. 2.

32. Quoted in K. A. B. Jones-Quartey, *A Life of Azikiwe* (Baltimore: Penguin Books, 1965), p. 123.

33. "Hands off Abyssinia!" *Labour Monthly* 17, no. 9 (Sept. 1935), p. 534.

34. Vol. 12, no. 8 (Aug. 1935), p. 230.

35. "Negroes and the Ethiopian Crisis," *The Christian Century* 52, no. 47 (20 Nov. 1935): 1485.

CHAPTER 2

1. "Aithiopika," *Hermes* 87 (1959): 38.

2. *The Prester John of the Indies,* ed. C. F. Beckingham and G. W. B. Huntingford (Cambridge University Press, 1961), 1: 34.

3. *The Ethiopians: An Introduction to Country and People* (London: Oxford University Press, 1960), pp. 32, 46.

4. Ibid., p. 116.

5. For example, one of the few courses ever offered in an American university on the history of Ethiopia, a course first offered at Columbia University in the spring of 1936 (doubtless in response to interest in Ethiopia awakened by the Italo-Ethiopian War) was listed in the curriculum as "Semitic 102."

After writing this chapter I received a copy of the program of the Fourth International Conference of Ethiopian Studies held at Rome in April 1972. The program indicates that the dominance of the "old-school" approach to Ethiopian studies is by no means a thing of the past: of thirty-four papers in the historical section, all but three reflected the Semitist perspective; of nineteen papers in the linguistic section, fifteen dealt with one or more Ethio-Semitic languages, and not a single paper was devoted to analyzing one of the several dozen Cushitic and Omotic languages of Ethiopia.

6. *Ethiopia Today* (Stanford University Press, 1968), p. 36.

7. *The Study of Total Societies,* ed. Samuel Z. Klausner (New York: Anchor Books, 1967), p. 100.

8. I refer above all to the formulations developed by Talcott Parsons during the last decade. See his *Societies: Comparative and Evolutionary Perspectives,* and *The System of Modern Societies* (Englewood Cliffs, N.J.: Prentice-Hall, 1966 and 1971, respectively), and references therein. See also Marshall D. Sahlins and Elman R. Service, eds., *Evolution and Culture* (Ann Arbor: University of Michigan Press, 1960), and other references for chapter 11 cited in the bibliography of this volume.

CHAPTER 3

1. See Harold Fleming, "The Classification of West Cushitic within Hamito-Semitic," in *Eastern African History,* ed. D. F. McCall (New York: Praeger, 1969), pp. 3–27; Fleming, "Classification of Cushitic and Omotic Languages," in M. L. Bender et al., *Language in Ethiopia,* (Oxford University Press, 1974); and M. L. Bender, *The Position of Omotic in Afroasiatic* (The Hague: Mouton, forthcoming).

2. This reconstruction follows a line of analysis presented in per-

sonal communications from Professor Gene Gragg, departments of Linguistics and Near Eastern Languages and Literatures, the University of Chicago. An alternative reconstruction of the genealogy of North Ethio-Semitic languages, deriving Tigre and Tigrinya from a common ancestor and making Ge'ez a separate "dead-end" language, has been presented by Robert Hetzron in "Ethiopian Semitic: Studies in Classification," *Journal of Semitic Studies Monograph Series* 2 (Manchester: University Press, 1972).

3. It is not known whether the intrusion of Sudanic cultures came about through an invasion of Sudanic peoples into parts of Greater Ethiopia already settled by Cushitic and Omotic peoples or by an invasion from the latter into parts of western Ethiopia previously settled by the Pre-Nilotes and Nilotes. A. E. Jensen and his associates at the Frobenius Institut, on whose work this reconstruction of the Sudanic influences is largely based, attribute the Sudanic physical and cultural characteristics of the southwest Ethiopians to the presence of previously established Pre-Nilotic and later Nilotic peoples; G. P. Murdock stresses the possibility of a Sudanic invasion.

4. Wolf Leslau, "The Meaning of ARAB in Ethiopia," *Muslim World* 30 (1949): 307–8.

5. The question of an early Judaic intrusion remains somewhat controversial, though the many lines of evidence assembled by Edward Ullendorff constitute a formidable argument on behalf of this hypothesis. The evidence for a pre-Christian Jewish presence in Ethiopia includes Ethiopian traditions, which attribute Hebrew names to Aksumite kings before the period of their conversion to Christianity, and philological studies which indicate that Hebraic Aramaic texts were among those used by Ethiopians in translating the Old Testament into Ge'ez. See Edward Ullendorff, *Ethiopia and the Bible* (London: Oxford University Press, 1968).

6. "The Many Worlds of Ethiopia," *African Affairs* 68 (Jan. 1969): 49–54.

7. The population estimates in this section are based primarily on the figures for those speaking the respective languages of the peoples in question as mother tongues presented in Bender et al., *Language in Ethiopia.*

Chapter 4

1. M. Abir, "Caravan Trade and History in the Northern Parts of East Africa," *Paideuma* 14 (1968): 170.

2. Manoel de Almeida, "The History of High Ethiopia or Abassia," in *Some Records of Ethiopia, 1593–1646,* ed. C. F. Beckingham and G. W. B. Huntingford (London: Hakluyt, 1954), 56–57.

3. *Anthropology* (New York: Harcourt Brace, 1948), p. 724.

4. Eike Haberland, *Untersuchungen zum Äthiopischen Königtum* (Wiesbaden: Franz Steiner Verlag, 1965), p. 293.

5. See Donald N. Levine, "The Concept of Masculinity in Ethiopian Culture," *International Journal of Social Psychiatry* 12 (1966): 17–23. Haberland interprets the glorification of outstanding warriors and hunters as an instance of a more general pan-Ethiopian value orientation, the glorification of outstanding individual achievement. He finds this "merit system" manifest in heroic activities of many sorts: attainment of great wealth, procreation of many children, lavish entertainment of numerous guests, as well as killing of fearsome enemies and wild beasts. He further sees this emphasis on individual achievement as precluding the ascription of status on a strictly hereditary basis; but this latter point, though valid to some extent, must be sharply qualified by a realization that hereditary ascription of status is important in most Ethiopian tribes as well: male primogeniture as the basis for king selection in several tribes, the privileged status of certain lineages, caste-group affiliation, and so on. See his *Untersuchungen*, chap. 4.

6. Enrico Cerulli, *La lingua e la storia di Harar* (Rome, 1936), p. 322.

7. Amnon Orent, "Dual Organization in Southern Ethiopia," *Ethnology* 9 (July 1970): 228–33.

8. Werner Munzinger, *Ostafrikanische Studien* (Schaffhausen, 1864), p. 245.

9. Herbert Lewis, "Wealth, Influence, and Prestige among the Shoa Galla," in *Social Stratification in Africa*, ed. Arthur Tuden and Leonard Plotnicov (New York: Free Press, 1970), p. 182 ff.

10. Haberland, *Untersuchungen*, 114–33; 293–300.

11. William Shack, *The Gurage* (London: Oxford University Press, 1966), p. 136.

12. See Eike Haberland, "Äthiopische Dachaufsätze," *Jahrbuch des Museums für Völkerkunde zu Leipzig*, vol. 18 (1960).

13. Eike Haberland, *Galla Süd-Äthiopiens* (Stuttgart: W. Kohlhammer, 1963), pp. 7, 36.

14. R. Sauter, "Où en est notre connaissance des églises rupestres d'Ethiopie," *Annales d'Ethiopie* 5 (1963), 235–92.

15. J. Spencer Trimingham, *Islam in Ethiopia* (London: Oxford University Press, 1952), p. 263.

16. Richard Pankhurst, "Gabata and Related Board Games of Ethiopia and the Horn of Africa," *Ethiopia Observer* 14, no. 3 (1971), pp. 154–206.

17. *Storia della letteratura etiopica* (Milan, 1956), pp. 12–13.

18. Marilyn Heldman, "Miniatures of the Gospels of Princess Zir Ganela, an Ethiopic Manuscript Dated A.D. 1400/01" (Ph.D. disserta-

tion, Washington University, Department of Art and Archaeology, August 1972), p. 82, n. 48.

19. *Africa: Its Peoples and Their Culture History* (New York: McGraw-Hill, 1959), chap. 22. I shall follow Murdock's general line of interpretation here while acknowledging (1) that the Sudanic agricultural complex may well have originated in the area of eastern Sudan and western Ethiopia, not in West Africa as Murdock argues; and (2) that the Pre-Nilotes may represent an earlier settlement in western Ethiopia subsequently subjugated by the Cushites, rather than an invading element. This would not greatly affect my general point about the characteristic way Ethiopians responded to external cultures.

20. Enrico Cerulli, *Etiopia Occidentale* (Rome, 1932), 1: 240.

21. *Islam in Ethiopia,* p. 211.

CHAPTER 5

1. The striking parallel between these consequences of the Arab expansion for Ethiopia and the comparable situation in southern Europe, as portrayed in Henri Pirenne's *Mohammed and Charlemagne* (New York: Barns and Noble, 1955), has been called to my attention in a personal communication from Harold Marcus.

2. A subsequent northward migration of Agew tribes into Eritrea, involving the Zagwa and Adkeme Melga, resulted from the overthrow of the Zagwe Dynasty in the thirteenth century. See Conti-Rossini, "La seconda migrazione Agau dell'Eritrea," *Rivista degli studi orientali 4* (1912): 559–651.

3. See M. L. Bender, "Searching for Creolization in South Ethio-Semitic," unpublished manuscript, September 1972, Southern Illinois University, Carbondale.

4. "The Amharic Language," in M. L. Bender, et al., *Language in Ethiopia* (Oxford University Press, 1974). It should also be noted that a number of distinctive Cushitic features, such as the use of subject-object-verb sentence order, compound verbs, consecutive gerunds, and cleft sentences, are found in Amharic but not in Ge'ez.

5. The church of Saint Stephen was built on an island of Lake Hayq. This later became the center of a famous monastery called Debra Hayq. The other church, Debra Egziabher, Mount of the Lord, was built on a mountain overlooking the lake.

6. See Haberland, *Untersuchungen,* p. 241.

7. Ibid., chap. 4.

CHAPTER 6

1. *Islam in Ethiopia,* p. 48 ff.

2. *Church and State in Ethiopia, 1270–1527* (Oxford: Clarendon Press, 1972), pp. 80 ff., 128.

3. *Some Records of Ethiopia, 1593–1646*, p. 126.
4. Ibid., p. 122.
5. Ibid., p. 137.
6. In the social sphere the elementary units are either persons or status-roles. In the cultural sphere the elementary units are symbols.

CHAPTER 7

1. See David A. Hubbard, "The Literary Sources of the *Kebra Nagast*" (dissertation, University of Saint Andrews, 1956).
2. Budge, *The Queen of Sheba and Her Only Son Menyelek* (London, 1922), p. vii; Ullendorff, *The Ethiopians*, p. 144. Hubbard comments that as a repository of elements from many different literatures, the *Kibra Negest* "presents a literary reflection of the polychromic pattern of life which is Ethiopia" ("Literary Sources of the *Kebra Nagast*," p. 6).
3. *Voyage dans le Royaume de Choa* (Paris, 1841), 1: 204.
4. *Travels in Abyssinia* (London, 1868), p. 33.
5. *Storia d'Etiopia* (Milan, 1928), p. 319.
6. "Menilek and Oedipus: Further Observations on the Ethiopian National Epic., *Proceedings of the First United States Conference on Ethiopian Studies*, ed. Harold G. Marcus (forthcoming).
7. See *Societies: Evolutionary and Comparative Perspectives*, passim.
8. "The Identity Struggle," in *Intensive Family Therapy*, ed. Ivan Borzormenyi-Nagy and J. L. Framo (New York: Harper and Row, 1965). Wallace and Fogelson define identity as "any image, or set of images, either conscious or unconscious, which an individual has of himself." They conceive of a person's total identity as consisting of a number of analytically separable subsets of images. *Real identity* is a subset of images which the person believes, privately, to be a true present description of himself as he "really" is. *Ideal identity* is a subset of images which the person would like to be able to say was true but which he does not necessarily believe is true at present. *Feared identity* is a subset of images which the person would not like to have to say was true of himself at present and which he does not necessarily believe is true. *Claimed identity* is a subset of images which the person would like another party to believe is his real identity.
9. See Snowden, *Blacks in Antiquity*, chap. 9.
10. For an illuminating analysis of this concept which throws light on the meaning of the Ethiopian case, see Delbert R. Hillers, *Covenant: The History of a Biblical Idea* (Baltimore: Johns Hopkins Press, 1969).
11. "Legitimacy in Ethiopia," paper presented at the 1964 meetings

of the American Political Science Association (mimeographed, Department of Sociology, University of Chicago).

12. *Liber Axumae,* ed. C. Conti Rossini (*Corpus Scriptorum Christianorum Orientalium,* scr. Aeth., ser. alt., 8; Paris, 1910), 67,72 (text).

13. See Eike Haberland, "Die Fest-Inthronisation in Aksum," in *Untersuchungen,* pp. 90–103.

CHAPTER 8

1. "Social Stratification in Traditional Amhara Society," in *Social Stratification in Africa,* ed. Arthur Tuden and Leonard Plotnicov (New York: Free Press, 1970), p. 199.

2. *The Life of Tekla Haymanot,* ed. and trans. E. Wallis Budge (London, 1906), p. 384.

3. See D. Levine, "Ethiopia: Identity, Authority, and Realism," in *Political Culture and Political Development,* ed. Lucien Pye and Sidney Verba (Princeton: Princeton University Press, 1965).

4. After the reorganization of the Imperial Ethiopian Government in 1942, many traditional activities of the local lords were assumed by agents of the central government reporting to the ministries of Interior, Finance, and Justice.

5. See D. Levine, *Wax and Gold* (Chicago: University of Chicago Press, 1965), chap. 5; and Hoben, "Social Stratification in Traditional Amhara Society."

6. See Taddesse Tamrat, "Some notes on the fifteenth century Stephanite 'heresy' in the Ethiopian Church," *Rassegna di Studi Etiopici* 22 (1958): 103–15.

7. *Douze ans de séjour dans la Haute-Ethiopie* (Paris, 1868), p. 374.

8. "Social Stratification in Traditional Amhara Society," p. 194.

9. See *Wax and Gold,* chaps. 4 and 5.

CHAPTER 9

1. Present-day Guji appear to differ from the Borana in this respect. John Hinnant reports that there is less tension among Guji brothers, since there is effective pressure on the firstborn to distribute the family patrimony equitably, and that Guji families where all the married sons have separate homesteads are rare.

2. This is not to say that de facto divorce does not occur. Among the Guji, at least, Hinnant has confirmed that, although divorce remains illegal, it is possible for a man to drive a wife out of his house, and wives sometimes run away and resist pressures to return.

3. This is currently the case among the Borana. Among the Guji, women cut the dry grass for the house roof but men build the houses.

4. The traditional moiety organization in Guji appears by now to have lost all importance, but a new dual division between Akaku and Dalata, regarded as senior and junior clans, now pervades the Guji descent system.

5. This account of the *gada* is based almost exclusively on the Borana material presented by Legesse and Haberland.

6. *Voyage dans le Royaume de Choa,* 1: 175.

7. This ceremony, known as *daga kora* ("he climbs the stones"), is described by Karl Eric Knutsson in *Authority and Change: A Study of the Kallu Institution among the Macha Galla of Ethiopia* (Göteborg: Etnografiska Museet, 1967), pp. 174–75.

8. "Wealth, Influence, and Prestige among the Shoa Galla," in *Social Stratification in Africa,* ed. Arthur Tuden and Leonard Plotnicov (New York: Free Press, 1970), p. 173.

9. "The Folk-Literature of the Galla of Southern Abyssinia," *Varia Africana* (Cambridge, Mass.: Harvard University Press, 1922), 3: 141 ff.

10. P. W. Schmidt, "Die Religion der Galla," *Annali Lateranensi* 1 (1937): 138.

11. M. Borello, "Proverbi Galla," *Rassegna di studi etiopici* 5 (1947): 118.

12. P. Paulitschke, *Ethnographie Nordost-Afrikas* (Berlin, 1893), p. 14.

13. Herbert Lewis, "Wealth, Influence and Prestige among the Shoa Galla." See also the superb monograph by Karl Eric Knutsson, *Authority and Change,* for a detailed account of the organization, functions, and historical development of the *qallu* institution among the Mecha Galla.

14. Knutsson, *Authority and Change,* p. 180.

Chapter 10

1. The Galla verses are taken from Cerulli, "Folk-Literature of the Galla," pp. 103, 101, and 67. The Amhara verses are from my own field notes.

2. *Some Records of Ethiopia,* p. 127.

3. *Les noms propres, les noms de bâptème et l'étude généalogique des rois d'Ethiopie (XIII-XX° siecles) à travers leurs noms patronymiques* (mimeographed monograph; Belgrade, 1966).

4. *King of Kings: Tewodros of Ethiopia* (Addis Abeba-Nairobi: Oxford University Press, 1966), p. 49.

5. *Travels to Discover the Source of the Blue Nile* (Dublin, 1791), book 3.

6. "The Process of Re-unification of the Ethiopian Empire, 1868–1889, 2 vols. (Ph.D. dissertation, Oxford University, 1971), 2: 561.

7. Otto Klineberg and Marisa Zavalloni, *Nationalism and Tribalism among African Students* (The Hague: Mouton, 1969), chap. 7.

8. "Wealth, Influence, and Prestige among the Shoa Galla," p. 165.

CHAPTER 11

1. *The Majangir: Ecology and Society of a Southwest Ethiopian People* (Cambridge: Cambridge University Press, 1971), p. 5.

2. "If, however, in certain cases, peoples tied by no bond, even regarding themselves as enemies, exchange products in a more or less regular manner, it is necessary to see in these facts only simple relations of *mutualism* having nothing in common with the division of labor"; Emile Durkheim, *The Division of Labor in Society,* trans. George Simpson (Glencoe, Ill.: Free Press, 1947), pp. 281–82.

3. "The Status of Craftsmen among the Konso of South-west Ethiopia," *Africa* 38, no. 3 (July 1968): 268.

4. See Herbert Lewis, "Historical Problems in Ethiopia and the Horn of Africa," *Annals of the New York Academy of Sciences* 6, no. 2 (1962): 510–11.

5. *Ancient Semitic Civilization* (New York: Putnam's, 1957), pp. 235–36.

6. A patrimonial system is one in which a political domain is treated as one large household. Political authority is regarded as a personal possession of the ruler, and retainers are supported from the ruler's own table or supply stores. When a patrimonial empire becomes highly decentralized, it is commonly referred to as a feudal system.

In a bureaucratic system, there is a principled separation between private and official spheres. The bureaucratic officer is supported by norms and salaries which render him more independent of the political ruler and more oriented to the proper exercise of his function, the needs of his clients, and his personal advancement in a prestructured career line.

Both patrimonial and feudal systems represent the same evolutionary modality, an order in which a specialized political sphere operates with relative autonomy from the spheres of kinship and religion, but where *within* the political sphere there is little or no functional specialization. In a bureaucratic system roles are differentiated to some extent within the political sphere. In the patrimonial and feudal systems labor and loyalties are owed on a personal basis to one's lord or patron; in a bureaucratic system to the societal center or to an open market. There is a rough correspondence between the modalities of the patrimonial and historical bureaucratic empires and what Parsons, in *Societies: Comparative and Evolutionary Perspectives,* has called the "archaic" and "advanced intermediate" stages of evolutionary development.

The standard sociological sources on the contrast between patrimonial and bureaucratic systems are Max Weber, *Economy and Society,* ed. G. Roth and C. Wittich, 3 vols. (New York: Bedminster Press, 1968), and S. N. Eisenstadt, *The Political Systems of Empires* (New York: Fress Press, 1963).

7. The significance of the ensete monoculture as the center around which a complex of social, political, economic, and ritual practices are organized was first recognized by William A. Shack, "Some Aspects of Ecology and Social Structure in the Ensete Complex in South-west Ethiopia," *Journal of the Royal Anthropological Institute* 93, part 1 (1963): 72–79.

8. *Islam in Ethiopia,* p. 175.

9. *The Konso of Ethiopia* (Oxford: Clarendon Press, 1972), p. 22.

10. Of the Guji, John Hinnant writes in a personal communication: "Cattle and cattle products are at the dead center of traditional Guji ritual. Each Gada ceremony reiterates the ties between cattle and men. The welfare of cattle is a prime concern of rituals of affliction. . . . Clearly, they are well on the way to becoming agriculturalists who keep domestic herds. Yet, in their minds, status, well-being, and life itself are completely involved with cattle. They govern their lives by the needs of cattle, and will abandon an area if cattle do not thrive there. They are unhappy if plant food does not grow well in an area, but will remain if the cattle are healthy. They love to talk about cattle and grow bored when crops are discussed at length."

11. The Gurage are also divided among pagans, Christians, and Muslims, though because of their smaller numbers and relative isolation they do not appear so fully integrated into the national Christian and Islamic communities.

12. The policies of Haile Sellassie I thus exhibit an exact parallel to the characteristic policies of rulers in the historic bureaucratic empires as delineated by Eisenstadt in *The Political Systems of Empires,* chap. 7. For additional material on the developments described in this paragraph, see Christopher Clapham, *Haile-Selassie's Government* (New York: Frederick A. Praeger, 1969); Levine, *Wax and Gold,* pp. 177–17; and Marjery Perham, *The Government of Ethiopia,* 2d ed. (Evanston, Ill.: Northwestern University Press, 1969).

13. This is an important accomplishment of the Pax Amharica that is often obscured by reports of the decimation and enslavement of many of the conquered peoples in the two decades following Menilek's conquests and by more recent accounts of sporadic brutality on the part of members of provincial police garrisons. Reliable reports from the Borana, Guji, Gurage, Konso, Dorze, and other tribes make it clear that the intersocietal warfare and raiding that was formerly a common

fact of life has now almost completely disappeared, with a consequent increase in productivity and trade in all cases.

14. See, for example, Leon Mayhew, "Ascription in Modern Societies," *Sociological Inquiry,* vol. 38, no. 2 (Spring 1968); reprinted in *The Logic of Social Hierarchies,* ed. Edward Laumann, Paul Siegel, and Robert Hodge (Chicago: Markham, 1971), pp. 308–23.

15. Perhaps the time has come to pursue more rigorously the question whether man in the most differentiated kinds of societies has need for certain forms of experience which are practiced with grace by peoples in holistically specialized societies. To say this is neither to patronize or idealize the "primitives" nor to abandon modernity, but to recognize the possibility that there may be some significant affinities between peoples living at the two ends of the evolutionary continuum. The point would hold whether or not one argues that members of modern societies who feel strong affinities with primitive cultures are those with weak internal differentiation which renders them relatively unfit for the disciplines of highly differentiated societies. As Durkheim would say, they simply represent in exaggerated form propensities and yearnings found in much smaller doses among the more normal members of their society.

Premonitions of such affinities were voiced by a few evolutionary theorists in the nineteenth century. Most evolutionary theorists, to be sure, conceived of the evolutionary process as one in which primitive forms were more or less continually being replaced by more advanced forms. A contrary motif appears, however, among those who suggest certain respects in which societies in the most advanced states of specialization are likely to return to very primitive structures. Comte foresees in the positive polity a return to a degree of impulsivity and a kind of polytheistic orientation that marked the human species before its long ascent toward scientific mastery. Marx prophesies a return to what he imagined were forms of communal ownership and unalienated humanity in primitive society. Spencer envisages a return to the highly individualistic forms of social life he thought existed at the dawn of social evolution. Veblen visualizes an abandonment of the predatory and emulative habits of historic societies to the workmanlike and gregarious habits of man before the Fall. Whatever the validity of such conceptions as prophecies, they may be taken as expressions of an abiding sentiment among some members of industrialized societies that may be worthy of further exploration.

Bibliography

Part 1 is designed to introduce the general reader to a select list of basic works on Ethiopia. Part 2 contains selected references related to the special topics of the chapters, with particular emphasis on recent titles not likely to be cited in other bibliographies.

PART 1

History and Polity

A good general survey of the whole of Ethiopian history does not yet exist. Part 2 of J. Spencer Trimingham's *Islam in Ethiopia* (published by Oxford University Press in 1952 and reissued by Frank Cass of London in 1965), though dated in certain respects, remains the best text available. Jean Doresse, *Ethiopia* (New York: G. P. Putnam's, 1959) is a very readable nonacademic survey and offers a magnificent selection of plates. For a fuller treatment of the ancient and medieval periods, Doresse's *L'empire du Prêtre-Jean,* 2 vols. (Paris: Plon, 1957) is choice.

Marjery Perham's *The Government of Ethiopia* (Evanston: Northwestern University Press, 1969 [1948]) remains the outstanding introduction to the historical and contemporary condition of the Ethiopian state. The second edition of this work contains addenda on develpments in Ethiopia from 1946 to 1968. Other titles on Ethiopian politics are listed below under chapter 2, "Modernization" Studies.

On the Italo-Ethiopian War, the most useful single work is perhaps Angelo Del Boca, *The Ethiopian War, 1935–1941,* trans. P. D. Cummins (Chicago: University of Chicago Press, 1969), originally published as *La guerra d'Abissinia* (Milan: Feltrinelli, 1965).

Culture

For an introduction to the art and architecture of northern Ethiopia, David Buxton's *The Abyssinians* (New York: Praeger, 1970) can be recommended. For a much more sumptuous presentation, see the two volumes by George Gerster, *L'art éthiopien* (Boston: Newbury Books, 1969) and *Churches in Rock* (London: Phaidon, 1970), as well as Jules Leroy, *Ethiopian Painting* (New York: Praeger, 1967).

A set of three long-playing records prepared by the gifted musicologist Jean Jenkins offers annotated selections from the music of the central highlands, the desert nomads, and the peoples of Eritrea (London: Tangent Records, TGM 101–2–3). Michael Powne, *Ethiopian Music* (London: Oxford University Press, 1966), is of some limited value.

On the literature, religion, and world view of the Christian Ethiopians, see Edward Ullendorff, *The Ethiopians* (London: Oxford University Press, 1960; 2d ed., 1965); Enrico Cerulli, *Storia della letteratura etiopica* (Milan: Nuova Academia Editrice, 1956; 2d ed., 1961); and Donald N. Levine, *Wax and Gold: Tradition and Innovation in Ethiopian Culture* (Chicago: University of Chicago Press, 1965; Phoenix paperback edition, with a new preface by the author, 1972).

A thorough discussion of the Judaic elements in Ethiopian Christian culture is to be found in Edward Ullendorff, *Ethiopia and the Bible* (London: Oxford University Press, 1968). Parts 3 and 4 of Trimingham's *Islam in Ethiopia* discuss the beliefs and practices of Ethiopia's Muslim peoples, and B. W. Andrzejewski and I. M. Lewis have produced *Somali Poetry: An Introduction* (Oxford, Clarendon Press, 1964). A general introduction to the religious systems and folk cultures of Ethiopian peoples who are not followers of one of the three Semitic religions does not exist.

Travelers' Literature and Fiction

The travelers' literature on Ethiopia is particularly rich and informative. Richard Pankhurst has edited a delightful sampler of this material: *Travellers in Ethiopia* (London: Oxford University Press, 1965). The following titles can be especially recommended: Francesco Alvarez, *The Prester John of the Indies,* ed. C. F. Beckingham and G. W. B. Huntingford; 2 vols. (Cambridge University Press, 1961); Arnauld d'Abbadie, *Douze ans de séjour dans la Haute-Ethiopie* (Paris, 1868); James Bruce, *Travels to Discover the Source of the Nile,* selected, edited, and with an introduction by C. F. Beckingham (Edinburgh: University of Edinburgh Press, 1964); Major Cornwallis Harris, *The Highlands of Aethiopia,* 3 vols. (London, 1844); and Walter Plowden, *Travels in Abyssinia* (London, 1868).

Two recent novels reveal a good deal about the contemporary Ethiopian scene: Edmund P. Murray, *Kulubi* (New York: Crown, 1973) and Daniachew Worku, *The Thirteenth Sun* (London: Heineman, 1973).

Bibliographies

Jean Doresse, *L'empire du Prêtre-Jean* (1: 283–97, and 2: 333–51) provides a helpful guide to the standard historical materials. See also

Maurice de Coppet's edition of Guebre Sellassie, *Chronique du regne de Menelik II* (Paris: Maisonneuve, 1932), 2: 633–710. Robert L. Hess, *Ethiopia* (Ithaca: Cornell University Press, 1970) includes a conspectus of the limited and rather uneven materials dealing with contemporary Ethiopia. Two invaluable specialized tools are Wolf Leslau, *An Annotated Bibliography of the Semitic Language of Ethiopia* (The Hague: Mouton, 1965) and Harold G. Marcus, *The Modern History of Ethiopia and the Horn of Africa: A Select and Annotated Bibliography* (Stanford: Hoover Institution Press, 1972).

PART 2

CHAPTER 1

Images of Ethiopia in Antiquity

Hable-Selassie, Sergew. *Beziehungen Äthiopiens zur Griechisch-Romischen Welt.* Bonn: Rudolf Habelt, 1964.

Snowden, Frank M., Jr. *Blacks in Antiquity: Ethiopians in the Greco-Roman Experience.* Cambridge: Harvard University Press, 1970.

Thompson, L. A. "Eastern Africa and the Graeco-Roman World." In *Africa in Classical Antiquity,* ed. L. A. Thompson and J. Ferguson. Ibadan: Ibadan University Press, 1969, pp. 26–61.

Medieval Images

Bevan, W. L., and Phillott, H. W. *Medieval Geography.* London, 1873.

Cerulli, Enrico. *Etiopi in Palestina.* 2 vols. Rome, 1943.

———. "Preteianni." *Encyclopedia Italiana.*

Ross, Sir E. Denison. "Prester John and the Empire of Ethiopia." In *Travel and Travellers of the Middle Ages,* ed. A. P. Newton. London: Kegan Paul, 1926.

CHAPTER 2

"Classical" Ethiopian Studies

Conti-Rossini, Carlo. *Storia d'Etiopia,* Milan, 1928; chap. 1.

Hammerschmidt, Ernst. *Äthiopistik an deutschen Universitäten.* Wiesbaden: Franz Steiner, 1968.

Ullendorff, Edward. *The Ethiopians,* London: Oxford University Press, 1960, chap. 1.

A Museum of Peoples

Note: anthropological monographs on individual peoples are listed with the references for chapters 3 and 4 according to ethnic group category.

"Modernization" Studies

Bequele, Assefa, and Chole, Eshetu. *A Profile of the Ethiopian Economy.* Nairobi: Oxford University Press, 1969.

Clapham, Christopher. *Haile-Selassie's Government.* New York: Praeger, 1969.

Ginzberg, Eli, and Smith, Herbert A. *Manpower Strategy for Developing Countries: Lessons from Ethiopia.* New York: Columbia University Press, 1967.

Hoben, Allan. "Social Anthropology and Development Planning: A Case Study in Ethiopian Land Reform Policy." *Journal of Modern African Studies* 10, no. 4 (1972): 561–82.

Korten, David C., with Korten, Frances F. *Planned Change in a Traditional Society: Psychological Problems of Modernization in Ethiopia.* New York: Praeger, 1972.

Levine, Donald N. "Class Consciousness and Class Solidarity in the New Ethiopian Elites." In *The New Elites of Tropical Africa,* ed. Peter Lloyd, pp. 312–27. London: International African Institute, 1966.

———. "Ethiopia: Identity, Authority, and Realism." In *Political Culture and Political Development,* ed. L. Pye and S. Verba. Princeton: Princeton University Press, 1965.

———. "The Military in Ethiopian Politics." In *The Military Intervenes: Case Studies in Political Development,* ed. Henry Bienen, pp. 5–34. New York: Russell Sage, 1968.

———. *Wax and Gold: Tradition and Innovation in Ethiopian Culture.* Chicago: University of Chicago Press, 1965.

Markakis, John, and Beyene, Asmelash. "Representative Institutions in Ethiopia." *Journal of Modern African Studies* 5, no. 2 (1967): 193–219.

Messing, Simon. "Changing Ethiopia." *Middle East Journal* 9 (1955): 413–52.

Schwab, Peter. *Decision-Making in Ethiopia.* Cranbury, N.J.: Fairleigh Dickinson University Press, 1972.

Chapters 3 and 4
Prehistory

Anfray, Francis. "Aspects de l'archéologie éthiopienne." *Journal of African History* 9 (1968): 34.

Clark, J. Desmond. *The Prehistory of Africa.* New York: Praeger, 1970.

Diakonoff, I. M. *Semito-Hamitic Languages.* Moscow: Nauka, 1965.

Drewes, A. J. *Inscriptions de l'Ethiopie antique.* Leiden: Brill, 1962.

Hudson, Grover. "The Semitic Prehistory of Ethiopia." In *Current Trends in Ethiopian Linguistics and Philology,* ed. M. L. Bender and R. Hetzron, forthcoming.

Irvine, A. K. "On the Identity of Ḥabashat in the South Arabian Inscriptions." *Journal of Semitic Studies* 10 (1965): 178–96.

Linguistic Surveys

Bender, M. L. "The Languages of Ethiopia." In *Anthropological Linguistics* 13, no. 5 (May 1971): 165–288.

Bender, M. L.; Bowen, J. D.; Cooper, R. L.; Ferguson, C. A.; et al., *Language in Ethiopia.* London: Oxford University Press, 1973.

Tucker, A. N., and Bryan, M. A. *The Non-Bantu Languages of North-Eastern Africa.* London: Oxford University Press, 1956.

Ullendorff, Edward. *The Semitic Languages of Ethiopia.* London: Taylor's Foreign Press, 1955.

Ethnographic Surveys (cited hereafter by abbreviations)

AFR = Murdock, George P. *Africa: Its Peoples and Their Culture History.* New York: McGraw-Hill, 1959.

IIE = Trimingham, J. S., *Islam in Ethiopia,* London: Frank Cass, 1965, part 3.

NWE = Simoons, Frederick J. *Northwest Ethiopia: Peoples and Economy.* Madison: University of Wisconsin Press, 1960.

NEA = International African Institute, *Ethnographic Survey of Africa,* volumes on *North Eastern Africa:*

- NEA/ I. = Lewis, I. M. *Peoples of the Horn of Africa.* 1970 (1955).
- NEA/ II. = Huntingford, G. W. B. *The Galla of Ethiopia and the Kingdoms of Kefa and Janjero.* 1955.
- NEA/III. = Cerulli, Ernesta. *Peoples of South-West Ethiopia and Its Borderland.* 1956.
- NEA/IV. = Shack, William A. *Amhara, Tigriña, and Related Peoples.* 1974.

VSA = Frobenius Institut, *Völker Süd-Äthiopiens:*

- VSA/ I. = Jensen, A. E., et al. *Altvölker Süd-Äthiopiens.* 1959.
- VSA/ II. = Haberland, Eike, et al. *Galla Sür-Äthiopiens.* 1963.
- VSA/III. = Straube, H., et al. *Westkuschitische Völker Süd-Äthiopiens.* 1963.

See also Cerulli, Enrico. *Etiopia Occidentale.* 2 vols. Rome, 1932–33.

Conti-Rossini, Carlo. *Etiopia e Genti d'Etiopia.* Florence, 1937.

North Eritrean Peoples

Munzinger, W. *Ostafrikanische Studien.* Schaffhausen, 1864.

Littman, Enno. *Tales, Customs, Names and Dirges of the Tigrē Tribes.* 5 vols. Leyden, 1910.

AFR, pp. 314–18.
IIE, pp. 49–51, 153–70.

Agew Peoples

Biru, Teqebba; Adal, Zena; and Cowley, Roger. "The Kunfäl People and Their Language." *Journal of Ethiopian Studies* 9, no. 2 (July 1971): 99–106.

Conti-Rossini, C. *La langue des Kemant en Abyssinie.* Vienna, 1912.

Gamst, Frederick C. *The Qemant: A Pagan-Hebraic Peasantry of Ethiopia.* New York: Holt, Rinehart, and Winston, 1969.

Hess, Robert L. "Toward a History of the Falasha," In *Eastern African History,* ed. D. McCall et al., chap. 4. New York: Praeger, 1969.

Hetzron, Robert. *The Verbal System of Southern Agaw.* University of California Press, 1969.

Leslau, Wolf. *Falasha Anthology.* New York: Shocken, 1969 (1951).

NWE, pp. 34–45; see also NEA/IV.

Amhara-Tigrean Peoples

See references above (Part 1) and below (chapters 5, 7, and 8).
See also NEA/IV, and NWE, pp. 24–31.

Core Islamic Peoples

Cerulli, Enrico. *La lingua e la storia di Harar.* Rome, 1936.

Chedeville, E. "Quelques faits de l'organisation sociale des 'Afar.'" *Africa* 36 (1966): 173–96.

Doresse, Jean. *Histoire sommaire de le corne orientale de l'Afrique.* Paris: Librairie Orientaliste Paul Geuthner, 1971.

Lewis, I. M. *A Pastoral Democracy.* London: Oxford University Press, 1961.

Parker, Enid. "Afar Stories, Riddles and Proverbs." *Journal of Ethiopian Studies* 9, no. 2 (1971): 219–87.

Savard, George. "War Chants in Praise of Ancient Afar Heroes." *Journal of Ethiopian Studies* 3, no. 1 (Jan. 1965): 105–8.

NEA/II (Afar, Saho, Somali).

NEA/IV (Argobba, Harari).

Galla Peoples

See references below for chapters 5 and 9.
See also NEA/II.

Lacustrine Peoples

Almagor, Uri. "Name-Oxen and Ox-Names among the Dassanetch of Southwest Ethiopia." *Paideuma* 18 (1972): 79–96.

———. "The Social Organization of the Dassanetch of the Lower Omo." (Ph.D. dissertation, Manchester University, 1971).
———. "Tribal Sections, Territory and Myth: Dassanetch Responses to Variable Ecological Conditions," *Asian and African Studies* 8, no. 2 (1972): 185–206.
Carr, Claudia. "Societal/Environmental Interactions as a System: The Dasanetch of Southwest Ethiopia." University of Chicago Monographs in Geography. In press.
Hallpike, Christopher R. *The Konso of Ethiopia: a Study of the Values of a Cushitic People.* Oxford: Clarendon Press, 1972.
Hamer, John. "Spirit Possession and Its Socio-Psychological Implications among the Sidamo of Southwest Ethiopia." *Ethnology* 5, no. 4 (Oct. 1966): 392–408.
———. "Sidamo Generational Class Cycles: A Political Gerontocracy." *Africa* 40, no. 1 (Jan. 1970): 50–70.
———. "Voluntary Associations as Structures of Change among the Sidamo of South-West Ethiopia." *Anthropological Quarterly* 40, no. 2: 73–91.
Leslau, Wolf. "Ethiopic Documents: Gurage." *Viking Fund Publications in Anthropology* 13 (1950): 1–176.
Shack, Dorothy N. "Nutritional Processes and Personality Development among the Gurage." *Ethnology* 8, no. 3 (July 1969): 292–300.
Shack, William S. "Religious Ideas and Social Action in Gurage Bond-Friendship." *Africa* 33, no. 3 (July 1963): 198–208.
———. *The Gurage: A People of the Ensete Culture.* (London: Oxford University Press, 1966).
———. "Hunger, Anxiety, and Ritual: Deprivation and Spirit Possession among the Gurage of Ethiopia." *Man* 6, no. 1 (Mar. 1971): 30–43.
Simone, Antonio. *I Sidamo* (Bologna: A. Cacciari, 1939).
NEA/III, pp. 51–68 (Konso group), pp. 118–32 (Sidamo group); NEA/IV (Gafat, Gurage).
VSA/I, chaps. 12–13 (Tsamako, Arbore); VSA/II, chaps. E.11 (Hadiyya), K (Zway).

Omotic Peoples

Haberland, Eike. "Das Königtum von Wolamo." *Untersuchungen zum äthiopischen Königtum,* ch. 6. Wiesbaden: Franz Steiner, 1965.
Montandon, G. *Au pays Ghimirra.* Paris, 1913.
Olmstead, Judith. "Agricultural Land and Social Stratification in the Gamu Highlands of Southern Ethiopia." *Proceedings of the First United States Conference on Ethiopian Studies.* Ed. Harold G. Marcus, forthcoming.

Orent, Amnon. "Lineage Structure and the Supernatural: The Kafa of Southwest Ethiopia." Ph.D. dissertation, Boston University, 1969.

Sperber, Dan. "Paradoxes of Seniority among the Dorze." *Proceedings of the First United States Conference on Ethiopian Studies.* Ed. Harold G. Marcus, forthcoming.

NEA/II (Kefa, Janjero); NEA/III, pp. 89–117 (Gimira-Maji and Ometo groups).

VSA/I, chaps. 1–4, 6, 9–11 (Ari-Banna group), 5, 7–8 (Ometo group); VSA/II, chap. L (East Ometo cluster); VSA/III, chaps. 1 (Sheko), 2–4 (Ometo group), and 5 (Janjero).

Sudanic Peoples

Conti-Rossini, C. "Popoli dell'Etiopia occidentale." *Rendiconti della Reale Accademia dei Lincei* 28 (1919): 251–85, 319–25 (Gumuz and Berta).

Evans-Pritchard, E. E. "Further Observations on the Political System of the Anuak." *Sudan Notes and Records* 28 (1947): 62–97.

———. *Kinship and Marriage among the Nuer.* London: Oxford University Press, 1951.

———. *The Nuer.* London: Oxford University Press, 1940.

———. "The Political System of the Anuak." In *Monographs on Social Anthropology,* 4:1–164. London: London School of Economics, 1940.

Grottanelli, V. L. *I Mao.* Rome, 1940.

———. "I Pre-Niloti." *Annali Lateranensi* 12 (1948): 282–326.

Lyth, R. E. "The Suri Tribe." *Sudan Notes and Records* 28 (1947): 104–14.

Stauder, Jack. *The Majangir: Ecology and Society of a Southwest Ethiopian People.* Cambridge University Press, 1971.

Tucci, G. "I Baria e i Cunama." *Rivista di Etnografia* 4 (1950): 49–75.

AFR, chaps. 21 ("Prenilotes"), 43 ("Nilotes").

IIE, pp. 216–20 (Nara, Kunama, Berta).

NEA/III, pp. 11–50.

NWE, pp. 52–56 (Gumuz).

VSA/I, chap. 14 (Bodi).

Caste Groups

Cerulli, Enrico. "The Folk-Literature of the Galla of Southern Abyssinia." *Varia Africana* 3 (Cambridge: Harvard University Press, 1922): 200–14.

Hallpike, C. R. "The Status of Craftsmen among the Konso of Southwest Ethiopia." *Africa* 38, no. 3 (July1968):258–69.

Lewis, Herbert S. "Historical Problems in Ethiopia and the Horn of

Africa." *Annals of the New York Academy of Sciences* 96, no. 2 (1962): 508–11.
———. "Occupational Caste in Ethiopia." In *Social Stratification in Africa,* ed. A. Tuden and L. Plotnicov, pp. 182–85. New York: Free Press, 1970.
Shack, William A. "Notes on Occupational Castes Among the Gurage of Southwest Ethiopia." *Man* 54 (1964): 50–52.
NWE, pp. 45–52; 174–189.
NEA and VSA, passim.

CHAPTER 4
Trade and Markets

Abir, Mordechai. "Southern Ethiopia." In *Pre-Colonial African Trade,* ed. D. Birmingham and R. Gray, chap. 6. Oxford University Press, 1970.
———. "Caravan Trade and History in the Northern Parts of East Africa." *Paideuma* 14 (1968): 155–72.
Bohannan, Paul, and Dalton, George. eds. *Markets in Africa.* Evanston: Northwestern University Press, 1962, chapters by I. M. Lewis (Somali), Simon Messing (Amhara), and Richard Kluckhohn (Konso).
Kürchhof, D. "Alte und neue Handelsstrassen und Handelsmittelpunkte an den afrikanischen Küster des Roten Meeres und des Golfes von Aden, Sowie in deren Hinterländern." *Geographische Zeitschrift* 14 (1908): 251–67, 312–27.
Pankhurst, Richard. *An Introduction to the Economic History of Ethiopia.* London: Lalibela House, 1961, pp. 307–21.
Simoons, Frederick. *Northwest Ethiopia* (NWE), pp. 192–210.
Tamrat, Tadesse. *Church and State in Ethiopia, 1270–1527.* Oxford: Clarendon Press, 1972, pp. 80–89.

CHAPTER 5
Early Expansions

Doresse, Jean. *L'empire du Prêtre-Jean.* Vol. I. Paris: Plon, 1957.
Conti-Rossini, C. *Storia d'Etiopia.* Milan, 1928; chap. 12.
Lewis, I. M. "The Somali Conquest of the Horn of Africa." *Journal of African History* 1, no. 2 (1960): 213–29.

Amhara Expansion

Tamrat, Tadesse. *Church and State in Ethiopia, 1270–1527.* Oxford: Clarendon Press, 1972.

Oromo Origins and Expansion

Beckingham, C. F., and Huntingford, G. W. B. *Some Records of Ethiopia.* London: Hakluyt, 1954.

Haberland, Eike. *Galla Süd-Äthiopiens* (=VSA/II).

Lewis, Herbert. "The Origins of the Galla and Somali." *Journal of African History* 7, no. 1 (1966): 27–46.

Reunification in the Nineteenth Century

Abir, Mordechai. *Ethiopia: The Era of the Princes.* New York: Praeger, 1968.

Gabre-Sellassie, Zewde. "The Process of Re-unification of the Ethiopian Empire, 1868–1889." 2 vols. Ph.D. dissertation, Oxford University, 1971.

Marcus, Harold. *The Life and Times of Menilek II.* Oxford: Clarendon, 1974.

Pankhurst, Richard K. *An Introduction to the Economic History of Ethiopia, 1800–1935.* Addis Ababa: Haile Sellassie I University Press, 1968.

Rubenson, Sven. *King of Kings: Tewodros of Ethiopia.* Addis Abeba: Oxford University Press, 1966.

CHAPTER 7
The Kibre Negest

Bezold, Carl. "Kebra Nagast: Die Herrlichkeit der Könige." *Abhandlungen der königlich Bayerischen Akademie der Wissenschaften* (München). Phil. Class, vol. 23, part 1 (1905). Munich, 1909.

Budge, E. A. Wallis. *The Queen of Sheba and Her Only Son Menyelek.* London, 1922.

Cerulli, Enrico. *Storia della letteratura etiopica.* Milan, 1956, pp. 43–52.

Chastel, A. "La legende de la Reine de Saba." *Revue de l'histoire des religions* 119 (1939): 204–25; 120 (1939): 27–44; 160–74.

Doresse, Jean. *L'empire du Prêtre-Jean.* Vol. 1. Paris: Plon, 1957; chap. 8.

Haberland, Eike. *Untersuchungen zum äthiopischen Königtum.* Wiesbaden: Franz Steiner, 1965; chap. 1.

Hubbard, David. "The Literary Sources of the *Kebra Nagast.*" Ph.D. dissertation, University of St. Andrews, Scotland, 1956.

Jones, A. and Monroe, Elizabeth. *A History of Ethiopia.* Oxford: Clarendon Press, 1955 (1935); chap. 3.

Levine, Donald N. "Menilek and Oedipus: Further Observations on the Ethiopian National Epic." *Proceedings of the First United States Conference on Ethiopian Studies.* Ed. Harold G. Marcus, forthcoming.

Littmann, Enno. "The Legend of the Queen of Sheba in the Tradition of Axum." In *Bibliotheca Abessinica.* Vol. I. Leyden: Brill, 1904.

Perham, Marjery. *The Government of Ethiopia.* Evanston: Northwestern University Press, 1969 (1948); pp. 35–36, 69–71, app. B.

Ullendorff, Edward. *Ethiopia and the Bible.* London: Oxford University Press, 1968.

CHAPTER 8
The Amhara (-Tigrean) System

Bauer, Dan Franz. "Land, Leadership and Legitimacy among the Inderta Tigray of Ethiopia." Ph.D. dissertation, University of Rochester, 1972.

Hoben, Allan. *Land Tenure among the Amhara of Ethiopia.* Chicago: University of Chicago Press, 1973.

———. "Social Stratification in Traditional Amhara Society." In *Social Stratification in Africa,* ed. Arthur Tuden and Leonard Plotnicov. New York: Free Press, 1970.

Hoben, Susan. "Situational Constraints among the Amhara of Ethiopia." Ph.D. dissertation, University of Rochester, 1972.

Levine, Donald N. *Wax and Gold.* Chicago: University of Chicago Press, 1965.

Messing, Simon. "The Highland-Plateau Amhara of Ethiopia." Ph.D. dissertation, University of Pennsylvania, 1957.

Reminick, Ronald. "The Manze Amhara of Ethiopia: A Study of Authority, Masculinity, and Sociality." Ph.D. dissertation, University of Chicago, 1973.

Weissleder, Wolfgang. "The Political Ecology of Amhara Domination." Ph.D. dissertation, University of Chicago, 1965.

Young, Allan. "Medical Beliefs and Practices of Begemder Amhara." Ph.D. dissertation, University of Pennsylvania, 1970.

CHAPTER 9
The Oromo System

Baxter, P. T. W. "Repetition in Certain Boran Ceremonies." In *African Systems of Thought,* ed. M. Fortes and P. Dieterlen. London: Oxford University Press, 1965.

Cerulli, Enrico. "I riti della iniziazione nella tribu Galla." *Rivista degli studi orientali* 9 (1921–23): 48–95.

Haberland, Eike. *Galla Süd-Äthiopiens* (VSA/II).

Hoffman, Hans. "Markov Chains in Ethiopia." In *Explorations in Mathematical Anthropology,* ed. Paul Kay. Cambridge: MIT Press, 1971.

Knutsson, Karl Eric. *Authority and Change: A Study of the Kalla Institution among the Macha Galla of Ethiopia.* Göteborg: Etnografiska Museet, 1967.

Legesse, Asmarom. "Class Systems Based on Time." *Journal of Ethiopian Studies* 1, no. 2 (1963): 1–29.

———. *Gada: Three Approaches to the Study of African Society.* New York: Free Press, 1973.

Chapter 11
Evolutionary Theory

Bellah, Robert. "Religious Evolution." *American Sociological Review* 29 (June 1964): 358–74.

Eisenstadt, S. N. "Social Change, Differentiation, and Evolution." *American Sociological Review* 29 (June 1964): 375–85.

———. "Social Evolution." *International Encyclopedia of the Social Sciences.*

Fried, Morton H. *The Evolution of Political Society.* New York: Random House, 1967.

Harris, Marvin. *The Rise of Anthropological Theory.* New York: Thomas Y. Crowell, 1968.

Parsons, Talcott. "Evolutionary Universals in Society." *American Sociological Review* 29 (June 1964): 339–57.

———. *Societies: Evolutionary and Comparative Perspectives.* Englewood Cliffs, N.J.: Prentice-Hall, 1966.

———. "Some Considerations on the Theory of Social Change." *Rural Sociology* 26 (Sept. 1961): 219–39.

———. *The System of Modern Societies.* Englewod Cliffs, N.J.: Prentice-Hall, 1971.

Peel, J. D. Y. "Spencer and the Neo-Evolutionists." *Sociology* 3 (1969): 173–91.

Sahlins, Marshall D., and Service, Elman R. *Evolution and Culture.* Ann Arbor: University of Michigan Press, 1960.

Service, Elman R. "Cultural Evolution." *International Encyclopedia of the Social Sciences.*

———. *Primtive Social Organization: An Evolutionary Perspective.* New York: Random House, 1962.

Index

Abbadie, Arnauld d', 123, 200
Abba dula, 137, 144, 145
Abba gada, 137, 147
Abir, Mordechai, 43
Abun, 120, 121, 127
Abuna Tewoflos, 127
Adal, 175
Adam, Guillaume, 7
Addis Ababa, 12, 22
Adwa, 12, 13, 109, 110
Aeschylus, 1
Aethiopika, 5
Afar, 30, 37, 42, 46, 47, 48, 51, 52, 54, 55, 56, 60–63, 78, 130, 177, 178, 182
Afkala, 43
Afro-Asiatic, 27–28
Afro-Mediterranean, 26, 28
Agew peoples: as ethnic category, 34, 37; expansion of, 70–71; listed, 189. *See also* Cushites, Central
Aksum, 2, 3, 4, 5, 6–7, 30, 32, 41, 42, 70–72, 88, 92, 93, 109, 110–12, 160, 171, 173, 184
Aksumites, 30, 32, 70, 71, 87, 100, 110, 111
Alabdu, 136
Ali I, Ras, 83–84
Almeida, Manoel de, 10
Alvarez, Francesco, 10, 16
Amarro, 45, 51, 61, 63
Amde Siyon, 73, 74, 88, 100, 108
Amhara: expansion, 72–75, 88, 148–52, 171–75, 179; homeland, 72–73, 76; interactional patterns, 122–26, 148–50, 154–55, 163; kinship system, 114, 116–17, 119, 120; language, 30, 46, 72, 82, 160; pan-Ethiopian traits of, 47–64, 67; political institutions, 114–15, 118–22, 126–27, 146–64, 165, 171–75, 179–80, 181, 184–85; religious institutions, 115–16, 120–22, 150–51, 159–60, 163; systemic structural features, 117–27, 146–64, 171–75, 179–80, 184–85
Amhara-Tigrean peoples: as ethnic category, 35, 37; listed, 189; political culture of, 118, 136; political resurgence of, 90, 155–61, 165, 182. *See also* Amhara; Habesha; Tigreans
Amharic, 30, 46, 72, 82, 160
Angot, 42, 75, 78, 82
Ankober, 42
Anyuak, 31, 39
Arbore, 43, 52, 61
Aregawi, Abba, 110
Argobba, 30, 37, 62
Arwe, King, 49
Ariosto, Ludovico, 8
Aristotle, 2
Arsi, 49, 50, 52, 53, 60–63, 135, 136, 143, 178
Athanasius, 3
Augustine, Saint, 2, 10
Azariah, 98, 102
Azikiwe, Nnamdi, 13

Bab-el-Mandab, 28, 31
Bahrey, 89, 130, 135, 154, 155

Bakaffa, 83
Bale, 44, 73, 78
Banna, 55
Barbarossa, Frederick, 8
Barettuma, 130
Barya, 56
Basketo, 58, 63
Baxter, P. T. W., 139
Bedawie, 29, 36
Beja, 36, 44, 70–71, 72, 73, 130
Beni Amer, 36, 52, 53, 60–63
Berta, 30, 56
Bet Asgede, 62, 63
Bet Juk, 56
Bet Mala, 36
Beyne-Lekhem. *See* Menilek I
Bezold, Karl, 95
Bieber, Friedrich, 42
Bilin, 48, 54, 60, 62, 73
Bishoftu, Lake, rites at, 44
Blemmyes, 10, 29
Bogos, 42
Bonga, 41
Borana, 43, 49, 50, 53, 55, 56, 57, 58, 60–63, 128, 129, 135, 136, 139, 140, 140–43, 144, 147, 162, 168. *See also* Galla peoples; Oromo
Boulding, Kenneth, 24
Bruce, James, 10–11, 16, 43, 53, 93, 157
Budge, Wallis, 94–95, 100
Burji, 52, 62, 63
Byzantine influence: cultural, 33, 65; political, 7, 106

Cambyses, 1, 4, 12
Caste groups: as ethnic category, 39; evolutionary significance of, 169–70; in relational network, 45–46, 170; listed, 195–97; as pan-Ethiopian, 56–57, 62
Cerulli, Enrico, 24, 53, 64–65, 95, 97, 139–40
Christianity, 32, 44, 65, 72, 74–75, 82, 88, 109, 110, 119, 150–52, 160, 173, 178
Cohen, Marcel, 18
Comnenus I, 8
Constantius II, 7
Conti-Rossini, Carlo, 19–20, 24, 100
Core Islamic peoples: as ethnic category, 34, 37–38; listed, 189
"Creative incorporation," 64–68
Cultural relativism, 20–22
Cushites, Central, 24, 29. *See also* Agew peoples
Cushites, Eastern, 29, 30, 37, 47. *See also* Galla peoples; Lacustrine peoples
Cushites, Northern, 29, 30. *See also* North Eritrean peoples
Cushitic language family, 19, 27–28

Damot, 74, 75, 78, 82, 119
Danquah, J. B., 13
Darimu, 131
Dasenech, 20–21, 47
Dawit I, 108, 159
Debre Tabor, 4
Dembiya, 75, 78
Derasa, 46, 62, 162
Dewaro, 44, 73, 77, 78
Diakonoff, I. M., 28
Dillman, August, 17
Domitius, 96
Doresse, Jean, 100
Dorze, 20, 46, 50, 51, 54, 56, 57, 58, 60–63
Du Bois, W. E. B., 14
Durkheim, Emile, 169
Dwane, James, 13

Egypt, 1, 7, 12, 87
Eisenstadt, S. N., 174, 179, 209
Era of the Judges (Princes), 83, 159–60
Eritrea, 77, 109, 161
Ethiopian studies: history of, 16–17; scholarly approaches to, 17–25
Ethnikon, 3
Evil eye, 49
Evolution, social: adaptive radia-

tion in, 167, 184; as basis for new scholarly image, 25; defined, 166; law of evolutionary potential in, 176; modalities of, in Ethiopia, 166–85; principle of evolutionary complementarity in, 182, 185
Ewostatewos (Eustathius), Saint, 74–75, 83
Ezana, 173

Falasha, 32, 46, 49, 53, 59, 60–63, 67, 73, 77, 173
Fatigar, 73
Fikkere Iyesus, 157, 159
Florence, Council of, 8
Fogelson, Raymond, 103
Food taboos, 53
Fortunatus, Venantius, 3
Fried, Morton, 173
Frobenius Institut, 20, 202
Fulani, 78

Gabre-Sellasie, Zewde, 160–61
Gabriel, Saint, 44, 48
Gada system, 30, 132–34, 137, 142–44, 145, 152, 158, 162, 164, 176
Gafat, 30
Galawdewos, 77
Galla peoples: as ethnic category, 38; listed, 190. *See also* Arsi; Borana; Guji; Mecha; Oromo; Tulema
Gallinya, 38, 46, 84
Garvey, Marcus, 14
Gebeta, 64
Ge'ez, 16, 17, 19, 24, 30, 70, 101, 157
Gerima, Abba, 110
Gobena, Ras, 85
Gobeze, Wagshum, 159
Gona, 130
Gonder, 41, 44, 45, 82, 84, 119, 174
Grañ, Ahmad, 76–77, 78, 88, 135
Grass, ritual use of, 51
Greater Ethiopia: boundaries of, 26–27; as culture area, 46–68; ethnic composition of, 33–39; ethnic differentiation in, 28–30; ethnic interactions within, 40–46; external influences on, 30–33; political unification of, 69–86; prehistory of, 27–28; social evolution within, 165–85
Gregorios, Abba, 16, 93
Gregory of Nyasa, 104
Gregory Thaumaturgus, 96
Gregory the Illuminator, 96
Guidi, Ignazio, 18
Guji, 46, 50, 51, 52, 53, 54, 55, 60–63, 128, 129, 130, 135, 136, 143, 144, 162, 178
Gult rights, 114–15, 120
Guma, 42
Gurage, 20, 30, 42, 43, 44, 45, 46, 51, 52, 54, 55, 56, 58, 59, 60–63, 77, 81, 177, 178, 182. *See also* Lacustrine peoples

Habab, 56
Haberland, Eike, 57, 58, 64, 75, 128, 203
Habesha (Abyssinian), 118, 199
Hadiyya, 44, 48, 52, 53, 58, 60–62, 73, 108
Haile Melekot, 158
Haile Sellassie I, 9, 14, 45, 175, 179–80
Hairstyles, 58–59
Hallo, 136
Hallpike, C. R., 169, 170, 178
Hamasien, 42
Haoulti, 29
Harari, 20, 30, 37–38, 54, 62, 63
Harer, 32–33, 41, 76, 81
Harerge, 27, 44, 51
Harris, Cornwallis, 11
Hauda, 170
Haynes, George Edmund, 14
Heldman, Marilyn, 65
Heliodorus, 5
Henry IV, 6
Heraclius, 7

Héricourt, Charles Rochet d', 93, 95, 135, 200
Herodotus, 1, 4–5
Himyar, 100
Hindlip, Lord, 11
Hinnant, John, 128, 162, 206, 209
Hirmata, 42
Hoben, Allan, 24, 114–15, 124
Homer, 1, 3–4
Homes, construction of, 59
Hotten, John, 3
Household: Amhara, 113–14, 116, 117, 119, 123–24; Oromo, 129–30
Hubbard, David, 94, 95, 108

Ibna el-Hakim. *See* Menilek I
Ifat, 44, 73
Iliad, 3–4
Images of Ethiopia: as ethnic museum, 19–22; as evolving system, 23–24; as fabulous kingdom, 6–9; as independent state, 12–14; as pious people, 3–6; as remote place, 1–3; as savage people, 9–11; as Semitic outpost, 17–19; as underdeveloped country, 22–23
Inarya, 42, 43, 77
India, 1, 5
Insignia of authority, 57–58
International African Institute, 20
Islam: diffusion of, 43–44, 66, 71, 165; and national ideology, 151–52. *See also* Muslim
Islam in Ethiopia, 19
Istifanos, Saint, 121–22
Italy, 11, 12, 13, 14, 17, 85, 86, 87, 161
Ittu, 135, 145
Iyasu I, 83, 111
Iyasu II, 83
Iyesus Moa, 74
Iyoas I, 83

Jabarti, 37, 42
Jamaica, 13
Janjero, 42, 45, 49, 53, 57, 58, 61, 62
Jensen, Adolf, 202
Jimma (Galla), 21, 42
Johnson, Samuel, 5
Justin I, 7, 99
Justinian, 7

Kaleb, 7
Kasa (Tewodros II), 84, 157, 158
Kasa (Yohannes IV), 159
Kasmati Wali, 83
Kefa, 20, 42, 43, 45, 49, 54, 56, 57, 60–63, 88, 175
Kembata, 59, 67, 73
Kenya, 11, 78
Kenyatta, Jomo, 14
Kibre Negest: compared with *Aeneid,* 101; as national epic, 100–101; objective of, 95; as reflecting identity struggle, 101–9, 118; as societal script, 101, 113, 118, 124, 151–52, 156, 158, 159, 160, 161, 172; sources of, 93; structure of, 95–99; style of, 93–94; as Tigrean product, 109–12
Kimant, 20, 32, 48, 49, 52, 53, 55, 60–63
Kinship: Amhara, 116–17, 119, 120; Oromo, 129–31, 136, 137, 138
Kitab al-Fara'id, 54
Konso, 20, 43, 49, 50, 51, 52, 54, 56, 57, 58, 60–63, 170, 175, 177–78, 182
Konta, 42, 45
Kontoma, 131
Kroeber, Alfred, 47
Kulubi, 44, 51, 212
Kush, 1, 12

Lacustrine peoples: as ethnic category, 38; listed, 191–92; in trading networks, 42, 43
Lalibela, King, 58

Lasta, 42, 71, 75, 76, 119, 156, 160
Leach, Edmund, 56
Legesse, Asmarom, 24, 78, 128, 130, 137, 140, 142
Lesky, Albin, 15
Lewis, Herbert, 21, 56, 139, 140, 162, 169
Liqanos, Abba, 110
Ludolf, Job, 16, 93
Luther, Ernest, 22–23

Majangir, 20, 52, 60, 61, 168, 177, 178, 182
Makeda (Queen of Sheba), 9, 93, 97–98, 100, 108, 109, 111
Mani, 7
Mao, 51
Markets, 41–43, 114
Masculinity, cult of, 53–55, 152–54
Matara, 29
Mecha, 20, 135, 136, 139, 140
Mediterranean cultures, influence of, 33
Mekouria, Tekle-Tsadik, 156
Mela, Pomponius, 10
Menander, 2
Menilek I, 98, 100, 102, 104–7, 158
Menilek II, 9, 13, 21, 26, 42, 45, 81, 85, 88, 90, 156, 158, 160, 179, 185
Menz, 73, 75, 118
Meroe, 2, 4, 12
Mikael Sehul, Ras, 159
Missionaries, 74–75, 151
Monasteries, 109, 120, 159
Monks, 5–6, 16, 44, 111
Moroda Bakere, 85
Moscati, Sabatino, 172
Moses, Father, 6, 104
Muhammad Ali, 84
Muhammad Ali, Imam (Ras Mikael), 85
Murdock, G. P., 65–66, 202, 204
Muslim: beliefs about Ethiopians, 5, 15; military expansions, 15, 44, 70, 76–78, 90; traders, 42–43, 46. *See also* Islam

Nao, 67
Napata, 1, 4
New Testament, 2, 93–94, 109
Nguni, 78
Nicene Council, 96
Nile, 3, 7, 9
Nilo-Saharan, 19
Nilotic peoples, 31, 39
"Nine Saints," 109–10
Nkrumah, Kwame, 13
Noeldeke, Theodore, 18
North Eritrean peoples: as ethnic category, 36–37; listed, 188
Nubia, 1, 4, 6, 12, 70
Nuer, 31, 39, 178

Odyssey, The, 1, 4
Old Testament, 5, 10, 93–94, 99, 104–5, 108, 109
Olla, 130, 164
Ometo peoples, 42; listed, 193
Omotic language family, 27, 28, 29
Omotic peoples: Amhara influence on, 74, 75; as ethnic category, 38–39; listed, 192–94; in trading networks, 42, 43
Oriental Semitic cultural influences, 31–33, 66–67, 172
Oromo: expansion, 78–80, 152–55; homeland, 78, 79; interactional patterns, 138–41, 149–50, 154–55, 161–64; kinship, 129–31, 136, 137, 138; systemic structural features, 129–45, 146–48, 150–56, 158, 161–64, 183, 184. *See also* *Gada* system; Galla peoples

Padmore, George, 13
Palladius, 5
Pan-Ethiopian traits: defined, 64; listed in tables, 60–63; origins of, 46–47. *See also* Caste groups; Food taboos; Insignia

Pan-Ethiopian traits (*continued*) of authority; Masculinity; Religious symbolism; Stratification patterns
Parish, 115–16, 117, 118, 120, 123, 124
Park, Robert E., 143
Parsons, Talcott, 101, 110, 181, 208
Pax Amharica, 209
Pentellewon, Abba, 110
Perham, Marjery, 3
Phallic symbols, 46, 54
Philotheus, 100
Pilgrimages, 44, 50–51
Placidus, Lactantius, 4
Pliny (the Elder), 6, 10
Plowden, Walter, 95
Poggibonsi, Niccolò da, 7
Poles, central mainstay, 59
Portugal, 8, 33, 65, 77
Praetorius, Franz, 24
Pre-Nilotes, 30–31, 65, 66
Prester John, 8–9, 15

Qabena, 42
Qallu, 49, 131, 136, 137, 138, 140, 144–45

Rainmaking, 52–53
Ramusio, 16
Rastafarians, 14
Raya, 42
Religious symbolism: beliefs, 47–50, 103–9, 151–52; rituals, 50–53
Rubenson, Sven, 157
Rufinus, 5

Sabacos, 4
Sabaean cultural influence, 18, 31–32
Sabbo, 131
Sacrifice, animal, 51
Safara, 42, 43
Sahle Maryam, 158
Sahle Sellassie, 11, 84, 135, 158
Sahlins, Marshall, 167
Saho, 30, 37, 70
Said, Mohammed, 13
Scetis, Desert of, 5
Scythians, 2, 3
Seignory, 114–15, 116, 117, 123
Semiramis, 12
Semitic studies, 17–19, 201
Seraqo, 74
Serpents, beliefs about, 49–50
Sertsa Dingil, 77, 82, 89–90, 111, 152
Service, Elman, 176
Seqota, 42
Shack, William, 24, 209
Sheba, Queen of. *See* Makeda
Sheko, 52, 60, 63, 168
Siculus, Diodorus, 4, 6, 9–10, 12, 16
Sidamo, 20–21, 43, 49, 50, 51, 52, 53, 55, 57, 60–63, 64, 162
Simoons, Frederick, 41
Sixtus IV, 16
Slavery, 11, 56, 156
Snowden, Frank M., Jr., 2
Solinus, 10
Solomon, King, 97–100, 102, 105, 109, 111
Solomonid Dynasty, 72, 73, 75, 76, 77, 85, 90, 95, 100, 108, 110, 150, 151, 156, 158, 159, 175
Somali, 19, 20, 30, 37, 42, 44, 48, 51, 52, 57, 58, 60–63, 70, 71, 78, 79, 80, 81, 88, 130, 145
Stauder, Jack, 168
Stephanus of Byzantium, 3, 4
Strabo, 10
Stratification patterns, 55–57. *See also* Caste groups
Sudan, 12, 30, 42, 67, 86, 87
Sudanic peoples: cultural impact of, 30–31, 35; as ethnic category, 35, 39; listed, 194–95
Sumner, William Graham, 143
Supernatural beings, 47–50
Susneyos, 111

Tamrat, Tadesse, 88
Tekle Haymanot, Saint, 74, 119
Tewodros I, 157
Tewodros II, 84, 85, 86, 90, 156–58, 159, 160, 179
Tewoflos, Abuna, 127
Tigray (province), 30, 37, 42, 44, 75, 76, 83, 84, 109, 110, 111, 118, 119, 156, 160
Tigre (language), 18, 20, 30, 36
Tigrean: contributions to Ethiopian society, 92, 110–12, 159–61, 183, 185; people, 44, 92, 162; relationship to *Kibre Negest,* 93, 100–101, 103, 109–10. *See also* Amhara-Tigrean peoples
Tigrinya, 18, 24, 30, 37, 92, 109
Timbaro, 42
Trees, sacred, 52
Trimingham, J. Spencer, 19, 67, 77, 88, 177
Tulema, 139, 145
Turkey, 75–77, 88

Ullendorff, Edward, 18–19, 95
Urreta, Luis de, 12

Waj, 78
Wallace, Anthony, 103
Warner, W. Lloyd, 21
Wax and Gold, 24
Weber, Max, 179, 208–9
Wegera, 75
Weissleder, Wolfgang, 113
Welamo, 20, 42, 44, 50, 53, 61, 63
Wello (Galla), 144
Wello (province), 156
Winstanley, William, 11
Women, status of, 54–55
Woysitsu, 136

Ya' ibike Igzi, 100
Yeha, 29
Yejju, 42, 67, 83, 90, 144, 156
Yemen, 70, 100
Yikunno Amlak, 73, 95, 100, 111
Yishaq, 93, 101, 108, 111
Yohannes I, 121
Yohannes IV, 26, 43, 45, 85, 86, 88, 90, 121, 156, 160–61, 179, 185

Zagwe Dynasty, 42, 71, 73, 111, 171
Zar, 47–49
Zeila, 42
Zera Ya'iqob, 43, 45, 74, 85, 88, 108, 111, 121, 122, 173
Zulu, 13